Peter M. Hamm

Continuity & Change

Among Canadian Mennonite Brethren

Wilfrid Laurier University Press

*Religion and Identity: Social-Scientific
Studies in Religion, 3*
Hans Mol, editor

Canadian Cataloguing in Publication Data

Hamm, Peter Martin
  Continuity and change among Canadian Mennonite
Brethren

(Religion and identity ; 3)
Bibliography: p.
Includes index.
ISBN 0-88920-189-7

1. Mennonite Brethren Church of North America –
Canada.   2. Mennonites – Canada.   I. Title.
II. Series.

BX8118.5.H35 1987   289.7′71   C86-094791-2

WILFRID LAURIER UNIVERSITY PRESS
Waterloo, Ontario, Canada   N2L 3C5

87 88 89 90 4 3 2 1

Cover design by Polygon Design Limited

Printed in Canada

To Betty
Richard and Barbara
Carolyn and Gregory

Contents

Part Three: Sacralization of Identity

Part Four: Secularization Process

Part Five: Viability of Sectarianism

List of Figure and Tables

Abbreviations

AFCL   *Anabaptists Four Centuries Later*

GCYB   *Year Book of the General Conference of Mennonite Brethren Churches*

HMBC   *A History of the Mennonite Brethren Church*

IMH   *Introduction to Mennonite History*

JSSR   *Journal for the Scientific Study of Religion*

K-J   *Konferenz-Jugendblatt*

MBBC   Mennonite Brethren Bible College

MBH   *Mennonite Brethren Herald*

MO   *Mennonite Observer*

MQR   *Mennonite Quarterly Review*

MR   *Mennonitische Rundschau*

RAV   *The Recovery of the Anabaptist Vision*

Voice   *The Voice*

YB   *Year Book of the Canadian Conference of the Mennonite Brethren Churches of North America*

Preface

The casual observer cannot help but notice the flow of vehicles to a Mennonite Brethren Church at the hour of worship on a Sunday morning. This external indicator of religious vitality measured in terms of church attendance is indicative of other measures, less easily defined, which reflect the continuity of a religious phenomenon despite the changes which the passing of generations may encounter. From the mid-1920s, when large numbers of Mennonite Brethren immigrated to Canada from Russia, this sectarian immigrant people has been prospering in numbers as well as in socio-economic status. More astute observers will be led to question the viability of such a religious movement which increasingly accommodates itself to its host society. More particularly, such observers look for factors which have enabled it to change without losing its vitality. They search for the key variable to account for the dynamic of sectarianism in the so-called post-Christian era.

To examine the viability of such a sectarian group, the author hypothesizes that specific, empirically measurable factors contributed to the continuity of the movement. These synthesizing components of continuity are viewed as sacralizing the identity of the sectarian group. At the same time, specifically measurable factors bring about change and lead to secularization, viewed here as loss of religiosity and/or conformity to the world. The study hypothesizes that for a sectarian movement to persist both integration, represented by the sacralization process, and differentiation, represented by the secularization process, must occur, the dialectic of the two forces guarding against overly restrictive rigidity and excessive adaptability.

While the analysis of the Canadian Mennonite Brethren becomes a case study to test the utility of an identity theory of religion, which hinges on the integration/differentiation dialectic, it is more than simply an experiment in the sociology of religion. It is, at the same time, a serious self-study in religious sociology, by which the author seeks to gain a better understanding of the processes of growth and decline, of continuity and change, and of the ongoing tension resulting from the religious movement's confrontation with society. To understand this task, the author engages the tools which assure as detached and analytical a study as possible. Not only are sociological categories of thought and its heuristic devices employed, but basically two types of source materials are utilized—empirical data derived largely from the 1972 Church Member Profile[1] of five Mennonite and Brethren in Christ churches, and historical data retrieved from Conference year books, periodicals, and theological writings. The study, thus, attempts the two-fold task of analysing the religious movement from without, that is, testing a theory of religion by the application of empirical measures derived from the secondary analysis of data, and assessing its progress from within, whereby representative spokespersons of the religious group are given a serious hearing as they interpret their own sectarian struggle with the world. It is the combination of these external and internal measures of the viability of the movement which constitutes the explanation for the persistence of the Mennonite Brethren one-half century after their immigration to Canada.

This book has been published with the help of a grant from the Canadian Federation for the Humanities, using funds provided by the Social Sciences and Humanities Research Council of Canada.

---

1 These raw data are not to be confused with the use of the same data by J. Howard Kauffman and Leland D. Harder in their book, *Anabaptism Four Centuries Later* (Scottdale: Herald Press, 1975). This study devised its own cross-tabulations and makes comparisons of Canadian Mennonite Brethren with three North American Mennonite groups.

Part One

THEORETICAL FRAMEWORK

I

Sectarianism

There are those social analysts who view religion as outmoded for this "world come of age," and there are those prophets of religion who not only welcome secularization as a liberating movement, but also predict religion's imminent demise. And yet, religion persists. It was observed by Max Weber that there is no known human society without something which modern social scientists would classify as religion (Weber, 1969, 14-17), and Talcott Parsons maintains that modern anthropologists have completely confirmed that belief in the supernatural is universal (Weber, 1969, xxviii). There are also those prophets, therefore, either who see a place for "honest religion" for "secular man" (Newbigin, 1966) or who, in fact, maintain that man is quite "unsecular" (Greeley, 1974), and thus support Durkheim's notion that "there is something eternal in religion . . ." (Durkheim, 1965, 474). Perhaps the "new direction" of the traditional religious symbolism, which Robert Bellah foresees in the post-modern age (Bellah, 1964, 358-74), is not the "invisible religion" of Thomas Luckmann (Luckmann, 1967), but the persistence of earlier forms of religion. No doubt, one such expression of religion could be that of sectarianism.

1. The Persistence of Sectarianism

In the last sentence of the conclusion of his well-known work, *Religion in Secular Society*, Bryan R. Wilson predicts that in response to the growing institutionalism, impersonality, and bureaucracy of modern society, religion will find new functions to perform. However, that would not be the religion of ecumenism, but the religion of the sects. Increasingly studies have shown that sects and the more evangelical and orthodox Protestant denominations have gained in both influence and numbers at the expense of the liberal and adjustable churches. Peter Berger, while not speaking of growth, admits the continuing evidence of religion. "There is scattered evidence," he submits, "that secularization may not be as all-embracing as some have thought, that

2

the supernatural, banished from cognitive respectability by the intellectual authorities, may survive in hidden nooks and crannies of the culture. Some, for that matter, are not all that hidden" (Berger, 1971, 39). The following treatise hypothesizes such a viability for sectarianism, but, first, more needs to be said about sectarian studies as such.

2. The Need for This Field of Study

Some thirty years ago, Peter Berger suggested that there were few areas in the sociology of religion that were of greater interest than that of sectarianism. This was so, not because of his interest in delving into the more picturesque aspects of religious life, whether in some backward rural area or the religious underworld of the modern metropolis, but because "in the deepening analysis of sectarianism, its structure and dynamics, the sociology of religion may make a formidable contribution to the general effort of the social sciences to understand the inner forces of our society" (Berger, 1955, 467). He then deplored that the study of sectarianism had been characterized by a mass of empirical data with little or no theoretical orientation. In conclusion, he expressed the need for carefully worked out monographs on a number of sectarian movements and a systematic investigation of the processes within these movements. The proposed study of the Canadian Mennonite Brethren Church encompasses such an analysis, most prominently the processes of sacralization and secularization and the religious vitality which results from the interaction of these forces.

3. The Methodology Adopted for Such a Study

That aspect of the scientific study of religion known as the discipline of the sociology of religion concerns itself, on the one hand, with the ways in which society, culture, and the individual influence religion—influence its origin, its doctrine, its practices, the types of groups that express it, and their kinds of leadership. On the other hand, it is also the study of the ways in which religion affects society, culture, and the individual. To pursue such a scientific study, social scientists, as much as possible, must avoid the mixture of value judgments and science. Only then can they fulfill the requirements of a social science, that is, the prediction of the hypothetical or actual recurrence of social phenomena (Becker, 1968, 97). Otherwise, they become social philosophers or pseudo-sociologists. To be scientific they must devise tools which are as value-free as possible and can readily be employed in their study of religious phenomena. Moreover, contrary to ideographic historians who seek to describe the unique and the particular, sociologists need to generalize in order to advance a theory which interprets society. To make such generalizations, on the basis of which they will make predictions about social phenomena, they construct a "pure" or "ideal" type which becomes such a tool or heuristic device against which to project a more precisely measurable reality. Their prediction can then be made within the framework provided by constructive typology. However, such construction of a type requires, first, the proposal of a highly provisional hypothesis; then, studying a number of instances to construct a set of typical circumstances; and, lastly, constructing a hypothetical "ideal" type. Furthermore, the data of social phenomena are not susceptible to experimental manipulation (except for limited "controlled" situations in a totalitarian setting), but the use of undated and non-localized types allows social scientists to make predictions given certain circumstances. As a result, then, of the construction of such a type, which type is not itself an hypothesis, they can employ the type in testing the proximity of occurrences of social phenomena. It is not intended, however, that a given construct be exactly found in "external" nature. At best, it can only approximate the ideal.

The church-sect typology is such a tool for sociologists. Where it has been abused, its critics have rightfully derogated this device. However, abuse does not rule out the legitimacy of proper use. When Max Weber and Ernst Troeltsch first used the church-sect typology, they appropriately thought in terms of "ideal types" or "constructs" against which to measure religious phenomena. Although the polar ends of the hypothetical continuum were "pure" church and "pure" sect, Troeltsch did not rule out the simultaneous occurrence of these trends in the history of the church. And Peter Berger suggested that sectarianism was, indeed, a process that might also occur within the social structure of a church (Berger, 1958, 43). One might deduce that "churchness" is also a process which characterizes a developing sect.

If ideographic historians, with their concern for the particular detail in a given time and place, are not the model for sociologists, one may well question the place for such an elaborate historical framework that this study proposes for the religious movement under study. First, one must admit the need for some historical background, since a religious movement which can date its time and place of origin is also part of a cultural milieu within a particular time and place of history. To recognize the social, economic, political, and religious factors at work may elucidate the causes which gave rise to the movement and the unique shape the movement assumes. To do without the historical background may well limit one's understanding of the essence of the movement itself. Secondly, one must hasten to add that sociology of religion is not to be confused with social history nor with the history of the social gospel. Both of these may supply data for the sociology of religion, but they raise different questions. Sociology of religion will seek to support a proposed hypothesis or generalization for which it needs a careful understanding of historical components. And for this, the historic background is essential. Thirdly, Anabaptists have repeatedly been cited as the classic example of sectarianism. To study the persistent, sectarian nature of this twentieth-century Anabaptist movement, it will be helpful to recall the norms of beliefs and practice of its ideal as these were rediscovered to be the New Testament ideals both at the time of the beginning of the Anabaptist movement in the sixteenth century, as well as in the more recent appearance of the Mennonite Brethren Church in the nineteenth century. Tensions which gave rise to the schism between church and sect both in the sixteenth and nineteenth centuries are present in the movement today. The two chapters on Anabaptist and Mennonite Brethren beginnings, therefore, not only provide a historical setting for the contemporary movement, but lay the groundwork for an understanding of the processes of sacralization and secularization within the movement from 1925 to 1975.

Two sections of the treatise, with five chapters in each, form the body of the component data for analysing change and continuity. What kind of data, then, are required for such a study? Tracing change or lack of change through time makes at least two demands upon the data. The information must in some manner be measurable, whether quantitatively or qualitatively, and must be comparable, that is, there must be similar kinds of data with which to make valid comparisons. Most accurate for purposes of measurement, of course, would be an extensive survey with a similar questionnaire administered at two or more points in time. In the absence of such a survey, which can be conducted for the present but cannot be administered retroactively in history, other supporting evidence will need to be discovered, evidence which is sufficiently specific and "measurable," as well as recurring in some form, in order to trace the change through time. A limited amount of "hard core" empirical data are available, including extensive empirical testing of specific indices.[1]

The analysis will not merely be descriptive in supplying data to demonstrate continuity and change. It will be shown that both sacralization and secularization are ongoing processes between which a

---

1 Many of the statistical data used for this study are taken from the Church Member Profile, a survey of five Mennonite and Brethren in Christ denominations conducted in 1972. Permission to do a secondary analysis was kindly granted by the directors, Dr. J. Howard Kauffman of Goshen College, Goshen, Indiana, and Dr. Leland D. Harder of Mennonite Biblical Seminary, Elkhart, Indiana. Their own findings are summarized in the work of Howard Kauffman and Leland Harder, *Anabaptists Four Centuries Later* (hereafter *AFCL*): *A Profile of Five Mennonite and Brethren in Christ Denominations* (Scottdale: Herald Press, 1975).

dialectic occurs. While sacralization inhibits progress, impedes social change, and eternalizes norms, secularization erodes boundaries, dislodges stable structures, and destroys identity. Therefore, for a religious movement to remain viable, there will need to be a continued tension between sacralization and secularization. Harold Fallding has well stated that "secularization is the analytical process that has sacralization for the complementary synthesizing process. They make a dialectic. Secularization, through the operation of reason, breaks down; sacralization, through the operation of faith, builds up" (Fallding, 1974, 210). In a similar vein, Calvin Redekop maintains that sect development is not simply an unfolding of a predetermined course of events. Rather, it is the "outcome of a continuing *dialectic* between sect and host society" (Redekop, 1974, 347). The conclusion of the study comes to grips with the impact of this dialectic.

4. A Critique of the Church-Sect Typology

Studies of sectarianism are invariably confronted with the church-sect typology, first popularized by Max Weber and Ernst Troeltsch. Some scholars have indiscriminately used their dichotomous typology or conveniently expanded it. Others have totally rejected it, while still others have understood its utility and cautiously employed it. Since the initial stage of the religious movement under study so closely fits Troeltsch's portrayal of a sect, it is well to review his typology and the subsequent critique it has generated.

Troeltsch's typology was based on Weber's distinction of institutions capable of exercising authority and of his theory of charisma. The church, Weber explained, emerged out of a hierocracy with a professional priesthood, with claims of universal domination, with rationalized dogmas and rites, and with a compulsory organization (Weber, 1968, 1164-66). As a result, the church becomes the bearer of an office charisma to preserve the dignity of the organization, not a community of personally charismatic individuals like a sect. Weber's basic distinction between church and sect, then, rests on the compulsory-voluntary aspect. He notes, "As a rule, it (the church) is not joined voluntarily, like an association, but its members are born into it" (Weber, 1968, 1164). Elsewhere, to illustrate such voluntary association, Weber refers to the introduction of adult baptism by the Anabaptists in Zurich (Weber, 1974, 313-14). Important, also, is Weber's notion of the "routinization (*Veraltaeglichung*) of charisma" to explain sect development. When a social relationship based on personal allegiance to a charismatic figure becomes a permanent one, the charismatic power is traditionalized or rationalized (legalized) (Weber, 1964, 358-73). Thus, a sect tends to pass away with the generation that first constituted it, since the new generation enshrines the charisma in a traditional or legalistic order. However limited Weber's church-sect typology may have been in its restriction to the principle of voluntariness, the strength of his distinction was in its sociological analysis of the structural differences, rather than in providing a theological explanation of the difference; moreover, his dichotomy stimulated further investigation.

Troeltsch built upon Weber's distinction between church and sect, but separated both from mysticism. He undertook a more theological analysis in his amplified distinction. Troeltsch saw the Reformation as the culmination of the church-sect distinction, although both forms were present from the beginning of Christian history. The church type was based on the idea of grace administered to an organization of masses, while the sect was based on the idea of law governing a small "holy community" set aside from the world. More specifically, in Troeltsch's own summary, the church is an "institution which has been endowed with grace and salvation as the result of the work of Redemption; it is able to receive the masses, and to adjust to the world," while the sect is "a voluntary society, composed of strict and definite Christian believers bound to each other by the fact that all have experienced 'the new birth'" (Troeltsch, 1960, II, 993). Figure 1-1 illustrates in summary form the contrasts between church and sect as depicted by Troeltsch.

Troeltsch's typology has received much attention by sociologists, historians, and theologians. Usually his two categories were too polarized, so in-between positions on the continuum were devised. Joachim Wach, from a more theological perspective (with a reminder that religious bodies are first worshipping communities), has avoided the word "church" altogether and recognized three distinct bodies sociologically: (1) the ecclesiastical bodies, appealing to the ideal of the true ecclesia (especially expanded by Calvin) as a middle position between Rome and the left wing of the Reformation; (2) the independent bodies or denominations, especially the American church form; and (3) the sect, rigidly exclusive (not even including the right wing of the Anabaptists) (Wach, 1972, 191-98). Howard Becker expanded Troeltsch's typology to include four constructs: ecclesia, sect, denomination (sect at an advanced stage), and cult; and suggested a hypothetical cycle of cult, sect, denomination, and ecclesia (Wiese and Becker, 1932, 624-28). Milton Yinger found these elaborations inadequate and refined the typology according to two criteria, the degree of universality and the degree of emphasis on social integration: (1) the universal church (combining both church and sect tendencies); (2) the ecclesia (encompassing the boundaries of society as in established national churches); (3) class church or denomination (limited by class, racial, and regional boundaries, yet not withdrawing from the social order);

(4) the established sect (an outgrowth of the sect, in its continued protest resisting for many generations the disintegrating effects of improved economic status, mobility, persecution, and education); (5) the sect (as in Troeltsch's terms, responding to their host society by acceptance, aggression, or avoidance); and (6) the cult (connoting mystical experience, lack of organization, and presence of charismatic leaders) (Yinger, 1969, 147-55). Yinger's classification is of special interest in its application to an Anabaptist sect, since Mennonites have frequently been referred to as an "established sect" (Harder, 1962, 12-15).

Figure I-1
Summary of Church-Sect Typology as Portrayed by Ernst Troeltsch

Criterion of Judgment	Church Characteristic	Sect Characteristic
Starting point	Sacerdotal office of apostolic church	Jesus and primitive church
Access to divine	Objective possession of grace	Individual effort and subjective holiness
Source of legitimation	Sacerdotal and sacramental office	Gospel and primitive church ideal
Membership	Ascriptive status, by birth	Achieved status, by voluntary adherence
Commitment	Differential, especially by monks and priests	Total commitment from all
Asceticism	Confined to monastic orders	Principle of separation for all
Class appeal	Dominant class (upper and ruling)	Lower and oppressed
Organizational response	Hierarchical and traditional	Egalitarian and radical
Attitude to world	Compromise	Separate from and in tension with
Attitude to state	Utilize state and social order	Oppose or avoid state

More important than merely stimulating typological refinement, Troeltsch's church-sect distinction led to productive studies of sect development. Most prominent among these was the work of H. Richard Niebuhr. Writing as a theologian rather than sociologist, he maintained that sects, defined rigorously, cannot last beyond the founding generation, since family life, increasing wealth and respecta-bility, and routinization lead to accommodation and result in denomi-nations. Niebuhr astutely observes, "Rarely does a second generation hold the convictions it has inherited with a fervor equal to that of its fathers, who fashioned these convictions in the heat of conflict and at the risk of martyrdom" (Niebuhr, 1972, 20). The aptness of this insight will be tested in the study of the Mennonite Brethren sect.

Social scientists have recently more rigorously critiqued the typology and rejected it altogether. Eric Goode raised three basic problems with the church-sect dimension: its definition (more enumerations are "notoriously useless"), empirical correlates (a construct and actual fact never coincide), and the association of its defining elements (e.g., social class position). He concluded that "unless it undergoes a radical revi-sion which is universally accepted by researchers and theorists in the field, church-sect must be seen as a dead concept, obsolete, sterile, and archaic" (Goode, 1967, 69-77). This harsh judgment is largely shared by Nicholas J. Demerath III in his reply to Goode, and he further faulted the typology with lack of logical elegance, irrelevant variables, lack of systematic cohesiveness, and arbitrariness. In addition, it is both culture-bound to the West and institution-bound. Demerath con-sequently called for the abandonment of this Weberian scheme (De-merath III, 1967, 77-84). Allan W. Eister argues that even as a heuristic device, the church-sect conceptualization faltered, the initial clarity of Weber having been confused. The major weaknesses are (1) the unre-liability of listing characteristics attributed to types; (2) the failure to recognize the difference between Weber's and Troeltsch's conceptions of the intents of churches and sects vis-a-vis the "world"; and (3) the impetus in the construction and proper use of types, namely the ten-dency to dichotomous constructs (Eister, 1967, 85-90). Eister noted that not all, nor even the majority of, sects are lower class or "protest groups."

These more radical critiques, however, have not terminated the discussion on church-sect typology. Already in 1961, David O. Moberg summarized the major criticisms of the typology as follows: (1) no American religious bodies are pure churches; (2) "church" and "sect" are value-laden terms; (3) the typology is inconsistent with theological definitions of the church; (4) evolution of religious bodies is not consis-tently from sect to church; (5) the types are not religiously defined, and details in distinctions between them are not accurate; (6) applications of Troeltsch's typology omit his minor categories; (7) internal roles within the religious bodies have been minimized; (8) illustrating a theory is not testing it. He concluded that the criticisms are based upon incomplete understanding of typological analysis, misinterpreting sociological generalizations by assuming they must have universal applicability, and insufficient research which apply the concepts (Moberg, 1961, 47-58). Church-sect typology is thus not invalidated, but with discernment can be applied to other than Christian religions. Moberg, in fact, encouraged cross-cultural and cross-religious research on the basis of this typology. In 1971, Benton Johnson reopened the discussion reminding the critics that Troeltsch did not mean the typology to be universally applicable, that it was not highly formalized (but merely that Troeltsch's reading of history suggested clusters in two different directions), and that Troeltsch built no theory around his typology, but simply helped bring conceptual order to such historical data. While Johnson noted a shortcoming in subsequent theory on sect development, namely, that sect growth always leads to the compromising of religious purity and distinctiveness, he proposed that the reverse may be true, that sects may have a strong impact on their environment. He encouraged research on how religious bodies actually adapt themselves to their environment (Johnson, 1971, 124-37). Calvin Redekop similarly made a plea for a "new look at sect development." He argued that at the heart of sectarian protests is "perceived dissonance between the *actual* or *real* and what is considered *ideal*" (Redekop, 1974, 346-52). Redekop purported the following: (1) the degree to which a sect's protest strikes at the central and sacred values of a society will have a strong bearing on its future prospects; (2) societies differ in their ability to tolerate and integrate radical protests; and (3) sects differ in their strategies for confronting the evils against which they are protesting. Important for this study is Redekop's further statement that "sect development is not simply an unfolding of a predetermined course of events. Rather, it is the outcome of a continuing *dialectic* between sect and host society" (Redekop, 1974, 347). Since this study concerns itself with this dialectic, it is appropriate to note the applicability of the church-sect typology to a study of the Canadian Mennonite Brethren Church in the light of the foregoing critique of the typology. First, however, one needs to define sectarianism more closely.

5. A Definition of Sectarianism and Its Applicability to Mennonite Brethren

In a non-sociological discussion, the word "sectarian" has pejorative overtones which adherents of such a religious group do not find complimentary. The word is sometimes used to denote a type of warfare among religious groups because of their differences. It refers also to esoteric religious beliefs which the established religion would frown upon. Moreover, it implies a querulous attitude of intolerance resulting in secession from a larger religious body. The popular *Web-

ster's Seventh New Collegiate Dictionary refers to a sectarian as a "narrow or bigoted person." Little wonder that adherents of such smaller Christian denominations resent being called by this derisive term. Troeltsch may have been wiser from a theological standpoint to have avoided Weber's terminology and, instead, employed the distinction "institutional" versus "voluntary" church, a possibility he considered. Theologically, such "sectarian" groups rightly argue that they are the church as well and ought not to be defined vis-a-vis the church.

From a sociological standpoint, the term "sectarian" conveys the notion of dissent, which was at the root of Weber's and Troeltsch's distinction and continues to be for those who persist in its use today. It refers to a particular type of religious organization which stands in protest. At the base of Weber's distinction was the compulsory-voluntary aspect of religious sociation, the voluntary as in protest to being born into the church. In Troeltsch's more theological distinction, the sectarian stance of separation from the world, among other variables, was a protest to the compromise with the world. Johnson's single variable dealt with acceptance of the social environment in which a sect exists. The non-acceptance of this environment is sectarian protest. Similarly, Bryan Wilson defines sects mainly in terms of their response to the world, thus, in the form of protest (Wilson, 1966, 179). This protest is likewise the result, according to Redekop, of "perceived dissonance between the actual or real and what is considered ideal." From this perspective, identifying with such a protest group is commendatory for the adherent of a sectarian group and the term in fact becomes a compliment. The stage is thus set for a workable definition.

The definition of sectarianism for the purpose of this study can be stated as follows: sectarianism is a movement of religious protest against the social order, be it state, institution or society, or established religious organization, which results in voluntary separation from such environment to demonstrate the dissonance between what the group perceives as normative in matters of faith and practice and what it experiences as dominant in the social order. This definition has developed as a result of the influence of Weber, Troeltsch, Johnson, Wilson, Berger, and Redekop, as the foregoing discussion indicates, but is not simply an eclectic product of the same. It does focus deliberately on protest, voluntary separation, perception of dissonance between real and ideal, and on process.

Several scholars have devised their own typology of sectarianism to enable a clearer analysis of individual sectarian movements. Elmer T. Clark first devised such a classification with reference to small American sects according to the "mental make-up of the persons who find their spiritual cravings satisfied by the teaching or worship practices of the various bodies" (Clark, 1937, 22). This highly arbitrary scheme is based on alleged "psychological make-up and temperament" without clear-cut indices of measurement, resulting in the following seven groups: the pessimistic or Adventist, the perfectionist subjectivist, the charismatic or Pentecostal, the communistic, the legalistic or objectivist, the egocentric or New Thought, and esoteric or mystic sects. According to Clark, the Mennonites as a body belong to the legalistic or objectivist sects because of their separatist emphasis. Clark's typology is to be questioned not only for its lack of clear indices constituting the "psychological make-up," but for his arbitrary classification of sects into this mold. More useful is Bryan Wilson's typology of sects, initially of four groups and expanded to seven (Wilson, 1959, 3-15; 1973, 22-30). These seven "responses to the world" to indicate the degree of tension with the world are the conversionist, revolutionist, introversionist, manipulationist, thaumaturgical (magical), reformist, and utopian. According to his typology, Mennonite Brethren today would be primarily conversionist in which "salvation is seen not as available through objective agencies but only by a profoundly felt, supernaturally wrought transformation of the self" (Wilson, 1973, 22). To a degree they fit the introversionist type because of their tendency, especially in the early stages of sect development, to withdraw from the world. The intent of this study, however, is not so much to classify Mennonite Brethren within a sectarian typology, but to study them as a sect which is undergoing change. The more fundamental question is: Can the Mennonite Brethren generally be classified as a sect?

The church-sect typology as a whole is, indeed, applicable to the Mennonite Brethren. The criticisms that the typology is not universally valid nor its variables relevant simply does not apply when using this heuristic device with Mennonites. From the outset of the use of this typology, the Anabaptist movement was generally illustrative of precisely Troeltsch's variables (Gerth and Mills, 1974, 313-14; Weber, 1958, 145; Troeltsch, 1960, II, 691-706), and Mennonite Brethren sought to recover this Anabaptist vision, as chapter four will show. Moreover, church historians who have specialized in Reformation history view the Anabaptists as sectarian in their "left-wing" or "radical" Reformation stance (Williams, 1962; Littell, 1972). More important, perhaps, is that Mennonite and Mennonite Brethren scholars—including theologians, historians, and sociologists—view themselves as dissenters, and thus fit the protesting nature of the sect. Theologian John H. Yoder viewed the sixteenth-century Anabaptists in terms of "prophetic dissent" from the Reformers (Hershberger, 1962, 93-104). Victor Adrian viewed the nineteenth-century beginning of the Mennonite Brethren church as born of two sectarian movements, Anabaptist and Pietist (Adrian, 1965). To focus on the sectarian stance in his recent history of Mennonites in Canada, Mennonite historian Frank H. Epp uses the subtitle,

"The History of a Separate People" (Epp, 1974). And Mennonite Brethren historian John A. Toews, in his most recent *A History of the Mennonite Brethren Church*, depicts the beginnings of the Mennonite Brethren in the nineteenth century as a return to the believers' church following a "decline" of Mennonitism to a "parish church" (Toews, 1975). Finally, sociologists Kauffman and Harder not only indicate that historically the Anabaptists were the best example of the sect-type, but show that, in a measure of voluntariness, the contemporary Mennonite Brethren Church scored highest among the five Anabaptist groups measured. They maintain:

While Mennonites have indeed become acculturated and have assimilated many of the values of the larger culture, they have *not* returned to the "churchly type" of morals and ethics. As long as they continue to challenge the social order by refusing to bear arms, swear oaths, pay war taxes, and discriminate against other minorities, their self-identity as a twentieth-century Anabaptist family of churches will be ideologically as well as historically continuous with their sixteenth-century forebears (Kauffman and Harder, 1975, 27).

Perhaps the fitness of the Mennonite Brethren to the summary by Kauffman and Harder would be questioned by some Mennonite Brethren because of their greater compromise to the social order. Nonetheless, to view the Canadian Mennonite Brethren Church as a sectarian movement can be useful in order more rigorously to examine its dissenting stance within a protesting group of churches, not merely from a theological and historical perspective, but particularly from a sociological vantage point. Such an approach, then, does not concern itself with the exact location on the church-sect continuum, nor where in a sectarian typology they may find themselves. Neither does the sociological use of sectarianism deny their being a church from a theological standpoint. It simply serves as a convenient tool to enable an analysis of continuity and change and to understand better the dialectic which makes this movement viable.

II

Religious Continuity and Change

Sects do not suddenly emerge on the spectrum of religious movements merely to flourish momentarily and fade away nor to occupy a stable niche in a predictable environment without being subject to change. Contrary to the hypothesis of Niebuhr, many sectarian groups continue beyond the second generation. One need not look far to find examples of such petrifaction in sectarianism. More frequently, however, one observes development within sects, change towards the church-type from which they orginally seceded. The intriguing question which follows is this: how much change can a given sect tolerate before it has accommodated itself so completely to the host society that it has, for all intents and purposes, lost its sectness? The following chapter, in preparation for later chapters which analyse the degree of continuity and change, looks more closely at these two processes, designated as sacralization and secularization, as they are treated in sociological literature. Not only are sacralization and secularization examined as religious phenomena as such, but the unique interaction of these forces is noted as resulting in a dialectic which, in fact, makes such sectarian movements viable.

1. The Process of Sacralization

The term "sacralization," used to designate the continuity of a religious movement, occurs only rarely in sociological literature. The occurrence of the phenomenon, however, is common in both classical and recent literature. To look more closely at the meaning of the term and the mechanisms of sacralization will facilitate isolating those primary components which characterize continuity in the recent history of the Canadian Mennonite Brethren Church.

Its Definition

In his recent book, *Identity and the Sacred*, Hans Mol uses the term "sacralization" to encompass his broad definition of religion: the sac-

14

ralization of identity (Mol, 1976, 1). However, his use does not mark the first occurrence of the term in sociological literature. Thomas O'Dea speaks of religion as sacralizing traditions, and in stating his functionalist theory of religion, he explains that "religion sacralizes the norms and values of established society, maintaining the dominance of group goals over individual wishes, and of group disciplines over individual impulses" (O'Dea, 1966, 14). Sacralization was used, then, to denote that which preserves, perpetuates, and promotes the group's ideals and norms. Andrew Greeley speaks of a "sacralizing tendency" in the human condition by which "the symbols even of a secular faith are so set apart from the profane, and eventually so cloaked with ritual and tradition, that they become in fact 'functionally sacred'" (Greeley, 1969, 11). Again, the "sacralizing tendency" includes the ideas of setting apart and preserving. Harold Fallding contrasts the synthesizing process of sacralization with the analysing process of secularization, thus forming a dialectic. He adds, "Secularization, through the operation of reason, breaks down; sacralization, through the operation of faith, builds up" (Fallding, 1974, 210).

Hans Mol incorporates these ideas in his explanation of the term. In a summary statement, he explains, "Sacralization is the process by means of which man has pre-eminently safeguarded and reinforced this complex of orderly interpretations of reality, rules and legitimations" (Mol, 1976, 15). In his further explanation of the concept, Mol refers to sacralization as "a sort of brake applied to unchecked infinite adaptations in symbolic systems ... which become increasingly more dysfunctional for the emotional security of personality and the integration of tribe or community." It is also close to the concept of "untouchability and awe, qualities which reinforce the rock (or better, which cement the sand) on which the house of identity is constructed" (Mol, 1976, 5). It safeguards identity, a system of meaning, or a definition of reality; and it modifies, obstructs, or legitimates change. Moreover, it is a process rather than a mere state of sacredness. The utility of this term in analysing change becomes apparent, for it not only includes the consolidating and stabilizing quality of setting apart, but also more readily allows the dialectic in its emphasis upon process, as will be explained below.

The Sacred in Sociological Literature

While this is not the place for a full discussion of the sacred in sociological literature, it may be appropriate to mention briefly the occurrence of this notion in both classical and more recent literature in order to relate it to the phenomenon of religion in general and to the concept of sacralization in particular. Robert Nisbet maintains that no concept is as suggestive of the underlying premises about the nature of humanity and society in the nineteenth century as the concept of the sacred. He shows that religion is necessary to society as an indispensable mechanism of integration of human beings and that it is a key element in understanding history and social change (Nisbet, 1966, 221). In addition to faith, doctrine, and precept, it is also rite and ceremony, community and authority, hierarchy and organization; and, for conservatives, it was the origin of all fundamental ideas in human thought and belief (Nisbet, 1966, 229-31). This is surely the case for Durkheim, Weber, and Simmel.

It was indeed radical for a positivist non-believer, such as Durkheim was, to attribute so much to the sacred, given the age in which he lived. Concerning the division of the world into two domains, Durkheim categorically announces it to be absolute. "In all the history of human thought there exists no other example of two categories of things so profoundly differentiated or so radically opposed to one another" (Durkheim, 1965, 53). The result is two worlds between which there is nothing in common. Despite the rejection of this duality by contemporary Mennonite Brethren theologians, it cannot be gainsaid that the doctrine of the two kingdoms of the early Anabaptists resembled Durkheim's distinction in no uncertain manner. However, to study the contemporary Canadian Mennonite Brethren Church and the interaction of the forces of change and continuity, Durkheim's distinction is too absolute, and Mol's notion of sacralization as a process seems more appropriate. Nonetheless, Durkheim's purely social explanation of the nature and function of religion, the emphasis on rites and collective acts rather than beliefs, and his demonstration that religion functioned by binding humans closer to society by communicating with other humans on a basis of shared concepts and specifying regulating ideas and social relations so that humans perceived them as absolute and obligatory (Budd, 1973, 39)—all these should be useful in understanding religious movements today.

For Max Weber the concept of the sacred was expressed in terms of charisma. Weber's understanding of the origin of charisma as a "certain quality of an individual personality by virtue of which he is set apart from ordinary men and treated as endowed with supernatural, superhuman ... qualities ... not accessible to the ordinary person" (Weber, 1964, 358-59) does not seem fully to apply to the Anabaptist emphasis upon the priesthood of all believers, especially in their rejection of the Roman ecclesiastical hierarchy. However, his further elaboration of the pristine shape of charismatic authority, "based on an emotional form of communal relationship" (Weber, 1964, 360), where there are no officials, no administrative hierarchy, but only disciples, believers, and followers, fits the Anabaptist pattern well. Even more so does Weber's notion of routinization of charisma apply to the sectarian

movement after its first generation with the process of "traditionaliza-
tion" that follows with transference of charisma from generation to
generation. George Simmel's understanding of the sacred is defined as
piety, "an emotion of the soul which turns into religion whenever it
projects itself into specific forms (Simmel, 1959, 24). Without religious
faith that piety evokes, society, for Simmel, is impossible. "I am sure
that without it society as we know could not exist" (Simmel, 1959,
33-34). The Mennonite Brethren Church has frequently been interpreted as part of the Pietistic tradition (Adrian, 1965). Thus, Simmel's
view of the sacred as piety should have an immediate appeal. However,
Simmel's broader understanding of piety in which "religious behavior
does not exclusively depend on religious contents, but . . . is a generally
human form of behavior which is realized under the stimulus not only
of transcendental objects but also of other motivations" (Nisbet, 1966,
262) would be less readily accepted. However, for this sociological
analysis of continuity in the church, it is a useful interpretation to keep
in mind, for it is these "other motivations" with which this study is
particularly concerned.

In more recent times, the views of O'Dea, Yinger, Bellah, Geertz,
Luckmann, and Berger have enlarged one's understanding of the
sacred, as they fluctuate from functionalist to substantive definitions of
religion. The functionalist theory sees religion concerned with those
experiences which transcend the mundane events of everyday existence involving belief in and response to some kind of beyond which
derive from "contingency, powerlessness, and scarcity," to use Thomas
O'Dea's three "breaking points" of human experience (O'Dea, 1966,
4-6, 13-14).

J. Milton Yinger, critical of functionalism's teleological approach,
examines the conflict theory as an alternative. Yinger refuses to accept,
without considerable qualification, that religion is an integrator of
society. Indeed, Yinger contends, the integrative function is at a very
minimum in a society where more than one religion is practised, when
"established expectancies" of the members of a society are frustrated,
when social change reduces the appeal of the ritual and belief systems,
when mobility from society to society is greatest, when society is sharply
divided into classes, and when outside pressures split a society (Yinger,
1970, 110-12). The protesting stance of sectarian movements certainly
represents conflict, and they surely pose as competition to prevailing
religious views. Yinger, hence, poses an integration-coercion model of
society as it relates to religion. He states, "An adequate view of society,
and of its parts, will see function and conflict together. They are not
opposites" (Yinger, 1970, 91). And this combination may be a useful
approach to examine the complex behaviour of change and continuity
in a sectarian movement.

Peter Berger goes on record preferring a substantive to a function-alist definition of religion (Berger, 1974, 125-33). Functionalism de-fines religion in terms of what is *does*, that is, in terms of its place in the social and/or psychological system, while a substantive definition de-fines religion in terms of what it *is*. Berger opposes functional defini-tions because of their ideological "interest in quasi-scientific legitima-tions of the avoidance of transcendence," that is, legitimations of a secularized world view. Berger adds, "Religion is absorbed into a night in which all cats are grey" (Berger, 1974, 128-29). Berger recommends, instead, the viewing of religion "from within," that is, from the standpoint of *Verstehen*, to use Max Weber's term. This requires seeing religious experience as breaching the realm of "paramount reality," the taken-for-granted world of common sense, and discovering the "finite provinces of meaning," namely, other realities than the ordinary, some of which will be "potential mediators of religious experience." The result is that the reality of everyday life is but an "outer court" of another reality, and "all mundane activity in everyday life is radically relativized, trivialized—the words of Ecclesiastes, reduced to 'vani-ty'"(Berger, 1974, 129-31). Almost a decade earlier Berger explained religion in terms of a human enterprise by which a sacred cosmos is established. As Berger explains in Appendix II of *The Sacred Canopy*, he deliberately speaks of religion as a human projection, in keeping with his approach of "methodological atheism" (Berger, 1969b, 25) and brackets all claims of ultimate truth. Yet two years later, in *A Rumour of Angels*, Berger elaborates these as "signals of transcendence," even though they may be reduced to a "rumour." These signals are humani-ty's propensity for order, the argument from play, from hope, from damnation, and from humour (Berger, 1969a, 70-92). These "theolog-ical possibilities: starting with man" suggest, according to Berger's more recent admission, that people continue to have religious experi-ences, and that "secularization appears to be less far-reaching and less inexorable than many theories of modern man had assumed." Indeed, he concludes, "the reports of God's demise have been somewhat exaggerated" (Berger, 1974, 132). The study of sacralization among Canadian Mennonite Brethren will confirm Berger's conclusion.

Mechanisms of Sacralization

Most sociologists do not find it difficult somehow to define the role of the sacred; fewer attempt to become specific with regards to how it operates and how it can be measured. To operationalize a study of religiosity, one needs to become precise in isolating variables which are in fact measurable. To do so, it is well to discover the mechanisms or dimensions of sacralization, following which one can devise scales of these dimensions which are based on specific measures.

Hans Mol isolates four mechanisms which sacralize identity both on the personal and social level—objectification, commitment, ritual, and myth (Mol, 1976, 11-13, 202-61). In effect, he has five or even six, since early in his book he deals with charisma and conversion. He states, "Both charisma and conversion are means by which religions continue to integrate in spite of their work being constantly undone by the forces of adaptation and change" (Mol, 1976, 54). For Mol, charisma is the "stripping" and "welding" function of a group or social level whereby an old identity is loosened and a new identity created and in which the charismatic leaders are mere catalysts from within the group. Conversion is to the person what charisma is to the social group, and it operates by first detaching from former patterns, by going through a stage of anomie, by attaching to a new focus of identity, and finally by being supported by a sympathetic group. For the continuing process of sacralization, Mol isolates the four mechanisms mentioned above. The objectification dimension is defined as "the tendency to sum up the variegated elements of mundane existence in a transcendental point of reference where they can appear more orderly, more consistent and more timeless" (Mol, 1976, 11, 206-14). It is thus a projection of order in a beyond and hence closely linked with the ability of human beings to think abstractly and to use symbols. It is a theodicy in which the contradictions, exceptions, and contingencies of this life can be understood as less arbitrary than the exigencies of life might suggest. Mol's second mechanism is commitment or emotional attachment to a specific focus of identity which "develops into awe which wraps the system in 'don't touch' sentiments" (Mol, 1976, 12-13, 216-32). Sacrifice is a form of commitment, according to Mol, which indicates priorities in a hierarchy of competing meanings. A third mechanism is ritual, which articulates and reiterates a system of meaning and thus restores, reinforces, and redirects identity (Mol, 1976, 13, 233-45). Rites of passage are but one example of such ritual in which the rites desacralize the old and sacralize the new identities. The fourth mechanism is myths, theology, and dreams, which interpret reality and sacralize through narration (Mol, 1976, 14, 246-61). Mol sees the sin/salvation theme of sectarian evangelical theology to be an instance of such sacralization. These mechanisms provide clues to an analysis of the process of sacralization which also characterizes the Canadian Mennonite Brethren Church.

Orrin Klapp's six criteria for the cultic, in which he includes "sacred sects," are somewhat similar. Without elaborating, one can summarize these as follows: enthusiasm for a central value, the element of the mystique (mysteries, esoteric knowledge), the celebration of the ritual, the role of the devotee, emphasis on identity change or redemption (satori, nirvana, enlightenment, salvation, rebirth, conversion), and solidarity of a fellowship or brotherhood (Klapp, 1969, 146-80). Most of these criteria apply to the Mennonite Brethren. Rosabeth Kanter, in her study of communes and utopias, isolated six major commitment mechanisms, each of which was further subdivided for providing more specific indices of measurement (Kanter, 1973, 72-125). Her major categories were sacrifice, investment, renunciation, communion, mortification, and transcendence. Again, these will offer clues to isolating components of sacralization among Mennonite Brethren. Perhaps most useful for general categories of analysis are Charles Glock's dimensions of religiosity (Glock, 1973, 9-11). These are the experiential (religious emotion), the ideological (beliefs), ritualistic (religious practices), intellectual (information on faith tenets and sacred scriptures), and consequential dimension (effects as seen in action or "works").

How then will the analysis of sacralization of Canadian Mennonite Brethren be operationalized? Since the intent of this study is not simply to measure degrees of religiosity but more generally to theorize on continuity and change or sacralization and secularization of a sectarian group, five areas have been chosen in order to include both historical material and empirical measurements as component data. These categories, which are separately treated in chapters five to nine, not only include Mol's and Glock's dimensions, but extend these to include organizational structures.

2. The Process of Secularization

If the term "sacralization" is only rarely found in sociological literature, it is quite the contrary with "secularization." In fact, Susan Budd maintains that it is the most important issue, theoretically and practically, in the sociology of religion (Budd, 1973, 119). So rich is the word in its range of meanings and so full of internal contradictions that it led David Martin to propose to abandon the concept, and Larry Shiner to look for an alternative (Martin, 1969, 9-22; Shiner, 1967, 207-20). It is necessary, therefore, before endeavouring an analysis of the process of secularization, in order to isolate variables, to look more closely at the meaning, for definition helps delimit the area of investigation.

Necessary Definitions

The meaning of secularization will depend, however, on one's definition of religion. If "secularization" presents difficulties, then "religion" defies all definition. Berger has emphasized the importance of a substantive definition of religion, that is, in terms of what religion *is*: the human enterprise by which the sacred cosmos is established. The consequences of opting for this definition of religion allows Berger, then, to speak of secularization in terms of a "shrinkage in the role of religion, both in social life and in individual consciousness" or "a progressive loss of plausibility to religious views of reality," to put it in sociology-of-knowledge terms (Berger, 1974, 132). Dobbelaere and Lauwers quote Norbeck, Kluegl, Pin, *et al.*, to suggest that a substantive definition of religion in our Western societies of today would be: "a system of beliefs and rituals relative to supernatural things which unite into a moral collectivity those who adhere to them" (Dobbelaere and Lauwers, 1973-74, 545). Admittedly, such a substantive definition has an ideological character, for it has restricted itself to things supernatural, but herein lies its relevance for a study of Mennonite Brethren.

Earlier in this chapter O'Dea and Yinger's explanations of the sacred were presented as functionalist. In an earlier work than the one cited, Yinger defines religion as "a system of beliefs and practices by means of which a group of people struggle with . . . the ultimate problems of human life" (Yinger, 1969a, 9). With such a definition, Yinger argues there is no secularization in the U.S.A. (Yinger, 1969b, 72). What changes one can witness are but the development of new religious forms. As a result, Yinger maintains, "the increase in religious activity and interest in the very context of supposed 'secularization' is paradoxical only to the sectarian not to the analyst" (Yinger, 1969b, 75). Again, one concludes with Dobbelaere and Lauwers that such a functionalist position has an ideological bias, and it was because of this bias that David Martin wanted the term eliminated. Apparently, to keep aloof from the ideological basis, one must avoid defining religion. And yet, the definition of religion is needed to delimit one's investigation. The only solution, according to Dobbelaere and Lauwers, is to determine the social context of the definition.

Before determining this social context, it may be helpful to propose a combination of a substantive and functionalist definition, deliberately chosen to serve the purpose of analysing both change and continuity among Mennonite Brethren. The closest model for such a definition is that of Durkheim: "A religion is a unified system of beliefs and practices relative to sacred things, that is to say, things set apart and forbidden—beliefs and practices which unite into one single moral community called a Church, all those who adhere to them" (Durkheim, 1965, 62). As Dobbelaere and Lauwers point out, the substantive part has to do with the essence of religion—"a unified system of beliefs and practices relative to sacred things," and the functional part shows what religion does—"unite into a single moral community . . . all those who adhere to them" (Dobbelaere and Lauwers, 1973-74, 537). The function of religion is to integrate into a cohesive collectivity. Similarly, the Mennonite Brethren emphasize strongly the transcendent in religion, which, for them, is its essence, and perceive themselves as a people of

God set apart from those who are not "Christian," and both their beliefs and practices accentuate this voluntary and deliberate separateness. At the same time, they are a brotherhood, a collectivity, integrated into a viable organized body which persists and grows generations after its beginnings. This is the social context in which a substantive-functional definition of religion is chosen, stated in those terms in which the group under study perceives itself as religious, and allowing thereby a more precise and thorough study of both change and secularization from its own perspective.

With such a definition of religion, although it straddles both substantive and functionalist elements, it is easier to define secularization. Bryan Wilson's definition of secularization conveys this narrower, substantive definition of religion: "the process whereby religious thinking, practice, and institutions lose social significance" (Wilson, 1966, xiv).

The need to distinguish between different kinds of secularization has been emphasized by both theologians and sociologists. Harvey Cox has clarified the difference between *secularism* and *secularization*. Both derive from the Latin *saeculum*, meaning "this present age" (Cox, 1971, 16), something vaguely inferior as opposed to the eternal "religious world" which is timeless. Initially, secularization referred to the process by which a "religious" priest was transferred to parish responsibility. Later the separation of pope and emperor institutionalized such secularization, and passing responsibilities from ecclesiastical to political authorities was designated "secularization." Most recently, secularization describes a process on the cultural level which is parallel to the political one, that is, the disappearance of religious symbols in the cultural sphere, such as freeing public schools from church control. Cox explains such secularization as a liberating development, "a historical process, almost certainly irreversible, in which society and culture are delivered from tutelage to religious control and closed metaphysical world views" (Cox, 1971, 18). On the other hand, *secularism* is the ideology, "a new closed world view which functions very much like a new religion. . . . It menaces the openness and freedom secularization has produced" (Cox, 1971, 18). Cox has made a helpful distinction, but still has not adequately explained secularization.

Milton Yinger, somewhat like Cox, distinguished between *secularism* which is the antithesis of religion and *secularization* which refers to a process in which belief and practice of a specific religious tradition decline in strength (Yinger, 1967, 19). In the same article, Yinger cautions one to distinguish between change in religious faith and decline of such faith.

Most serviceable in understanding the full range of meanings is Larry Shiner's study, "Concept of Secularization in Empirical Research" (Shiner, 1967, 207-20). Six types are differentiated and assessed, a summary of which follows:

(1) Decline of religion: the previously accepted symbols, doctrines, and institutions lose their prestige and influence; this culminates in a religionless society.

(2) Conformity with "this world": the religious group turns its attention from the supernatural and becomes more and more interested in "this world"; the culmination is total absorption in pragmatic tasks in which the religious group is indistinguishable from society.

(3) Disengagement of society from religion: society separates itself from religion to constitute an autonomous reality and limits religion to the sphere of private life; it culminates in purely inward religion.

(4) Transposition of religious beliefs and institutions: beliefs and institutions once viewed as grounded in divine power are transformed to purely human creation and responsibility; it culminates in a totally anthropologized religion.

(5) Desacralization of the world: the world is deprived of its sacred character through causal explanation and manipulation; it culminates in completely "rational" world with no supernatural phenomena.

(6) Movement from "sacred" to "secular" society: a general concept of social change culminating in a society based on rational and utilitarian considerations.

Shiner concludes that either the concept be dropped entirely or the term "differentiation" or "transposition" be used to incorporate the notions expressed in points 3, 4, and 5 above. However, as indicated above, this study of secularization, using Wilson's definition, incorporates points 1 and 2 above. At the same time, it recognizes the quite separate, yet closely allied phenomenon of social change as suggested in point 6. This does not rule out the use of the notion of differentiation, but, in keeping with the popular understanding of secularization among Mennonite Brethren, secularization will mean decline of religion and/or conformity to the world. This is also in keeping with Mennonite sociologists Kauffman and Harder who refer to secularization as "the exchange of sacred for profane values—the church's assimilation of the 'world,' defined theologically as a profane social reality fallen from the creative purposes of God" (Kauffman and Harder, 1975, 300).

An Analysis of the Secularization Process

With a workable definition of religion and a fairly precise understanding of secularization as a concept, one can proceed to analyse more closely the process itself. What are the causal factors? What transpires in the process? What is the response of institutional religion? These and more questions might be asked in such an analysis.

Most prominent among causal factors attributed to secularization is the process of change implicit to religion itself. It is not hard to trace such indications in ancient Judaism. Max Weber argued that the "disenchantment of the world" (*Entzauberung*) began in the Old Testament (Weber, 1969, 246-58). Harvey Cox sees Creation as "the disenchantment of nature," the Exodus as "the desacralization of politics," and the Sinai Covenant as "the deconsecration of values" (Cox, 1971, 19-32). Peter Berger likewise traces the roots of the "disenchantment of the world," commonly attributed to the Reformation, to ancient Judaism (Berger, 1969b, 115-20). Similarly, he contends, Christianity carried the seeds of the revolutionary impetus within itself, especially in its social formation. Here Marx and Engels would certainly find their roots (Marx and Engels, 1974, 97-118). Berger observes that Catholic Christianity may be seen as an "arresting and retrogressive step . . . although it preserved within it the secularizing potential" (Berger, 1969b, 124). In the Protestant Reformation he sees "a powerful re-emergence of precisely those secularizing forces that had been 'contained' by Catholicism, not only replicating the Old Testament in this, but going decisively beyond it" (Berger, 1969b, 124). Similarly, Werner Stark sees the seeds of decay in the virtuous qualities of sectarianism. With religious discipline and frugality come economic ascent and social respectability, all of which lead to compromise, especially with a change of generations (Stark, 1967, 271-87). O'Dea lists five kinds of human activity which influence secularization: work, war, exchange, government, learning and science (O'Dea, 1966, 80-86). These appear to relate more to Shiner's differentiation and transformation than to his decline and conformity to the world. Nonetheless, as Fallding observes, "Although secularization and profanity are not the same, the former shows a special vulnerability to the latter" (Fallding, 1974, 359).

One way of explaining what transpires in the secularization process is to think in terms of shift on the sect-church continuum. Karl Baehr has suggested a five-fold stage of re-entry or re-assimilation of Mennonites into the mainstream of society, representing the full shift from sect to church. These stages are summarized by Kauffman and Harder as follows:

Stage *one* is the conflict which first drives the sect into isolation, to escape persecution. Farming becomes the chief occupation of members because it provides a maximum of self-sufficiency and a minimum of contact with the hostile world. The sect becomes a closed community, characterized by distinctive dress, in-group marriage, and other devices.

Stage *two* is the cessation of overt conflict and the granting of formal religious freedom. Contact with the out-group is cautious, and comes primarily through the purchase and sale of commercial products.

Stage *three*, contact between the sect and society becomes more frequent. Through hard work and frugality and the peace that toleration brings, members become prosperous and begin to adapt their style to the ways of those around them.

Stage *four* is marked by differentiation within the sect between the conservatives, who fear the loss of the community's sacred values and want to enforce the old ways, and the liberals, who advocate change. There is also a new division between the "haves" and the "have-nots," and the former begin to deal with the latter according to the economic principles (rent, interest, mortgage, wages, foreclosures) of the larger society.

The *fifth* stage is a splintering of the sect, so that its variant groups, all claiming the same original label, contain all shadings along a continuum from withdrawal to accommodation. The most liberal group cannot be distinguished from the larger society except by name. The moderate group retains some distinctives from the world but finds the doctrine of nonconformity increasingly difficult to preserve. The conservative group maintains the old ways through strict discipline and the practice of excommunication (Kauffman and Harder, 1975, 298-99).

It is anticipated that the secularization among the Canadian Mennonite Brethren will closely follow the pattern taken by other Mennonite denominations.

Another way of viewing the process of secularization is to see it in terms of tension resulting from the secularization of culture, earlier expressed in O'Dea's five activities of work, war, exchange, government, and learning and science. The increased rationality results in a diminution of the sacred. The dialectic of this tension between religion and secularization is expressed admirably by O'Dea as five paradoxes of institutionalization of religion. These are summarized as follows:

(1) The dilemma of mixed motivation. This applies especially to single-mindedness given to charismatic leadership in the early stages of the movement and the subsequent shift to a stable set of statuses and roles with institutionalization (involving a stratified set of rewards in terms of prestige, life opportunities, and material compensations) and resulting lukewarmness.

(2) The symbolic dilemma: objectification versus alienation. Repetition of symbols devised to preserve the original experiences of the religious group results in ritual which routinizes and eventually alienates (the embodiment of the ultimate in empirical symbols causing diminution of the sense of ultimacy itself).

(3) The dilemma of administrative order: elaboration and alienation. With routinization of charisma, the accompanying formal organization and bureaucratic structure in time becomes dysfunctional and alienates.

(4) The dilemma of delimitation: concrete definition versus substitution of the letter for the spirit. Dangers of distortion of faith require definitions of dogma and morals, which concretization itself distorts for the symbol becomes "mechanistic and crude" (Mircea Eliade's "process of infantilization" of discursive sym-

bolism [Eliade, 1958, 444, 456]) seen especially in biblical fundamentalism.

(5) The dilemma of power: conversion versus coercion. Voluntarism and faith commitment through institutionalization are supplemented by public opinion, current ideas of respectability, consensual validation, and approval by accepted authority, so that eventually religion and secular power are coalesced and apparent religiosity conceals cynicism and unbelief (O'Dea, 1966, 90-97).

These five dilemmas not only provide clues to isolate variables which can further be tested empirically to trace the degree of secularization, but also draw attention to the dialectic implicit to the tension of a sect in its host environment.

To express the process of secularization in sociology-of-knowledge terminology, there is a disintegration of the traditional plausibility structures ("collection of people, procedures, and mental processes geared to the task of keeping a specific definition of reality going") in which "the status of objective reality begins to totter" (Berger, 1967, 10-11). This status is lost if the common social activity that served as its infrastructure disintegrates. Strongly integrated plausibility structures produce firm objectivations, but erosions of the structures result in de-objectification. And the sectarian strength of a movement will be determined by the degree of this erosion. The resulting problem posed by the process of de-objectification is simply: how to perpetuate an institution whose reality presuppositions are no longer taken for granted. This leads one to the question of sectarian response. However, stated in more theological terms, one can summarize the process of secularization by noting that decreased transcendence results in increased immanence in the symbol system.

In response to such secularization, sectarian groups have one of two choices basically, to take either a defensive or an accommodating stance. To follow the former means dissent from, and protest against, the world around. To proclaim old objectivities in a social environment that refuses to accept them results in retaining or constructing a sub-society which affirms the traditional values. To protect such a sub-society within a pluralistic milieu, one must maintain a separate identity. The extreme position of such withdrawal is what Bryan Wilson calls the introversionist sects (Wilson, 1973, 43-48) and Peter Berger, a ghetto (Berger, 1967, 10). To follow the latter, accommodation, is the more popular stance, but the question is: how far can one go? The practical answer is well stated by Peter Berger, "One then goes as far as one has to for the pastoral or evangelistic purpose at hand" (Berger, 1967, 11). The key difficulty is the tendency to escalate to the point where the traditional plausibility structure collapses. For the secular theologians (Harvey Cox, Paul van Buren, et al.), such accommodation has become total. Perhaps Harold Fallding has proffered too simple a solution when he suggests, "What modern man would need, if he chose to hold on to religion, is not to turn away from secularization but to baptize its fruits, grafting each innovation back onto the tree of his life and consecrating them all to the service of the whole" (Fallding, 1974, 359). Such accommodation is subject to the same escalation, unless very deliberate efforts are made to retain essential plausibility structures. The answer, it appears, is to avoid either extreme of defence or accommodation and to live with a tension between sectarian separateness and cultural compromise.

Isolating Variables

What, then, are the specific variables which require investigation to study secularization among Mennonite Brethren? On the one hand, one can simply analyse the countervailing forces of conflict which resist the sacralizing mechanisms. However, this approach could lead one to overlook additional spheres wherein secularization forces are at work. The countervailing negative forces are also factors of secularization, but these will be dealt with as part of the dialectic within sacralization. Chapters ten to fourteen look for a new cluster of independent variables. These are education, urbanization, occupational change, economic ascendancy, immigration and assimilation. It is anticipated that the primary thrust of these five factors will be secularizing, while the primary thrust of the factors isolated for sacralizing the identity will contribute towards continuity of the sectarian movement. The total effect of the interaction of these forces will be separately assessed in the final chapter.

3. A Statement of Hypothesis

Sectarian religiosity is a viable alternative among contemporary religious expressions, since it provides both the dynamic force and the structural form for a movement of religious dissent in its protest against "the world" or society at large, including the state, institutions of society, and the religious establishment.

More specifically, this study postulates the following:

(1) The synthetic process of sacralization accounts for the continuity of sectarianism in that it establishes boundaries, reinforces cohesion, safeguards identity, strengthens systems of meaning, and facilitates socialization.

(2) The analytic process of secularization accounts for change within sectarianism in that it is open to the disruptive influence of marginality, the relativizing impact of education, and the gradual ac-

commodation to the host culture as a result of economic ascendancy and upward social mobility, themselves the product of industrial urbanization and the Protestant ethic.

(3) The interaction of these processes is necessary to avoid rigidification in an excessively defensive stance and to avoid total accommodation to its environment, such dialectic furnishing the ongoing balance which is the outcome of tension between sect and society.

(4) The Canadian Mennonite Brethren Church is an example of such a viable sectarian movement, and it may well be the pattern for other evangelical denominations or movements of religious dissent.

Part Two

HISTORICAL BACKGROUND

III

The Anabaptist-Mennonite Movement

In their current identity crisis, Mennonite Brethren look for objectifications or reference points in history to legitimate their separate existence as a denomination. Not only do they look back to 1860—the time of their origin as a separate sect within the larger Mennonite body—and the circumstances which brought this about, but, in addition, they look back to the sixteenth century and the beginnings of Anabaptism. They ask similar questions about their origins as their founding fathers did, who deplored the decline of Mennonitism from a believers' church to a parish church and who realigned themselves anew to the "vision" of the sixteenth-century prototype. For an adequate historical framework, one needs to begin, therefore, with the sixteenth-century Protestant Reformation in Europe.

Before doing so, however, a note about nomenclature would be helpful. For some time, parliamentary parlance has been employed in designating the Anabaptist movement as the "left-wing of the Reformation" (Bainton, 1956, 43). More indicative is George H. Williams' use of "radical" to delineate the Anabaptist stance against magisterial or classical Protestantism (Williams, 1962). Among the dissidents of the Radical Reformation, Williams distinguishes the Anabaptists proper, the Spiritualists (such as Carlstadt, Muentzer, Schwenkfeld, and Franck) and the Evangelical Rationalists (such as Servetus and Erasmus). As subtypes of Anabaptism proper, he further distinguishes the revolutionary (also called "chiliastic" or "Maccabean," because of the Muenster debacle), the contemplative (such as John Denck and Adam Pastor), and evangelical Anabaptists (including Swiss Brethren, Moravian Hutterites, and Dutch and Low German Mennonites) (Williams, 1957, 19-31). It is the Swiss Brethren and Dutch Mennonites which constitute the founding fathers of the present-day Mennonite denominations. Among these, designated here as "Anabaptist-Mennonite," one must trace the origins of the Mennonite Brethren.

30

1. Anabaptist-Mennonite Beginnings: A Study of the First Generation (1525-c. 1550)

Whereas the Mennonite Brethren originated in Russia from the descendants of the Dutch Mennonites and whereas an independent origin for Swiss Brethren and Dutch Mennonites can persuasively be argued (Stayer *et al.*, 1975), it is deemed advisable to examine the origins of the Dutch Mennonites together with those of the Swiss and South German brethren, because of their common themes and subsequent associations.

Origins in Switzerland, Germany, and Netherlands

The radical reformers agreed with Luther in Germany and Zwingli in Switzerland on such cardinal doctrines of salvation as justification by faith through grace, but contended that the magisterial reformers did not complete their break with Roman Catholicism and establish a true believers' church signified by voluntary baptism upon confession of faith. They were partly indebted not only to the classical reformers for their radical notions, but also the humanism of Erasmus and possibly the asceticism of Groote's *Devotio Moderna* (Davis, 1974). Whatever the varied influences upon them, the radical reformers' primary court of appeal was the Bible itself, not any civil or ecclesiastical authority.

Anabaptism or the free-church movement, as it is also called, had its official beginning in the house of Felix Manz in Zurich, Switzerland, on January 21, 1525, when Conrad Grebel "re-baptized" George Blaurock, who, in turn, "re-baptized" the others present.[1] William Estep interprets this act as "the most revolutionary act of the Reformation" (Estep, 1963, 10), because no act so completely symbolized the break with Rome. As a result of the expository preaching of Zwingli, such university-trained theologians as Conrad Grebel (son of a Zurich councilman), Felix Manz (son of the canon of the Grossmuenster Cathedral), and Balthasar Hubmaier (former university rector), and such ecclesiastics as Simon Stumpf (pastor and spokesman for the group), Wilhelm Reublin (first Zurich priest to take a wife), and George Blaurock (a monk), rejected infant baptism and disagreed with Zwingli, when, because of resistance from the city council, he hesitated to abolish the mass (Dyck, 1967, 34). Overtly, the issue over the break was baptism and the mass; more basic was the question of authority and the

---

1 The term "Anabaptist" (*Wiedertaeufer*) is derived from such "re-baptism," which, of course, was not a "re-baptism" to the radical reformers, since they did not recognize infant baptism as valid. See Fritz Blanke, *Brothers in Christ* (Scottdale: Herald Press, 1961), for a detailed account of the first congregation which was subsequently formed at Zollikon, near Zurich.

true nature of the church. This open defiance of such ecclesiastics and civil authorities resulted in persecution of the leaders, so that by January 5, 1527, Felix Manz was forcibly drowned in the Limmat River near his own Grossmuenster Church and became the first martyr for the Anabaptist cause. Blaurock was executed two years later, and Hubmaier was burned at the stake in Vienna. Had Grebel not died of the plague, he would have likely met the same fate. Still others fled or were banished. While histories differ on the extent that the movement spread, the banishment of its leaders from Zurich resulted in the missionizing of St. Gall to the northeast, Basel to the northwest, and Bern to the southwest. Hubmaier, who wrote the most complete statement in early Anabaptism on the question of baptism, spread the movement to Waldshut, an Austrian possession some twenty miles from Zurich. Because of the loss of leaders and the danger of fragmentation, a group of Anabaptists met at Schleitheim in February of 1527, under the leadership of Michael Sattler (learned evangelist and former prior of a Benedictine monastery), to draft the first confession of faith. Sattler and his wife were executed shortly after.

In South Germany, it was Hans Denck (university-trained writer and educator influenced by Lutheran mystics Carlstadt and Muentzer) who spread the faith to Augsburg and Strassburg, and in Central Germany Hans Hut (bookbinder who was also influenced by mystics) preached and baptized in Franconia, Bavaria, Austria, and Moravia. It was in Moravia that Jacob Wiedemann organized communal living for Anabaptists. Strassburg, strategically located in South Germany, served as a more tolerant meeting place for dissenters. Here such leaders as Hubmaier, Sattler, Reublin, and especially Pilgram Marpeck (wealthy civil engineer) exercised their influence. Reformer Martin Bucer, differing from the more tolerant pastor, Matthew Zell, proposed severe treatment of the Anabaptists; yet Anabaptist conferences were conducted here repeatedly between 1554 and 1607. Marpeck opposed Bucer's interpretation of Scripture, arguing for the finality of the New Testament. He continued his ministry in other South German, Swiss, and Moravian cities, writing extensively (Klassen, 1968).

In the Netherlands in 1530, Melchior Hoffman, an uneducated but gifted Anabaptist, who not only had abandoned his Catholic and Lutheran affiliation, but had imbibed the influence of Zwingli and Carlstadt, preached a millennialism, the Great Tribulation presumably having begun in 1526 with the New Jerusalem to be centred in Strassburg. While Hoffman was imprisoned in Strassburg, his follower, Jan Matthijs, changed the location of the "New Jerusalem" to Muenster where he resorted to violence and polygamy in his aberration of the

Anabaptist faith.[2] Obbe and Dirk Philips repudiated the revolutionary Muensterites, and especially Menno Simons (Krahn, 1936; Bender,
1936) gave leadership to the new movement of peaceful Anabaptism.
Born at Witmarsum, Friesland, Menno became a Roman Catholic
priest at Pingjum, and because of questions about transsubstantiation
and infant baptism, he searched the New Testament for answers.
Dissatisfied with Catholicism and especially opposed to fanatical
Anabaptism, he finally sided with the peaceful Anabaptists in 1536
after his own brother had been killed in self-defence in the Muenster
tragedy. For twenty-five years Menno provided leadership for the
Dutch Anabaptists, preaching the gospel, instructing new converts,
organizing believers' churches, and defending the faith through such
writings as *The Foundation of Christian Doctrine* and *True Christian Faith*.
Mennonite Brethren historian J. A. Toews assesses his role as follows:

Judged by the personal sacrifice he made and by the principles which he
practiced in establishing churches according to the apostolic pattern, Menno
must be regarded as one of the noblest and most heroic Christians of his
age—and perhaps any age. He and his associate ministers were trailblazers and
pioneers in insisting on freedom of conscience, separation of church and state,
and the renunciation of war and violence (Toews, 1975, 10).

Predominant Themes of Early Anabaptist-Mennonite Sectarianism

The Anabaptist vision has been variously depicted, yet the biblical
nature of the church lies at the heart of these portrayals. Ernst
Troeltsch described its main characteristics in this manner:

emphasis on Believers' Baptism, a voluntary church, the precepts of the Sermon on the Mount, the rejection of the oath, of war, law, and authority, and,
finally, the most far-reaching mutual material help, and the equality of all
Church members, the election of elders and preachers by the local congregations, and, to a large extent, the unpaid character of the pastoral office...
(Troeltsch, 1960, II, 703).

This portrayal closely fits Troeltsch's earlier characterization of a sect.
A classic statement of the vision was given by Harold S. Bender to the
American Society of Church History in December 1943 (Bender, 1944,
3-24). To Bender, this vision consisted of (1) a new conception of the
essence of Christianity as discipleship, (2) a new conception of the

---

2 For an interpretation of the Muensterite tragedy, the comment of John H. Yoder is
   appropriate: "The revolution of Muenster, with which uninformed historians blacken
   the Anabaptist name, was not consistent Anabaptism; it was a reversion to the same
   heresy accepted by Lutherans and Catholics alike—the belief that political means can
   be used against God's enemies to oblige an entire society to do God's will." See *Peace
   Without Eschatology?* (Scottdale: Mennonite Publishing House, 1954), p. 15.

church as a brotherhood, and (3) a new ethic of love and non-resistance (Bender, 1962, 42-54). Bender fully realized that there were other contributions of the vision, such as the development of religious liberty; but he failed to note the missionizing dimension as a primary emphasis, unless it was implied in discipleship. Yet, Franklin H. Littell devotes a full chapter of his five-chapter dissertation, later published as *The Anabaptist View of the Church*, to the Great Commission. He notes that the Anabaptists were among the first to make the Commission binding upon all church members (Littell, 1972, 11). This is an important aspect of their sectarian stance, for, as Littell suggests, "In Biblical living, the tension between the 'church' and the 'world' is progressively overcome by the missionary outreach of the Christian community" (Littell, 1972, 136). As Littell's title indicates, he sees the Anabaptist distinction in terms of their understanding of the church. He understood the marks of the true church, as the Anabaptists reread these from the New Testament, as follows: (1) believers' baptism, administered to those who had repented; (2) spiritual government, in which the ban, by common consent, disciplines the believer, each believer having a definite role and responsibility in reaching a community decision; (3) community, mutual aid being demonstrated in an open economy, as among the Swiss Brethren and Dutch Mennonites, or as a closed economy, as among the Hutterian brethren; (4) Lord's Supper, symbolically interpreted as a memorial celebration and administered to the true community of believers; (5) separation of church and state, in which the believer refused participation in government, particularly in bearing arms (Littell, 1972, 82-108). These interpretations, helpful though they may be, do not present the vision as forthrightly as do the original sources.

The earliest document from the Swiss Brethren, written by Conrad Grebel some four months prior to the actual birth of Anabaptism, is sometimes referred to as the charter of the free church (Klaassen, 1973, 11). Among Grebel's concerns are those of believers' baptism, the separation of church and state, and the renunciation of war, as the following three fragmentary quotations from Grebel's letters indicate.

Concerning baptism:

It signifies that a man is dead and ought to be dead to sin and walks in newness of life and spirit, and that he shall certainly be saved if, according to this meaning, by inner baptism he lives his faith, as the scholars at Wittenberg say.... Also baptism does not save ... infant baptism is a senseless, blasphemous abomination, contrary to all Scripture (Williams, 1962, 80-81).

Concerning separation of church and state (as seen in his attack on Luther):

Be strong. Thou hast the Bible for defense against the idolatrous caution of Luther.... Do not act, teach, or establish anything according to human opinion, your own or that of others, and abolish again what has been so established; but establish and teach only the clear word and practice of God ... (Williams, 1962, 84-85).

Concerning renunciation of war:

Moreover, the gospel and its adherents are not to be protected by the sword, nor are they to protect themselves. . . . Neither do they use worldly sword or war, since all killing has ceased with them—unless, indeed, we would still be of the old law (Williams, 1962, 80).

This document demonstrates the rigorous separatism of Anabaptism from its earliest days.

The Schleitheim Confession of Faith very precisely states the distinctive concerns which the Anabaptists held over against the magisterial reformers and antinomian excesses to which the heterogeneous movement was vulnerable. Its seven statements are summarized as follows:

(1) Baptism is to be given to those who have repented, thus excluding infants.
(2) The ban (excommunication) is intended to purify the brotherhood, the true church being visible.
(3) The breaking of bread is for those united by baptism, excluding those who "follow the devil and the world."
(4) The separation of the visible body "from the evil and from the wickedness which the devil planted in the world ... we shall not have fellowship with them, the wicked. . . ."
(5) The pastor shall have good report, shall read, admonish, teach, warn, lead in prayer, and shall be supported by his church (thus, not an itinerant evangelist as were the leaders in the first year of the movement).
(6) The sword is ordained of God "outside the perfection of Christ," the Christian using only the ban "inside the perfection of Christ"; it is not appropriate for a Christian to serve as magistrate.
(7) The oath is forbade by Jesus in the New Testament, thus superseding the Old Testament practice (Hillerbrand, 1969, 129-36).

The Dutch Mennonites placed similar emphasis upon the establishment of a visible church with a voluntary membership based upon conversion and involving commitment to discipleship and holy living. In his "Reply to Gellius Faber," Menno characterizes the true church:

(1) an unadulterated, pure doctrine, including the responsibility of sharing the good news as demanded by the Great Commission;
(2) a scriptural use of the sacramental signs, baptism for those who by faith are born of God, and the Lord's Supper for those who have already experienced forgiveness, and who walk in love and unity;
(3) obedience to the Word, living a life of holiness and conformity to the life of Christ;

(4) unfeigned, brotherly love;

(5) a bold confession of God and Christ, despite persecution and difficulty;

(6) oppression and tribulation for the sake of the Lord's Word (Toews, 1975, 11-12).

John H. Yoder summarizes the Anabaptist vision as it emerged in the mid-1520s and survived as the church's involvement in society. The vision singles out those aspects in which the Anabaptists differed from other Protestants.

(1) Scripture alone takes precedence even over the authority of government.

(2) Unity in knowing God's will was worked by the Holy Spirit as believers gathered to study the Scriptures.

(3) Christ must be followed in life, not in childish mimicry, but in necessary obedience, as, for instance, the refusal to bear the sword.

(4) Love is demonstrated not only in pacifism, but in suffering servanthood or self-surrender (*Gelassenheit*).

(5) Baptism follows conversion and a determination to lead a new kind ·of life, and a commitment to brotherhood.

(6) Believers assume a moral responsibility for one another, the extreme instance of discipline being exclusion from the fellowship (ban).

(7) Community of goods was not interpreted in an absolute sense, with the exception of the Hutterian brothers, but with a sense of stewardship to God and his brethren (in this sense, no Christian can call his property his own) (Dyck, 1967, 103-10).

It is to this vision of the Anabaptists, the restitution of the primitive church, to which the Mennonite Brethren attempted to return in 1860.

Some Sociological Observations about Anabaptist-Mennonite Beginnings

In order to assess the degree of dissent or accommodation in subsequent generations, one must examine sociologically the first generation. Having defined sectarianism as a protest movement resulting in a voluntary separation from a dissonant environment, one can now better analyse Anabaptist-Mennonite beginnings in terms of a movement of dissent which attempts to restore what it perceives as normative.

The basis for dissent.   Typical of a sociological interpretation, Bryan Wilson suggests that whereas schisms ostensibly occur for doctrinal reasons, there are deeper causes (Wilson, 1966, 193). In fact, he suggests that sects thrive on separating from evil. On the contrary, histo-

rian J. A. Toews contends that "church renewal and new life movements cannot be explained simply in terms of an historical framework
of cause and effect" (Toews, 1975, 3), and theologian John H. Yoder
laments the "most glaring injustices of modern historiography" in the
failure to see "the movements of dissent within Protestantism as consistent, self-conscious, serious phenomena in their own light" (Hershberger, 1962, 93). Yoder then shows that the Anabaptist dissent, recorded in some forty "disputations" (exchanges of written arguments)
in the sixteenth century, had as its norm the Scriptures, its end in view
the church, its operational reality a visible body of believers, its ethical
relevance in discipleship, and as its eschatological realization the
church within the world, "a structural reality taking concrete form in
the demonic dimensions of economic and political life (Hershberger,
1962, 93-104). One may conclude that, notwithstanding the political
and socio-economic dimensions influencing it and generating from it,
the Anabaptist movement was one of religious dissent *sui generis*.

The ideal perceived. Most present-day Reformation scholars agree
that the Anabaptists held a "primitivist" view of the church. Yet Lutheran scholar, Hans Hillerbrand, maintains that all Reformers, including the Anabaptists, were in continuity with the old Catholic
Church, there being no difference between *reformatio* and *restitutio*
(Hillerbrand, 1971, 107-22). Franklin Littell has, however, convincingly
demonstrated in his examination of the sources that the Anabaptists
treated the New Testament and the apostolic church as normative
(Littell, 1972, 46-108). This radical departure, a third type as distinct
from Catholicism and magisterial Protestantism, led Walter Klaassen to
the intriguing title for his booklet, *Anabaptism: Neither Catholic nor
Protestant*, in which he states:

The word radical has been used adjectivally of Anabaptism because in its
reform of the church it went consciously and deliberately to primitive models
for guidance. Its cry was *Back to the Sources*; that is, back to the roots of
Christianity in the New Testament. The assumption was that what had hap-
pened between 325 and 1525 was mostly in error (Klaassen, 1973, 9).

The repeated attempt of the Mennonite Brethren to restore this ideal
of the New Testament is, therefore, a typically sixteenth-century
Anabaptist concern.

The separation necessitated. Such *restitution* required radical separation from the world, including the *corpus Christianum*, in which the
church was coextensive with society. In the account of the first "re-
baptism" by Grebel, in what may well be the oldest existing Anabaptist
document, the author concludes, "Thereby began separation from the
world and from its evil works" (Dyck, 1967, 34). And Menno Simons

similarly drew attention to such separation. "The entire evangelical Scriptures teach us that the church of Christ was and is, in doctrine, life, and worship, a people separated from the world" (Wenger, 1956, 679). This separatist tendency led also to its subsequent fragmentations, called by some *Taeuferkrankheit* (Anabaptist sickness). As Betty Scharf notes, sects were not known for fusion, but fission (Scharf, 1970, 109).

The voluntary aspect. Characteristic of Troeltsch's sect type, such separation was never compulsory, but entered into voluntarily. However, there was a merit requirement: conversion and baptism upon confession of faith, usually referred to as "believers' baptism." As Max Weber rightly interpreted, "This means that the religious community, the visible Church . . . was . . . solely a community of personal believers of the reborn, and only these. In other words, not as a Church but as a sect" (Weber, 1958, 144-45). In a lengthy footnote, Weber notes that the sectarian aspect of the Baptists (meaning Anabaptists) lay not only in their lack of relation to the state, but "it was because such a religious community could only be voluntarily organized as a sect, not compulsorily as a Church, if it did not wish to include the unregenerate and thus depart from the Early Christian ideal" (Weber, 1958, 254-55).

The role of charisma. The Anabaptist movement had its charismatic leaders, as the foregoing account has indicated, even if Weber's description of such charisma—"endowed with supernatural, superhuman . . . qualities . . . not accessible to the ordinary person"— does not fully apply (Weber, 1964, 358). Indeed, they were, almost without exception, highly educated and gifted leaders, and the movement suffered greatly through their systematic decimation by Roman Catholic ecclesiastics and magisterial reformers. It may have been a decided setback that the Anabaptists and especially the Swiss brethren who had such a promising start had no single leader over a longer period of time, the kind of role that might have been fulfilled by Grebel. It was the longer, almost single-handed leadership of Menno among the Dutch Mennonites which helped this faltering movement to survive.

Its democratic structure. With its emphasis upon the priesthood of all believers, the movement was egalitarian, not anarchic, as some of the less sympathetic critics have caricatured the Anabaptists (Oyer, 1964, 114-39). As Fritz Blanke observes, the Anabaptists recognized civil order, even though they refused to participate in government. "This is not anarchy; it is apolitism, withdrawal from responsibility for the life of the state" (Hershberger, 1962, 67-68). As the Schleitheim Confession indicates and Menno's practice demonstrates, they also believed in organizing congregations and ordaining leaders. This democratic structure of the sect was the antithesis of the hierarchical structure of the church type.

Socio-economic status and relative deprivation. One need not interpret Anabaptism as part of the class struggle, as does Friedrich Engels (Marx and Engels, 1974, 97-120) to support a relative deprivation view of sectarianism. To Richard Niebuhr, the Anabaptists were simply part of the socially and economically deprived in society (Niebuhr, 1972, 39). Littell similarly remarks that "the Anabaptist craftsmen transformed social misfortune into a religious vehicle, and 'glorified in living loose from the world'" (Littell, 1972, 124). These are popular interpretations, but not universally held. Fritz Blanke argues that it is impossible that Anabaptists were responsible for the Peasants' War, as schoolbook accounts commonly suggest, for it was predominantly an urban movement, with the sole exception of Zollikon (Blanke, 1961, 67). Robert Kreider would agree with Blanke. Examining the residences and occupations of 332 members recorded in court trials from 1525 to 1558, Kreider found the following occupational breakdown: clergy (41), nobility (11), merchants (16), schoolmasters (18), artisans (161), labourers (19), farmers and peasants (18), and others (48). On the basis of these data, Kreider concluded: (1) initially Anabaptism was an urban movement; (2) the rate of physical mobility was comparatively high; (3) transfer of occupations among them was quite common; (4) social and economic appeals to the disinherited were practically non-existent in their writings; and (5) the common denominator was not a proletarian status. And finally, Kreider concluded: "The data on hand does not support the generalization ... that the Anabaptists emerged essentially from the disinherited classes. Anabaptism in its early stages was heterogeneous in character with adherents from all vocations and classes. ... It was only after 1550 that Anabaptism became predominantly a rural movement" (Kreider, 1953, 43). The origin of the movement cannot, therefore, be explained in terms of economic and social deprivation. Roland Bainton apparently was right when he stated that they were Anabaptists not only because they were disinherited, but they were disinherited because they were Anabaptists (Bainton, 1956, 43).

2. From Believers' Church to Parish Church: A Study of the Subsequent Generations (c. 1550-c. 1850)

How then was the Anabaptist vision perpetuated and revitalized in subsequent generations? It appears that the Anabaptist-Mennonite movement encountered the same "routinization of charisma" (Weber,

1974, 313-14) which characterizes most religious movements beyond the first generation in their shift towards the church end of the sect-church continuum. And yet, the movement persisted. The following, very brief survey of the three hundred years of its history is not intended to be comprehensive, but simply to indicate the directions of its spread and the major forces of continuity and change which characterized it.

The Spread to Northern Europe and Russia

The persecution of the Swiss Brethren persisted until the Congress of Vienna in 1815. With the exception of the rural canton of Berne, the Brethren had either conformed to the militaristic demands of the state or emigrated to the Palatinate in South Germany or to Prussia. In Alsace, which was given to France in the Treaty of Westphalia in 1648, Jacob Ammann gave leadership to the Amish in the late seventeenth century, seceding from the Swiss and South German Mennonites because of his emphasis upon strict enforcement of the ban and simple clothing. The Palatinate, with its more tolerant attitude to religious dissenters, served as the crossroads for Mennonite refugees in the seventeenth and eighteenth centuries, and here Mennonites developed the reputation for being good farmers.

To the north in Belgium, where the missionary Leonard Bouwens had baptized 592 of his over 10,000 baptisms (recording exact date and place of each), with the exception of a brief period of relative freedom from 1576 to 1586, intense persecution by Roman Catholics forced most Anabaptists to flee by 1640. While Anabaptists, especially those coming from Belgium in 1567-1573, were repeatedly persecuted in England, even as early as 1535, it is difficult to distinguish them from other Protestant martyrs, and a permanent church group did not result, despite their influence. In the Netherlands, where Menno had consolidated the movement of peaceful Anabaptists, the movement suffered from internal division and economic prosperity, and membership declined from 160,000 in 1700 to some 27,000 in 1808, with one hundred congregations becoming extinct. By 1964, a partial recovery was indicated in the baptized membership of 40,000. For the growth and further spread of the movement, one must, therefore, look west and east. As for the west, large numbers of Mennonites and Amish emigrated to America in the eighteenth and nineteenth centuries (Dyck, 1967).

To trace the origin of the Mennonite Brethren Church, one must follow the move of the Anabaptist-Mennonites to the east, especially to its 250-year sojourn in the Vistula delta and approximately 100-year sojourn in Russia. The province of East Friesland in North Germany became the haven of persecuted Mennonites from the very beginning, Menno Simons spending much of his time there from 1536 to 1544. It was here at Emden in 1568 that the more moderate Waterlander Mennonites met to agree on a basis for working together, calling themselves *Doopsgezinde*, still used by Dutch Mennonites today. Eastward, in Schleswig-Holstein, Mennonite refugees settled on estates of noblemen. As Dutchmen, they knew about dikes and how to recover marshy lands, and congregations were founded near Hamburg. Because of greater religious toleration and the need for farming and irrigation skills, many Mennonites settled in the Vistula delta near Danzig from 1530s onwards, where, with the exception of those who went to Russia, large numbers remained until World War II (Ratzlaff, 1971). Also, smaller numbers came from Switzerland, Moravia, Bohemia, and Austria. Initially under Polish jurisdiction, the Vistula delta came under Prussian rule in 1772, and Frederick the Great's militarism created difficulty for the non-resistant Mennonites who refused to pay taxes to support the Lutheran state church. In addition, his successor in 1789 issued an edict denying land acquisition to Mennonites. The invitation from Catherine II of Russia in 1788 was, therefore, interpreted by Mennonites as a "special manifestation of divine providence" (Toews, 1975, 14).

In keeping with its colonial policy of granting a "charter of privileges" to entice immigrants, the Russian tsars (Paul I reaffirmed it in 1800) offered the Mennonites of Prussia an additional clause granting complete religious freedom and exemption from military service forever. After sending two men, Jacob Hoeppner and Johann Bartsch, to visit Russia and finalize an agreement with the government, eight families set out by wagon train on March 22, 1788. Other families joined shortly after, and a total of 228 families arrived a year later at the Chortitza River, a tributary of the Dnieper, in the Ukraine. This group of largely landless settlers, without any ministers or teachers among them, and increased to 400 families by 1800, established fifteen villages, farming some 89,100 acres of land. Governing themselves, with a *Schulze* (mayor) for each village and an *Oberschulze* for the entire colony, they endured great hardships in the initial years. In 1804 the Molotschna Colony, some one hundred miles to the southeast of Chortitza, near the Sea of Azov, was founded with some 365 families by 1806. This group increased to 1,200 families by 1835, settling in fifty-eight villages with an acreage of 324,000, despite the fact that the Prussian government feared the loss of its competent farmers and imposed a 10 percent tax on all immigrants. The second colony, having attracted the landed farmers, including teachers, ministers, and community leaders, was generally more prosperous. Johann Cornies was an outstanding leader among these in agricultural and educational reform. It was in these two colonies that the Mennonite Brethren Church originated almost simultaneously in the early 1860s. Two more colonies were later founded on the Volga, Am Trakt, in 1855 and Old Samara in 1859.

Continuity and Change in the Subsequent Generations

Two questions guide the following sociological analysis of continuity and change in subsequent generations and thereby focus more specifically on the background to the origin of the Mennonite Brethren Church. First, to what did the Mennonites of Prussia and Russia hold fast or in what did they persist in their dissent? Each of the terse answers could be greatly extended and documented.

Their industry and expertise as farmers.   Whether restoring war-devastated lands in the Palatinate or applying themselves to their farms or linen weaving in East Friesland, Mennonites soon gained a reputation for industry, frugality, honesty, and success. As a result, Prussia invited them for their land reclamation and irrigation skills, and later Russia invited them as model farmers (Dyck, 1967, 124-28). Their special success in the total economic development in South Russia in the first half of the nineteenth century, including the industrial development, has been ably researched by David G. Rempel at Stanford University (Rempel, 1933, 123-78).

Their mother tongue.   Until after 1750, the Mennonites in Prussia continued to speak Dutch and thereby resisted total assimilation into Prussian culture. Throughout their stay in Russia, they retained their newly assumed German "mother tongue" and identified themselves with Germans rather than Russian culture (Epp, 1962, 24-25). Thus, they succeeded through 300 years of history to isolate themselves from their host environment.

Their fissiparous tendencies.   Not only did new schisms over doctrinal and ethical issues arise in the Netherlands, such as Waterlanders versus followers of Menno in mid-sixteenth century, or the Sun versus the Lamb church in late eighteenth century, but such cultural schisms as Frisians versus Flemish, occurring just five years after Menno's death, continued into the mid-nineteenth century in Russia. By then new sectarian groups, such as Kleine Gemeinde (1814) and Mennonite Brethren (1860), emerged in an attempt to recapture the Anabaptist vision. As William Keeney notes, "It was the heritage of an age in which religious convictions ran deep, and tolerance was not a virtue" (Dyck, 1967, 96).

The principle of non-resistance. Contrary to the Netherlands, where non-resistance was compromised in their complete assimilation, Mennonites in both Prussia and Russia by and large observed this principle. In Russia, for example, the post of village constable was often turned over to a non-Mennonite. In Prussia the Mennonites had refused to pay taxes in support of the state church and the military establishment (both based on land ownership). Promised military exemption, whether by Prussia, Russia, and later Canada, was always an enticing factor in deciding to emigrate.

Their formal church participation. Although church discipline became increasingly lax, the ban was still enforced for grave public moral offences, such as adultery or physical assault. Church attendance remained compulsory, penalties being imposed for absentees. As Kreider observes, "The Mennonites brought to Russia . . . a faith which had acquired certain cultural accretions, which in turn had been absolutized and sanctified" (Kreider, 1951, 21). Apparently, the cultural accretions had been sacralized.

The genuinely religious core. Despite decline in religious fervour and accommodation to the church-type, there remained throughout a remnant, the *ecclesiola in ecclesia*, such as evangelist-preacher Bernhard Harder, who remained in the "old" church and diligently worked for reform from within and who lamented: "All that we have left is a dry formalism, a shell without a kernel, a church without living members" (Toews, 1975, 20). It was such a religious core, however, that made renewal on a much larger scale possible.

The second question has to do with change. What did the Prussian and Russian Mennonites abandon or to what extent did they accommodate to the host environment? Again, the answers are grossly oversimplified.

From persecuted to "die Stille im Lande." The bold witness of the sixteenth-century newly found vision, resulting in rigorous persecution, was transformed to a conventicle-type, *Stille-im-Lande* (the quiet in the land), reputation during the Prussian sojourn. The conversionist sect, to use Bryan Wilson's model, had become introversionist (Wilson, 1973, 22-30). And in Russia it was a "quietistic, non-missionary Mennonitism which sought to preserve an historic faith by formalistic, tradition-honored means" (Kreider, 1951, 21). Contrary to the case in the sixteenth century, government prohibitions to proselytize were either taken seriously or conveniently found to legitimize the quietistic stance.

From dispossessed to elite in socio-economic status. Scattered from their homes and occupations, sixteenth-century Anabaptists were largely landless refugees, and as such became serfs to the noblemen of Prussia. Eventually, a land-owning, wealthy elitist class emerged, and with the move to Russia many of the Prussian landless became property owners. Among these, by the turn of the nineteenth century, a capitalist class had emerged with 3 percent of the Mennonite population owning 30 percent of the lands and employing 22 percent of the Mennonite people (Krahn, 1935, 170). While but a few serfs in fact became noblemen, the socio-economic status of most Mennonites in Russian villages had surpassed that of the neighbouring Russian villages (Francis, 1955, 23).

From egalitarian to hierarchical in organization.   With rapid population growth and limited available land for expansion, about two-thirds of the inhabitants in Molotschna by 1860 were once again landless. Kreider observes, "No problem in the Mennonite colonies created such misunderstanding and class hatred as the land problem" (Kreider, 1953, 25). J. A. Toews refers to this social stratification as "approaching a caste system" (Toews, 1975, 18). Ecclesiastically, a hierarchy developed with elders and a convent of elders making decisions together with the *Schulze* (mayor) for the entire community, including such matters as education and civil affairs. To speak against an elder was considered a grave misdemeanour.

From separatism to coextension of church and society.   In keeping with their colonial policy, the Russian government granted the colonies a large measure of self-government, so that a "Mennonite Commonwealth" or "state within a state" developed (Toews, 1975, 15). The village assembly could dismiss citizens from the community for immoral conduct (Rempel, 1933, 117). Church concerns could thus be implemented by legal enforcement, and church and civil officials collaborated in such decision-making.

From aggressive leadership to failure in leadership.   Despite the large-scale decimation of first generation leaders, there were those Anabaptists who gave active leadership in evangelism and church-building. However, in 1789 a colony of 228 families was established at Chortitza without ministers or teachers. Johann Cornies, the agricultural entrepreneur and reformer, was an exception. The spiritual decline was blamed upon failure in religious leadership (Toews, 1975, 20). Few were the scholars and writers prior to the 1850s.

From spiritual vitality to decline and moral decay.   Sixteenth-century religious vigour, church discipline, and evangelistic fervour were transmuted in the mid-nineteenth century to spiritual lethargy, moral decay, and complacency with the status quo. German missionary David

Schlatter, who visited the colonies in 1825, reported on this state of degeneracy in the church (Goerz, 1949, 69-70). Robert Kreider explains: "Appraised from the perspective of the Anabaptist conception of the church, the Mennonites in Russia forfeited at the outset the possibility of being a brotherhood-type of church . . . they accepted a state of privileges which were bound to qualifications, not of faith, but of blood" (Kreider, 1953, 22). The Anabaptist understanding of a believers' church—a voluntary fellowship of regenerated believers— had become a parish (*Volkskirche*) or territorial (*Landeskirche*) church, in which church membership and citizenship were coextensive. The Mennonite church in Russia was rife for a "return to Menno" and another "restitution" of the New Testament model.

IV

Mennonite Brethren Beginnings

An analysis of a religious movement must take seriously its beginnings. Especially a study of continuity and change must clearly isolate those factors which reflect the pristine stance of the movement. The previous chapter portrayed the Anabaptist background within which the Mennonite Brethren have their roots and the Russian Mennonite setting from which the new sect was spawned. Particularly trenchant is the observation that the central belief of the Anabaptists—the notion of the believers' church—had gradually been transmuted, so that a parish church had developed in which the sectarian stance of the sixteenth century was virtually nullified. The situation was rife for reform or restitution. Which route would the new movement take?

The present chapter serves to highlight the norms of belief and practice characterizing the first generation and also to indicate the beginnings of significant change by the end of the second generation. It sets the stage for the following chapters which will assess sectarian viability on the basis of the dialectic of forces of sacralization and secularization from 1925 to 1975.

1. A New Secession and Its First Generation (1860-1885)

The renewal or awakening within Russian Mennonitism which resulted in the Mennonite Brethren church represents the path of *restitutio* (discontinuity with the past) rather than *reformatio* (continuity with the past). The secession marked a radical break from a church which had "fallen" into "institutionalized disobedience" (Dueck, 1972, 42-43). Not surprisingly then, as in the case of the sixteenth-century Anabaptists, there was rigorous opposition by both church and state. It took some time until the movement was officially recognized from without and effectively consolidated from within.

46

Influences Leading to the Religious Awakening

Antecedent to the Mennonite Brethren secession was that of the *Kleine Gemeinde*,[1] a group meeting for prayer and Bible study in private homes under the leadership of an ordained minister, Claas Reimer. Critical of the laxity in church discipline and formality of worship, they organized in 1814 as a separate group in the Molotschna colony in an attempt to restore Anabaptist Christianity. Mennonite Brethren historian J. A. Toews views their emphasis on personal experience and piety in keeping with the practice of early Mennonite Brethren (Toews, 1975, 27).

Somewhat later, in 1822, Tobias Voth, pietist teacher from Prussia, was invited by Johann Cornies to head the new *Vereinsschule* (an association school, usually for higher secondary and teacher training) in Ohrloff village, from which a large body of ultra-conservatives had withdrawn. Here Voth organized spontaneous prayer groups, sponsored mission meetings, and distributed Christian literature. P. M. Friesen credits Voth with having "given expression for the first time to something which we call 'brotherhood' (*Brudertum*) or intimate Christian fellowship" (Friesen, 1911, 79). A number of Lutheran pietists, led by Wilhelm Lange, had been especially influential in maintaining two Sunday services, a midweek meeting, mission festivals, Bible studies and prayer meetings, and the cause of temperance. The core of leaders of the Mennonite Brethren came from this prosperous and pious village (established only in 1835, and hence having a smaller landless class).

Perhaps no other single individual was as influential in bringing renewal as was Lutheran pietist Eduard Hugo Otto Wuest. Being dismissed from Neuenkirchen, Germany, for his pietistic zeal, Wuest accepted a pastorate of the Separatist Lutheran (Pietist) Church in Neuhoffnung, near Berdjansk, South Russia. From here he conducted evangelistic and missionary meetings in surrounding Lutheran and Mennonite churches. His evangelistic preaching of the free grace of God, however, was not followed up with a believers' church emphasis of the Anabaptists. Yet, all early Mennonite Brethren agree in their appreciation for the new life he brought in his call for personal commitment. The spiritual decline and the religious dearth, rather than socio-economic deprivation, provided the opportune setting for such spiritual influences of renewal to find a ready response among the landowning, educated upper middle-classes, as well as the landless, lower-classes.

---

1 The term means "small church." Today descendants of this group in Canada are called the Evangelical Mennonite Church.

Circumstances of the Secession

Following Wuest's death in 1859 conventicle groups in which they addressed each other as brothers, and were hence called "Brethren," met for Bible study and prayer. The estrangement from the existing Mennonite church with its mixture of believers and unbelievers led the group to conduct a separate observance of the Lord's Supper. At two church meetings of the Gnadenfeld church, the whole movement came under attack, and the leaders were asked to leave. As a result, Abraham Cornelson wrote a letter of secession and Johann Claassen called a Brotherhood meeting for Epiphany, January 6, 1860, at Elizabethtal. Here, at the home of Isaac Koop, the letter of secession was presented for voluntary signatures. Eighteen family heads signed that day and nine others on January 18. Their dissident stance is apparent: "For these reasons we herewith are completely severing ourselves from the corrupt church, but pray for our brethren that they might be saved" (Bekker, 1973, 43). Their confessional stance included: "According to our convictions from the Holy Scriptures, we are in full accord with our beloved Menno Simons regarding the articles of the Confession of Faith" (Bekker, 1973, 44). There then follows a statement concerning baptism, Lord's Supper, washing of feet, election of ministers, and use of the ban.

A similar movement, almost simultaneously yet independently, occurred in the Chortitza Colony as a result of a spiritual awakening begun through reading of Ludwig Hofacker's (German pietist) sermons and J. G. Oncken's (German Baptist) advice. On March 4, 1862, three brethren from the Einlage church of Chortitza were baptized in Molotschna, and another eighteen received baptism near Einlage one week later, March 11, 1862, the latter date considered their date of secession.

Immediate Opposition and Eventual Recognition

From the outset, opposition from the church members, represented through their spokesmen, the elders (more like bishops), and from the district and colonial government officials was intense. Five of the six elders at Molotschna insisted that the seceding members be turned over to the District Court for prosecution. The Colony Administrative Office (*Gebietsamt*), David Friesen, applied the Russian Penal Code dealing with secret societies, thereby prohibiting meetings with threats of imprisonment and banishment to Siberia. Representatives of the Brethren—Claassen, Cornelson, and Koop—appeared before the Colonial Inspector Andrea and were tricked into promising not to organize before receiving permission from the government. They kept their promise, and so the remaining brethren continued to struggle for survival without the official guidance of its most capable leaders. Claassen, however, made several trips to Petersburg to consult with higher officials—culminating with a petition to the tsar—eventually to secure government promise of freedom of worship without persecution and full exercise of civil rights and legal protection, which local officials had denied them. Only on May 30, 1866, was this granted. Claassen also secured permission for Mennonite Brethren to settle in a new colony, Kuban. In the meantime, however, many brethren had been molested, some forced to leave the colony, and especially school teachers lost their jobs (Lohrenz, 1950, 31-34). Recognition by Ohrloff church through its sympathetic elder, Johann Harder, had come by November 1862, when the Brethren promised to abide by the Confession of Faith of the Mennonite Church.

Consolidation and Early Development of the Brethren

The next twenty years following the official recognition by the Russian government were times of organization and consolidation, as well as fragmentation and spread of the movement. Organizationally, the movement in Molotschna lacked strong leadership, since its most capable candidates abided by their promise not to organize a church without official permission. The question of baptism only later became a controversy. Initially in Molotschna the mode of baptism was no issue, since the Document of Secession simply stressed believers' baptism. However, by September 1860, Bekker and Bartel baptized each other by immersion, after restudying the mode. Not until September 1863 did immersion become obligatory.[2] In Chortitza, with the strong Baptist influence, it was observed from the beginning. The first conference organization took place on May 14-16, 1872, when delegates from three congregations (Kuban, Molotschna, and Chortitza) representing over 600 members met for inspirational and business sessions. The major item of business was the establishment of an itinerant ministry for evangelism and church extension.

Most problematic for the young movement was the divisive impact of a "charismatic" movement, already active prior to 1860, called *die Froehliche Richtung* (literally, joyous movement). Manifesting itself in both Molotschna and Chortitza, because of Wuest's widespread impact (although Wuest himself objected to its excess), its excessive emotionalism (clapping and dancing), false freedom ("sister kiss"), and spiritual despotism (calling themselves "apostles") caused a number to be banned. It led the entire church to be accused of such excesses by its

---

2 In Winnipeg in 1963, this practice was modified, so that forms other than immersion were to be recognized, but upon confession of faith.

critics in the "old" Mennonite church. Claassen was instrumental in June 1865 in preparing resolutions of reform which delineated the church's prohibition of such excesses.

Despite this setback, the movement grew. In Molotschna, although about 465 members had been accepted into the church from 1860 to 1872, the initial years of harassment saw a more rapid growth than later, and only approximately 200 were members in 1872 because of a heavy migration to new settlements. Also a small group (about twenty) withdrew in 1872 because of the charismatic movement, refusing to accept the June reforms. But interest in missions revived, and by 1883 a huge church edifice was built in Rueckenau. Chortitza saw rapid growth from the outset; but Kuban, the new colony under Mennonite Brethren auspices, grew slowly. Several Mennonite Brethren families settled in the new colonies of Friedensfeld in 1867, Zagradowka in 1872, and on the Don River (they later became Baptists). Some 18,000 Mennonites migrated from Russia to United States (10,000) and Canada (8,000) between 1874 and 1880, because of the 1870 Imperial Decree which introduced universal military training (despite a clause allowing alternative service). Of these, about 400 (roughly one-third of Russian Mennonite Brethren) were Mennonite Brethren (Lohrenz, 1950, 42). By its twenty-fifth anniversary on January 6, 1885, its church statistics included the following: six main congregations, seventeen affiliated groups, seven houses for worship, four ordained elders, thirty-five other ministers, total membership of 1,800, with another 1,200 in America. General Conference historian Cornelius Krahn assesses the Mennonite Brethren contribution to Russian Mennonitism generally as follows: "What it gave the Russian Mennonites was a rebirth of personal piety, a living piety in which the individual believer receives assurance of the forgiveness of sins, and orders his life definitely according to the teachings of Christ, particularly the Sermon on the Mount" (Krahn, 1935, 173-74). This perceived ideal, the return to Menno and the New Testament, was indeed realized.

2. The Sectarian Stance of the First Generation

An analysis of the sectarian nature of the first generation of Mennonite Brethren may best be undertaken by ferreting out its theological distinctives and then comparing it sociologically with the first generation of Anabaptists in the sixteenth century.

Its Theological Distinctives

The first Mennonite Brethren confession of faith subscribed to by the whole Conference was adopted in 1902, some years after the passing of the first generation. In the interim, however, several documents were prepared as guidelines. The Molotschna Document of Secession included the following emphases to indicate its position over against the church from which it seceded. Yet it was not intended to be a complete confession of faith. The following are summary statements from the Document of Secession:

(1) Baptism was to be administered on genuine, living faith; not on a memorized faith.

(2) The Lord's Supper is a fellowship for believers, not a fellowship of believers and unbelievers.

(3) The practice of footwashing was to be observed.

(4) Ministers (preachers) are appointed by God alone or through the instrumentality of true believers.

(5) Carnal and unrepentant Christians must be banned from the fellowship of believers (Toews, 1975, 34-35).

Significant is the last article of the document, which states, "In all other articles of our confession, we are in full agreement with Menno Simons."

Perhaps most representative of the Mennonite Brethren stance through its more than a century of history are the distinctives identified by historian J. A. Toews, a summary of which follows:

(1) practical biblicism, turning to the Scriptures, not to construct systems of theology, but to find solutions to spiritual problems;

(2) experiential faith, the Christian life beginning with a radical inward renewal effected by a personal faith in Christ as Saviour and Lord;

(3) personal witnessing, the responsibility of every member, rather than a select group;

(4) Christian discipleship, the essence of new life, affecting ethical behaviour (refraining from drinking, smoking, dancing) and exhibited in non-resistance (pacifism);

(5) brotherhood emphasis, avoiding over-emphasis on the autonomy of the local church, yet preserving the fellowship of equals;

(6) evangelism and missions, an integral part of the church, becomes the responsibility of every member, including ministries of relief and welfare;

(7) Christ-centred eschatology, believing in a personal return of Christ, the spiritual kingdom having begun with the first coming (Toews, 1975, 368-74).

Its Sociological Interpretation

Viewed sociologically, there is a decided continuity with the first generation of Anabaptists, as the following similar outline for the analysis indicates:

The basis for dissent.   The Mennonite Brethren secession was, as well, a self-conscious movement of dissent *sui generis*. In a recent study of Mennonite Brethren origins, C. J. Dyck finds five parallels between 1525 (and 1536) and 1860: the issue of morality, church and state relationships, persecution, aberrations, and the sense of mission (Dyck, 1975). It might be argued that, if conditions in the state church were such that the Anabaptist dissent of the sixteenth century were warranted, then, by the same token, similar conditions in the larger Mennonite body being such in 1860 also necessitated a movement of dissent.

The perceived ideal.   Even as the movement in the sixteenth century was restitutionist in its attempt to recover the primitive church model, so the perceived ideal of the founders in 1860 was to return to the New Testament via the path of Menno. Four references are made to Menno in the Document of Secession which concludes with a statement of its being in accord with Menno.

The separation necessitated.   The Mennonite Church in Russia had become another *corpus Christianum* in which the church was coextensive with society and membership was virtually acquired by birth with all social, economic, or religious privileges enjoyed by virtue of membership of the group. C. J. Dyck admits, "This does not mean that a 'brotherhood type of church' *could* not have survived in the Russian context, but only that it *did* not" (Dyck, 1975, 5). The Brethren concluded, "Therefore, we herewith completely dissociate ourselves from these decadent churches . . ." (Toews, 1975, 34).

The voluntary aspect.   While the new secession was wholly voluntary, the entrance requirement, as with the sixteenth-century movement, was a conversion experience and, somewhat later, once Menno's own position had been restudied, baptism by immersion (Bekker, 1973, 70-72). The growth of such a voluntary movement is possibly the best argument for the validity of such voluntarism.

The role of charisma.   As Grebel gave leadership to the Swiss Brethren and Menno to the Dutch Anabaptists, so Eduard Wuest, although a Lutheran pietist who never became part of the movement (he died in 1859), helped precipitate the movement through his evangelistic preaching and promotion of conventicles of "brethren." Eminent historian P. M. Friesen regarded Menno as the first reformer and Wuest as the second (Friesen, 1911, 174). No doubt, Johann Claassen, although disqualified from holding office, was the unofficial leader of the early movement in his negotiations for freedom and recognition with both state and church.

Its democratic structure. The Mennonite Brethren movement was thoroughly egalitarian in which the laity participated in both worship and leadership. The focus on the individual and a personal relation to God was a direct result of Wuest's pietistic emphasis. Opposing the hierarchical control and failure of the ministers of the old church, the new movement also withstood despotism from within, as in the *Froehliche Richtung*. Yet it believed in electing and ordaining its own leaders, as the Document of Secession indicates.

Socio-economic status and relative deprivation. Evidence does not support socio-economic deprivation to account for the origin of the movement (Toews, 1975, 51-52). Historian C. J. Dyck agrees, "Economic factors were present but to see these as primary is to commit the same error present in contemporary Marxist historiography about Anabaptism" (Dyck, 1975, 8). Both landowning and influential, wealthy members of the community, as well as the landless and deprived, joined the new movement.

3. The Developments of the Second Generation and Beyond (1885-1925)

With the large-scale migration of Russian Mennonites to the United States and Canada in the 1870s, the story of the Mennonite Brethren after the first generation unfolds in two different locales, North America and Russia.

Developments in North America

Mennonite Brethren first came to Canada from the United States, where they had initially settled in Kansas, Nebraska, Minnesota, and South Dakota—some 200 families coming between 1874 and 1880, mainly from Molotschna and Kuban, but also a few from Chortitza and the Volga and Don River colonies (Lohrenz, 1950, 64). Ebenfeld, Kansas, claims the distinction of the first Mennonite Brethren congregation in North America, organized in 1874. It was in the Ebenezer church at Buhler, Kansas, that Elder Abraham Schellenberg ministered from 1879 onwards and extended his influence as Conference moderator and promoted missions, publication, and education. The Hillsboro congregation, organized in 1881, was to become one of the largest Mennonite Brethren churches with Conference headquarters located there—the foreign missions office there since its inception in 1885, Tabor College established in 1908, and the publishing house between 1909 and 1913. Henderson, Nebraska, hosted the first Conference of Mennonite Brethren churches in America in 1879. It was

Mountain Lake, Minnesota, from which Elder Heinrich Voth evangelized among the conservative Mennonites of Canada. South Dakota was the stronghold of the Krimmer Mennonite Brethren churches. From 1890 onwards, the United States Mennonite Brethren extended their frontiers northwards to North Dakota and Montana; westwards to Colorado, California, Oregon, and Washington (in 1937); and southwards to Oklahoma and Texas. To cooperate in missions, publication, and education, and to retain unity in theology and ethics, a Conference was organized, meeting annually from 1879 to 1909, and triennially thereafter. Eventually four district conferences emerged: Southern (Kansas, Oklahoma, Colorado, and Texas); Central (North and South Dakotas, Minnesota, Nebraska, Michigan, and Montana); Pacific (California, Oregon, and Washington); and Northern (later named Canadian).

To establish contacts for evangelism, Heinrich Voth (Minnesota) and David Dyck (Kansas) in 1884 first visited the conservative Mennonites in Manitoba, Canada, some 8,000 having immigrated in 1874-1880. Voth continued his ministry, establishing the first Mennonite Brethren church in Burwalde (later moved to Winkler), Manitoba, in 1888. From here the witness was extended to Plum Coulee in 1897 and Kronsgart in 1898, and Winnipeg in 1907. Workers were sent to Saskatchewan, where congregations were established in the Rosthern area in the north between 1901 and 1918 and the Herbert area in the south between 1904 and 1914. By 1924, fifty years after its beginning in North America, there was a total membership of 8,412 with 86 churches and 110 ordained ministers; of these, 1,763 were Canadian with 20 churches and 31 ministers (Lohrenz, 1950, 94). These *Kanadier* (that is, Canadians, to distinguish themselves from the *Russlaender* or Russian immigrants of a later time), who were partly assimilated into the North American culture, were soon to interact with the *Russlaender*. Little wonder there initially was a cultural gap.

Developments in Russia

The three decades prior to World War I have been referred to as the "Golden Age" of Mennonites in Russia in general, and of Mennonite Brethren in particular (Toews, 1975, 86). No longer persecuted and ostracized, Mennonite Brethren became actively involved, often in positions of leadership, in the socio-economic and cultural life of the larger Mennonite community. In 1902 a new Confession of Faith indicates their theological self-consciousness. New cooperative efforts with the Mennonite Church mark this period with regards to education, health and welfare, and alternative service (in lieu of military service). Publication received attention and involvement in foreign missions, its missionaries being sent under the American Baptist organization. Open communion (regardless of church affiliation) was increasingly practised, marriage was no longer strictly endogamous, and inter-church Faith Conferences were conducted. In 1905, a new fellowship advocating open communion formed the Allianz (Alliance) Church. Those of this group who emigrated to Canada in the 1920s were in time assimilated by the Canadian Mennonite Brethren Church.

This era of progress and prosperity ended abruptly with World War I and the Bolshevik Revolution. The war tested the Mennonite doctrine of non-resistance. Concession was granted by the church and agreement was effected with the government allowing the non-combatant medical corps (a civilian organization cooperating with the Red Cross) as a form of alternative military service for all able-bodied men up to the age of forty-five. Six thousand men served the corps with equal numbers in the forestry service. Once the revolution broke out, Mennonites reaffirmed their non-resistance stance, yet allowed it to be interpreted privately. As a result, a radical minority took up arms in the Self-Defense Corps (*Selbstschutz*). Under the roving Makhno, during the years of anarchy from 1918 to 1920, hundreds were killed (Ehrt, 1932, 113, 116). Unsanitary conditions produced by armed forces and robber bands resulted in the spread of typhus, cholera, syphilis, and malaria. Chortitza was especially hard hit, the population declining from 18,000 in 1917 to 13,000 in 1920 (Toews, 1967, 35-42). Molotschna and Zagradowka suffered similarly. Mennonite relief agencies from Europe and America responded generously to an appeal for help. The result was the inter-Mennonite relief agency, Mennonite Central Committee. Shortly after, in 1922, the Canadian Mennonite Board of Colonization was formed, an inter-Mennonite agency to negotiate and expedite immigration (Epp, 1962).

Just prior to the extensive emigration from Russia to Canada from 1923 to 1927, in which some 18,000 Mennonites (of various denominations) trekked to Canada, a spiritual renewal, accompanied by cooperative evangelism, swept through the Russian Mennonite villages. Historian J. A. Toews comments rather poignantly:

The immigrants who came to the new world had few earthly possessions, but they brought with them an enriched Christian experience and a new spiritual concern born in the harsh school of human suffering and in the warm atmosphere of religious revival. The Mennonite Brethren from this background who came to Canada had a decisive influence on the future development of their denomination in this country (Toews, 1975, 115).

4. An Assessment of Change and Continuity After Two Generations

In his popular study, *The Social Sources of Denominationalism*, H. Richard Niebuhr maintains, "By its very nature the sectarian type of organization is valid for only one generation" (Niebuhr, 1972, 19). Either Niebuhr's hypothesis is wrong or the Mennonite Brethren were not sectarian when they immigrated into Canada in large numbers in the mid-1920s. Change had indeed taken place since their beginnings some sixty-five years earlier, but the change was not so radical nor the secularization process so complete that Mennonite Brethren did not bear the major marks of their earlier sectarian stance. The dominant theme of their sectarian dissent after two generations is that of continuity rather than change.

The Mennonite immigrants from Russia in the mid-1920s came as a "purged" sect with all the traces of sectarian vitality which mark the first generation. It is not surprising, then, that there were some cultural differences between these *Russlaender* and the *Kanadier* brethren, who, also partly secularized through their fifty-year pilgrimage on the American and Canadian frontier, numbered only one-third the immigrant influx of Mennonite Brethren. No doubt, the immigrant influence would facilitate the perpetuation of the less prominent sectarian qualities of the *Kanadier*. Combining the experiences of the *Russlaender* and the *Kanadier*, one can then isolate the following components of continuity to explain the survival of sectarianism among Canadian Mennonite Brethren in the mid-1920s.

Redefinition of sectarian boundaries.   Once again sectarian boundaries were sharply delineated. The abrogation of the privilege of military exemption in 1870 was a major factor in the emigration of Russian Mennonites to America. Among these who emigrated were the forefathers of the *Kanadier*. The Bolshevik Revolution of 1917 and its aftermath of religious oppression again became a primary reason for emigration. Thus, the promise of religious freedom and the firm assurance of exemption from military service reinforced that stance of religious dissent which had been the very *raison d'être* of the sectarian group.

The stubborn clinging to non-resistance—more positively viewed, the ethic of love—was rooted in a system of meaning in which the New Testament was the final court of appeal and the ethic of Jesus the model. So also the calamities of the immigrants' last decade in Russia could be legitimated by a theodicy of the suffering church, not simply reliving the 1860s or the 1530s, but the experiences of the first-century church. Their education, vocations, and experiences in Russia not being readily transferable to their new environment, the Mennonite Brethren were highly motivated within the guidelines and normative frameworks which legitimated the utmost utility of their new-found freedoms and opportunities. The "Protestant ethic" had found a new market place in this immigrant group (Weber, 1958, chapter 5).

Cohesiveness of families and the ethnic group.   The solidarity found in both immigrant families and ethnic groups accounts for much of the continuity of sectarianism. Initially settling primarily on farms and homesteads, the immigrant family worked closely together to sustain their livelihood, and the community of immigrants worshipped together to provide for both their religious and social needs. In addition, the ethnic nature of the group, the German language having been retained by both the *Russlaender* as well as the *Kanadier* Mennonite Brethren, helped not only to unify the two groups but also to isolate them from their predominantly Anglo-Saxon environment.

Consolidating identities.   Fragile identities were strengthened and new identities consolidated through conversion and charisma. The *Kanadier* Mennonite Brethren were either immigrants from the American frontier (or descendants of the same) or the result of the evangelistic work among the conservative Mennonites. The spiritual revival among Mennonites in Russia, in which the Mennonite Brethren played a leading role, resulted in many conversions and increased membership. Such leaders as J. G. Wiens and A. H. Unruh in the Bible school movement, Adolf A. Reimer and Jacob J. Dyck in evangelism and missions, and C. F. Klassen and B. B. Janz in relief and emigration were greatly instrumental in consolidating the Russian Mennonite Brethren during times of greatest change just prior to their exodus.

Socialization through group worship and formal instruction.   Wherever a nucleus of Mennonite Brethren families moved, new congregations emerged. By 1924, the *Kanadier* had established twenty churches in Manitoba and Saskatchewan, and the incoming *Russlaender* greatly augmented the strength of these churches and organized new ones. Coming from some thirty-five to forty congregations in Russia, the new immigrants were regular in worship and Sunday school, the latter being an innovation brought into the Russian Mennonite Brethren by August Liebig, the German Baptist (Toews, 1975, 217). In addition to the weekly worship and education, there were Bible schools, both in Canada and Russia. Continuity of the sectarian vitality was facilitated through such socialization programs.

Integration through Conference structures.   Almost from the outset, conference sessions, in which delegates from all churches participated, united the Mennonite Brethren in action. In North America, sessions were held annually from 1879 to 1909, and triennially thereafter, to conduct such activities as missions, relief, publication, and higher education (Lohrenz, 1950, 71-77). Until 1954, the Canadians were organized as the Northern District, thereafter becoming the Canadian

Area Conference with equal status to the United States Area. In Russia conferences had been conducted since 1872. Especially meaningful were the inter-church Bible conferences begun in 1875. So also was the all-Mennonite conference conducted in 1910 to unify Mennonites in giving them a united voice before the government. Thus, Mennonite Brethren from Russia were accustomed to both denominational and inter-Mennonite conferences. They were prepared for integration with their fellow sectarians in conference structures on the new Canadian frontier.

Such, then, was the Canadian Mennonite Brethren Church in the mid-1920s, somewhat changed from its original sectarian position, but largely retaining its vitality. The stage is set, therefore, to examine more closely the extent to which these five components of continuity provide for sectarian viability in the next fifty years, 1925-1975.

Part Three

SACRALIZATION OF IDENTITY

V

Delineating Boundaries

The next five chapters test a central hypothesis of this study, namely, that the synthetic process of sacralization contributes to the continuity of sectarianism. To analyse the sacralization process, these chapters isolate the following components of continuity: the *boundaries* delineated by cognitive and normative frameworks, the *cohesion* enhanced by family solidarity and ethnicity, the *identity* consolidated through conversion and charisma, the *socialization* facilitated through weekly worship and formal instruction, and the *integration* provided by structural networks and service agencies. To isolate these components does not exhaust the number of variables nor does it maintain that the factors consistently and exclusively synthesize the religious group. Such would be over-simplifying the complex processes at work. Each of the components to be analysed has its own inherent, countervailing forces. For example, the belief system of Mennonite Brethren, while overwhelmingly continuous, has also been subject to change. These chapters examine the degree to which the sacralization has occurred and test the hypothesis that these factors are predominantly sacralizing in their total effect. Moreover, since the level of analysis is that of a group, not an individual nor the whole of society, the generalizations are applicable to the denomination as a whole; yet they allow for exceptions which apply to individuals within the group. At the same time, one individual, through his or her repeated leadership role, editorial influence, exegetical sermon, or historical interpretation influences the group as a whole. The cumulative effect of such individuals will be gleaned from the annual conference year books, quarterly or bimonthly religious journals, and weekly or biweekly denominational periodicals. These become the major source of information to explain the reason for the empirical observations.

To explain the need for boundaries, one must first understand the sociological nature of a group (Park and Burgess, 1970, 116). A group becomes a group through its associations with individuals and disassociation from the rest of society. It becomes real and palpable through a

60

bond of relationships inclusive enough to warrant its definition and exclusive enough to separate it from society. Its identity is defined by the boundaries which separate it both from self-orientations or from the more heterogeneous social whole. The sharpening of boundaries between in-group and out-group sociations helps to consolidate the group's identity. In the case of a sect, the group also acts as a buffer between personal and social identity, providing a competitive advantage between the amorphousness of the larger social whole and the anomie of self-orientation. At the same time, such groups provide for an interdependence with personal and social identities. As Hans Mol indicates: "Groups *both* provide individuals with possibilities for self-fulfilment, *and* constrict individual autonomy for the sake of group cohesion. Groups *both* reinforce many of the goals and values of society, *and* weaken societal cohesion through concerted protests and conflicitng systems of meaning" (Mol, 1976, 167). The Mennonite Brethren Church will be seen as a group which not only successfully competes with personal and social identities, but also espouses the interdependence which all three identities require.

1. Analysing the System of Meaning

Theoretically, the ideology or belief system of a sectarian group can be explained in terms of the meaning it provides for the movement. There needs to be a central value or Archimedean point which anchors a movement and provides the leverage for its encounter with a hostile environment. Talcott Parsons has conveniently applied the Archimedean dictum, "Give me a place to stand and I will move the world," to the transcendental God and the concept of salvation in the Protestant ethic (Parsons, 1949, 549). Similarly for Mennonite Brethren, the sacralizing mechanism of objectification, that is, the tendency to sum up the variegated elements of mundane existence in a transcendental frame of reference, to use Hans Mol's explanation (Mol, 1976, 206-14), gives not only meaning and order to their religious separateness, but the continuing dynamic despite ongoing change and accommodation to the world.

Methodologically, the present chapter begins its analysis of such religious beliefs by examining recent data derived from empirical measures.[1] These data measure the current degree of orthodoxy,

---

1 The data are extracted from a Church Member Profile, constructed by Howard Kauffman and Leland Harder, based on a questionnaire of some 342 questions given to 3,591 church members in five Mennonite and Brethren in Christ denominations in the U.S. and Canada in 1972. Of these, some 300 questions apply to Canadian Mennonite Brethren given to a scientifically selected random sample of fifteen local congregations with a sample population of 359. For further information about how the survey was conducted, see Kauffman and Harder, *AFCL*, Appendix I, pp. 364-85.

evangelicalism, and Anabaptism of representative Canadian Mennonite Brethren. To interpret the apparent retention of belief and doctrine, a flashback through half a century of ecclesiastical records will be followed. It will be shown that such sacralization of its transcendental frame of reference provided continuity for the sectarian group beyond the third generation.

Empirical Measures of Belief

Three groups of variables of belief are selected from the Church Member Profile. These variables measure the degree of orthodoxy, fundamentalism, and Anabaptism of Canadian Mennonite Brethren. Since few other similar measures are available for purposes of comparison, the responses of the Canadian Mennonite Brethren are compared not only with the larger Mennonite Brethren sample of North America, but also with the North American sample of the (Old) Mennonite Church and the General Conference Mennonite Church, the two largest Mennonite denominations. Only a few crude comparisons with other than Mennonite denominations can be attempted because of the lack of adequate data from other groups.

Orthodoxy. Table v-1 indicates the percentage of respondents choosing the most orthodox response, that is, those beliefs which have represented the central tenets of the Christian faith throughout its history. The first four columns of the table include the responses for six similar items of belief taken from the Glock and Stark study (Glock and Stark, 1969, 3-18). Although the time and circumstances of the survey of Glock and Stark differ from the Church Member Profile, the results constitute an interesting comparison. Significant in the results are the high responses for Mennonite Brethren, very nearly as orthodox as Southern Baptists. If one were to include the Mennonite Brethren who had doubts about God's existence, the total would be as high as Southern Baptists on that variable. The rating for Canadian Mennonite Brethren, given to the first decimal place, is slightly higher than for the North American Mennonite Brethren. The General Conference Mennonites represents that group from which the Mennonite Brethren seceded in 1860. In two items, belief in God and belief in Jesus, they are exceeded by Southern Baptists; in two, belief in miracles and in Christ's return, they significantly exceed the Baptists; and in two, belief in Satan and in life after death, they slightly exceed. In each response they significantly exceed the General Conference Mennonites, who themselves have high responses compared to other Christian groups.

Fundamentalism. More indicative of sectarianism than the belief in general orthodoxy is the group of variables suggesting fundamentalism. Table v-2 shows the percentage of respondents who gave the most conservative response possible with reference to five doctrines included in the creed of the World Christian Fundamentals Association (1919). Mennonite Brethren rank high in this fundamentalist scale, exceeding considerably the General Conference Mennonites, which again are significantly higher than Lutheran[2] or United Church of Christ.[3] Again, except for the question on creation, Canadian Mennonite Brethren are more conservative than the North American.

Table v-1

Measures of Orthodoxy

Belief	Percentage Response							
	RC[a] (n=545)	Prot. (n=2326)	CC (n=151)	SB (n=79)	MC (n=1202)	GC (n=614)	NAMB (n=712)	CMB (n=359)
God (really exists, no doubts about it)	81	71	41	99	89	86	92	93.5
Jesus (both human and divine, no doubt)	86	69	40	99	91	85	95	96.1
Miracles (supernatural, actually happened)	74	57	28	92	92	81	95	96.9
Christ's return (will actually return to earth)	47	44	13	94	91	83	97	98.3
Satan (personal devil, active in world today)	75	65	36	97	95	86	97	98.6
Life after death (definitely)	75	65	36	97	93	87	97	98.0
Resurrection (physical, historical fact)	-	-	-	-	92	86	96	97.7

Source: Church Member Profile, 1972; Glock and Stark, 1966.

a
  RC   = Roman Catholics
  Prot. = Protestants
  CC   = Congregational Church (now United Church of Christ)
  SB   = Southern Baptists
  MC   = (Old) Mennonite Church
  GC   = General Conference Mennonite Church
  NAMB = North American Mennonite Brethren (including U.S. and Canada)
  CMB   = Canadian Mennonite Brethren

2 In M. Strommen's fundamentalism-liberalism scale, Lutherans had the following percentage of most orthodox responses for similar questions: Bible, 24; Virgin birth, 40; Creation, 27; and Eternal punishment, 37. See M. Strommen et al., A Study of Generations (Minneapolis: Augsburg Press, 1972), pp. 378-81.

3 The United Church of Christ response is based on questions which are more general (e.g., "the Bible is the Word of God" and "hell is a just punishment for sinners"). The percentage response to three such questions was as follows: Bible, 67; Virgin birth, 58; Eternal punishment, 17. See T. Campbell and F. Fukuyama, The Fragmented Layman (Philadelphia: Pilgrim Press, 1970), p. 234.

Table v-2
Measures of Fundamentalism

Belief	Percentage Response			
	MC (n=1202)	GC (n=614)	NAMB (n=712)	CMB (n=359)
Bible (divinely inspired and infallible Word)	84	71	93	96.6
Virgin birth (Jesus was born of a virgin)	89	80	96	98.3
Creation (God created all in six days)	53	42	54	52.7
Flood (Noahic flood was universal)	84	71	90	93.0
Eternal punishment (for all who have not accepted Christ)	77	60	85	86.3

Source: Church Member Profile, 1972.

Anabaptism.   Indicators of Anabaptism are taken from Kauffman and Harder's scale constructed on the basis of twenty-two norms identified in H. S. Bender's famous "Anabaptist Vision." Table v-3 indicates the percentage of respondents agreeing or strongly agreeing with the given statements which were selected on the basis of an item analysis test. Mennonite Brethren are compared with the joint response of five Mennonite and Brethen in Christ groups (including Mennonite Brethren). Especially in non-resistance and separation of church and state, they lag behind other Anabaptists. In church discipline, they lead significantly. Ahead in doctrines relating to the believers' church notion, they lag in the practical expression of their Anabaptist distinctives. Canadian Mennonite Brethren are more Anabaptist than their American counterparts, especially in church discipline, the oath, and non-resistance.

These measures of Mennonite Brethren beliefs constitute a portrait not so much of the Mennonite Brethren ideal, or even of their Confession of Faith, as of the real; not what they prescribe, as much as what they in fact believe. They rank among the most orthodox of Christian groups, with the exception of belief in a six-day, twenty-four-hour-day creation; they rank high in fundamentalism; and compare favourably with other Mennonites on Anabaptism, although lagging in the practical expression of the same. After 115 years as a separate denomination, Mennonite Brethren have retained the most fundamental Christian beliefs as well as their own distinctives. How then does one account for such retention of beliefs?

Table v-3

Measures of Anabaptism

Belief	Percentage Agreeing or Strongly Agreeing		
	Anabaptists (n=3591)	NAMB (n=712)	CMBC (n=359)
Discipleship (following Jesus' life; ministry taking priority over security)	52	52	57.5
Suffering (obedience to Lordship of Christ results in criticism, persecution)	72	76	79.1
Baptism (reject paedo-baptism)	82	86	88.4
Church discipline (needed to restore, or in exceptions exclude, faltering members)	60	75	87.0
Oath (Christian not to swear oath as demanded by civil government)	66	64	79.8
Non-resistance (not to take part in war or war-promoting activities)	73	54	65.9
Church and state (certain offices in government not for Christians)	74	63	70.0
Litigation (disagree that lawsuits are permissible for Christians if claims legitimate)	36	42	37.8

Source: Church Member Profile, 1972.

Explaining the Continuity of Belief

While most theologians disagree over what one ought to believe, many would surely agree that religious belief itself is central to keeping a religious movement alive.

The following analysis of continuity of belief among Canadian Mennonite Brethren focuses as much on the process of *how* the belief concern is expressed and action is precipitated as on the actual beliefs. Rather than analysing the doctrinal formulations, as a theological enterprise might, this study is more concerned with the approach to the articulation of beliefs and seeks to discover why Mennonite Brethren so successfully perpetuated their ideology. Four separate, although not unrelated, answers are attempted.

Restorationist thinking.   Labelled by Franklin Littell as "primitivism" or "restitutionism" (Littell, 1972, 46-50), the stance of the Mennonite Brethren in their return to the sixteenth century and, more importantly, to the first century is here referred to as restorationist thinking. From the very beginning, Mennonite Brethren leaders and spokesmen have had a profound consciousness of their moorings in the past, and, as a consequence, their concern has been more with restoring something old than introducing something new. This attitude has lent permanency to their movement. The following instances are illustrations of such restorationist thinking.

The seceding brethren in 1860 explicitly prefaced and concluded the doctrinal statement within the secession document with a reminder that they were in "full agreement with Menno" (Bekker, 1973, 44, 46). In the official confession of faith, adopted by the General Conference in 1902, the authors express their attempt to recover the biblical concept of the church "as it was in the beginning—in the apostolic church." In tracing the heritage of the Mennonite Brethren Church through several centuries of dissenters, P. M. Friesen, an early Mennonite Brethren historian, states, "Menno Simons, boldly and humbly recovering that 'which was from the beginning,' has built an amazingly simple and comfortable house for us, in which we live 'on the foundation of the apostles and prophets, of which Jesus Christ is the cornerstone'" (Friesen, 1911, 40-41). The model for belief was obviously first-century Christianity.

Similar restorationist thinking has characterized the Mennonite Brethren in the last half century. In 1926 the *Mennonitische Rundschau* published the address of Russian Mennonite statesman, Benjamin Unruh, on the subject of non-resistance, to an all-Mennonite conference at Halbstadt, Russia, in 1917. This document, read in Canadian Mennonite homes in the mid-1920s, was a similar reminder of restorationist thinking. Unruh recognized the reformers as "restoring apostolic Christianity" (Unruh, 1926, 12). In 1949 a similar concern was expressed by a young theologian, John A. Toews (who in 1975 published the Mennonite Brethren history). In a Canadian Mennonite Brethren official bimonthly youth magazine, he stated, again with reference to non-resistance, that it is not a "Mennonite Doctrine," but a teaching of the Scriptures. "It is not a doctrine which originated with Menno Simons. . . . The roots of this teaching are found in the Gospel of Christ" (Toews, 1949, 13).

A new generation of theologians and spokesmen articulated similar views. Abram Dueck, instructor in historical theology at Mennonite Brethren Bible College, sees the Mennonite Brethren Church as "the result of the application of the restitution method" (Dueck, 1972, 43). Most recently, a young Mennonite Brethren theologian depicts the Anabaptists as "supremely a movement for the recovery of Jesus and His kingdom as the center of faith and church," and challenges them to "flesh out the New Testament heritage" from the present decadent

Mennonite Brethren reality (Toews, 1976, 2). These voices of Mennonite statesmen, theologians, and historians have inspired Mennonite Brethren through the past half century to continue to look back upon Menno and the first-century church for its pattern.

Biblicist orientation. More precisely, it was through a biblicist orientation that the New Testament vision was recaptured. Such biblicism is not necessarily to be understood in terms of a mechanistic view of inspiration or a hyper-literal interpretation of the Bible; rather the Bible was taken seriously and used extensively in defining a theological and ethical position.

Among the numerous indications of such biblicism, the practice of informal Bible studies (*Bibelstunden*), which gave rise to the movement itself, has been most continuous. These Bible studies were conducted weekly and became an integral part of the life of the church. Discussion of the text and prayer meetings were incorporated into these studies. The 1970 statistical report indicated that 94 of the 124 Canadian Mennonite Brethren churches observed a Wednesday night program, in addition to women's societies and boys' and girls' clubs (*Canadian Conference Year Book*, hereafter *YB*, 1970, 132). And the 1975 record shows that there were a total of 358 prayer/Bible study groups in the 122 reporting churches, an increase from 275 in the previous year (*YB*, 1975, 112). Apparently, Bible studies continue to be a vital part of church life among Canadian Mennonite Brethren.

Similarly, Bible conferences (*Bibelbesprechungen*), frequently a joint effort of several churches, provided for annual intensive studies of longer passages of Scripture or expositions of a book of the Bible. While the *Bibelbesprechung* has largely been abandoned, the Elmwood Mennonite Brethren Church in Winnipeg has retained this conference as an annual inter-Mennonite event for the post-Christmas holiday season. It conducted its forty-fifth conference in 1975. Reflecting on the legacy of the Elmwood Bible Conference, David D. Duerksen, English teacher and frequent contributor to periodicals, writes from the "divide of generations" and admonishes the younger generation to "retain the sincere piety and the unsophisticated love and reverence for the Bible as the inspired Word of God so evident in our elders" (Duerksen, 1968, 7, 18-19).

A further institutionalized form of this biblicism is the Bible school movement. Inheriting its models both from Russia and United States, the movement has continuously influenced the life of the church from the establishment of the first Bible school in Herbert in 1915 to the present. In 1975 there were 410 Mennonite Brethren students registered in post-high-school Bible studies in three Mennonite Brethren Bible schools.

Most persistent, however, in the continued influence upon the belief structure is the biblical preaching within the Mennonite Brethren churches. Besides the weekly preaching service, which the central place of the pulpit in Mennonite Brethren church architecture symbolizes, the itinerant ministry of J. W. Reimer (1860-1948), A. H. Unruh (1878-1961), and David Ewert (1922-) was known for its exegetical preaching.

The immediate impact of such biblicism is apparent in the increased lay Bible reading. Early Mennonite Brethren were reportedly recognized by the bulging coat pocket which contained a well-worn Bible (Wiebe, 1960). Such "radical reading" of the Bible had both its positive and negative effects. Daily reading and weekly study of the Bible resulted in informal discussion of its truths; memorization allowed for ready application personally or more forceful "witness" encounters using the exact Scripture quotation. In addition, however, it encouraged subjective understanding, literal interpretation, and arbitrary proof-texting (Ewert, 1960, 3-6). Whatever the beliefs such biblicism fostered, it strengthened the cognitive framework and permitted sharper delineation of group identities. Drawing attention to the "swing back to strengthening the original biblical theological and believers' community stakes," Driedger observes, "A sacred canopy, then as now, is the only means of survival in the changing urban laboratory of economic and political unrest" (Driedger, 1980, 133, 135).

Voluntarism. A third factor accounting for the persistence of religious belief is the vitality and renewal that comes through the voluntary association with a believers' church. Both the initial commitment and repeated deliberate, individual affirmations of the beliefs reinforced the boundaries of the religious group. This voluntarism has explicitly sociological dimensions: experiential faith is begun through a conversion experience; voluntary association is publicly witnessed through believers' baptism; continued membership requires active participation; and lapse of vitality or infidelity necessitates the exercise of discipline, including excommunication, by the group.

Prerequisite to the voluntarism associated with Mennonite Brethren church membership is repentance and regeneration, in keeping with the sixteenth-century Anabaptists and the nineteenth-century Mennonite Brethren emphasis. Symbolic of regeneration (referring to the spiritual transformation at the time of conversion) and proof of the voluntary commitment to the group is believers' baptism, given only after a test of eligibility. Such tests, however, were an examination not so much of one's knowledge of beliefs (as in a test of a catechism) as of the genuineness of the conversion experience and of a continuing Christian life. Most emphatic, therefore, for this Anabaptist denomination is the rejection of infant baptism. This has continued to be the official position not only of the Canadian Conference according to its Confession of Faith, but also for the inter-Mennonite community. Regarding the admission into church membership of those baptized by a mode other than immersion, there has been increased openness of the Canadian Mennonite Brethren Church, and a limited form of membership was approved by the General Conference decision of 1963 (*General Conference Year Book*, hereafter *GCYB*, 1963, 38). For full membership privileges, however, such as in ordination, immersion continues to be required.

Voluntarism does not suggest that church membership is optional, for with the decision to be baptized one also decides to join the local church. Only believers, therefore, who are baptized upon confession of faith can be members, and generally baptism is refused if church membership does not follow forthwith. This underscores the importance of the Christian community affirming the Christian experience, even as Berger and Luckmann have observed.

To have a conversion experience is nothing much. The real thing is to be able to keep on taking it seriously; to retain a sense of plausibility. *This* is where the religious community comes in. It provides the indispensable plausibility structure for the new reality. In other words, Saul may have become Paul in the aloneness of religious ecstasy, but he could *remain* Paul only in the context of the Christian community that recognized him as such and confirmed the "new being" in which he now located this identity (Berger and Luckmann, 1967, 158).

Mennonite Brethren, however, insist upon church membership, not merely for sociological reasons, but because of their biblical understanding of the church as a body of believers who have consciously entered into that fellowship and continue actively to participate.

Separatism. A fourth approach to a world view which has helped to perpetuate a tightly knit belief system is that of separatism, that is, a perceived disparity between the church and the world. The resulting dissent was uniquely part of the Anabaptist vision of reality, which George H. Williams has well recognized.

The whole Western world, not only the direct descendents of the Continental Anabaptists, not alone even the larger Protestant community, but all who cherish Western institutions and freedoms must acknowledge their indebtedness to the valor and the vision of the Anabaptists who glimpsed afresh the disparities between the church and the world, even when the latter construed itself as Christian (Williams and Mergal, 1957, 25).

The Mennonite Brethren had seceded from the larger Mennonite body in 1860 in order to separate genuine believers from nominal or non-believers, especially for purposes of intimate Christian fellowship, such as in the Lord's Supper. That Mennonite Brethren in Canada continued this separatist stance is apparent at the very first Canadian Conference held in Herbert, Saskatchewan, June 27 and 28, 1910. At this occasion, one of the pioneer ministers, Rev. Jacob Loepp of Dalmeny, preached on separation from the world (*YB*, 1910, 4). Subsequent decades of Canadian Mennonite Brethren history retained this motif.

Frequently the separatist emphasis was achieved by explicating the evils of society or the seriousness of the present era. The decade following World War II concentrated on another phase of separatism: worldliness. The emphasis was especially directed at youth and focused particularly on entertainments of the world. Rarely was materialism or economic self-sufficiency or failure to speak to issues of social injustice called into question. The youth magazine, *Das Konferenz-Jugendblatt*, was a helpful vehicle for such socialization. A sermon by A. H. Unruh, based on Romans 12:1, defined the world and worldliness, Satan having devised means for all types of people. After illustrating a number of such means—intimate friendships with non-believers, entertainments, business ventures, learning pursuits, and materialism—Unruh suggests two factors which can provide guidance for the believer: a conversion experience and a worthy calling (Unruh, 1951, 3-8). Typically, the last feature article of the last issue of the *Konferenz-Jugendblatt* was entitled, "Love not the World" (Voth, 1957, 29-30).

A younger generation of theologians likewise retained this theme in more academic journals. Biblical theologian David Ewert provided a New Testament word study on "The World" (Ewert, 1954, 6-9), and Anabaptist historian J. A. Toews lamented the neglect in the emphasis of a distinctive doctrine of the church and suggested as one of the remedies a greater understanding of separatism (Toews, 1953, 21-23). Toews provided a theological and historical framework for the conflicting issues of church and state (Toews, 1957, 2-5). F. C. Peters similarly addressed himself to the students and academic world in his sermon on "Living in the World as Strangers" (Peters, 1962, 1-3).

The dilemma of the separated church in an evil world has occupied Mennonite Brethren writers and theologians to the present time. Editor Harold Jantz has repeatedly depicted the church over against an unbelieving society. Writing in preparation for a Canadian Conference convened in 1966 in an arena in St. Catharines, Ontario, he stated:

The theme of the convention, "Separated unto God for Effective Witnessing," will strike a unique tone in the setting in which it will be expounded. It is precisely in the many entanglements that the arena symbolizes that we as Christians are seeking to understand the meaning of separation unto God. . . . The question will be on my mind whether we can enter into dozens of different vocations and professions and still practice the separated life which will give us a united church witness. . . . What does "separation unto God" have to do with political parties, labour movements, community associations and clubs, partnerships with non-believers, our friendships with non-believers, or our identification with the great power structures of our time be they financial, social, governmental or intellectual? (Jantz, 1966, 3).

Separatism, by now, had seemingly gained new aggressive overtures, not so much withdrawal from the world as confrontation with the world. The subsequent conference messages on separation bear out this emphasis (*YB*, 1966, 7-14). At the North American General Conference, held in Vancouver in 1969, moderator F. C. Peters addressed the assembly under the theme, "Quo Vadis: Mennonite Brethren Church?" In outlining the general purpose of the church, Peters accented the need to sustain the world, rebuke the world, and redeem the world (*GCYB*, 1969, 123-24). This was not an introversionist stance, but an aggressive, conversionist approach.

Thus, in 1975 the Canadian Mennonite Brethren Church was still firmly committed to its strongly orthodox, decidedly evangelical, and distinctly Anabaptist stance despite the many environmental and attitudinal changes. It has successfully delineated cognitive boundaries through its persistently restorationist thinking, its stubbornly biblicist orientation, its voluntary believers' church understanding, and its unchanging separatist stance.

2. Analysing the System of Ethics

With such insistence upon a believers' church and separatist stance, Anabaptists actually expect that being a Christian ought to make a difference in the ethical life of the church member, differences that are visible enough to be empirically measurable. Mennonite Brethren in particular have been known for their prescriptions and proscriptions. Does a further analysis of how Mennonite Brethren make ethical decisions indicate a legalistic moralism? Does the high priority for ethics on a personal level carry over to social ethics, or are Mennonite Brethren to be grouped with those evangelicals who have been principally concerned with individualistic salvation rather than (or even at the expense of) being concerned with social injustices? The remainder of the chapter will speak to these questions.

Empirical Measures of Ethics

The following data on moral issues and social ethics are taken from the Church Member Profile. Such moral issues are selected on which Mennonite Brethren have taken a particular stand or with which they have wrestled in recent times.

Table v-4 indicates the percentage of respondents answering "always wrong." Mennonite Brethren are generally seen to be more restrictive than the General Conference Mennonites, from whom they seceded, but roughly similar to the American Mennonite Church which had its origin in Switzerland and Germany. The greatest difference with General Conference Mennonites concerns drinking,[4] smoking, movies, dancing, and premarital sexual intercourse. Several of these practices that have been measured the forefathers objected to at the time of secession, namely, drinking and smoking. On issues such as hard drugs, extramarital sexual intercourse, reckless driving, or income tax evasion, there is great proximity in attitudes. Mennonite Brethren in Canada again are somewhat more conservative in all but one item, adult movies.

Table v-4
Moral Issues

Issues	Percentage Responding "Always Wrong"			
	MC (n=1202)	GC (n=614)	NAMB (n=712)	CMB (n=359)
Drinking alcoholic beverages (moderately)	56	35	51	52.5
Smoking tobacco	66	50	76	79.9
Use of hard drugs (LSD, heroin, etc.)	97	97	99	99.4
Attending movies rated for adults and children	19	10	25	26.4
Attending movies rated for adults	54	33	55	52.4
Premarital sexual intercourse	85	79	92	95.8
Extramarital sexual intercourse	86	86	86	86.5
Gambling (betting, gambling machines)	80	66	74	78.6
Social dancing	47	26	57	64.7
Reckless driving	88	91	90	91.0
Income tax evasion (not reporting all income)	90	89	94	96.1

Source: Church Member Profile, 1972.

Table v-5 is a comprehensive summary of responses among Mennonite churches on measures of pacifism, race relations, social welfare attitudes, anti-Communism, attitudes to labour unions, and other so-

4 Based on data gathered on a national study of Canadian Mennonites in 1977, Currie, Linden, and Driedger report that 68 percent of Mennonite Brethren are in fact total abstainers over against 47 percent for General Conference Mennonites (1980, 106).

cial concerns. Mennonite Brethren, ranking among the most restrictive in personal moral issues among Mennonite groups, are among the most lenient within these same groups when it comes to social ethics. The pacifist stance, in keeping with the earlier measures of Anabaptism, is considerably less rigorous than among the Mennonite Church or General Conference Mennonites, but Canadian Mennonite Brethren are more non-resistant than American. On racial issues they are inclined to believe in a biblical basis for separatism. They strongly believe in the Protestant ethics, poverty being caused by lack of discipline, and are reluctant for the government to provide a guaranteed income. Few would prohibit church members from joining labour unions. Most still believe that capital punishment is a necessary deterrent to crime. As Kauffman and Harder tested, fundamentalistic orthodoxy was negatively correlated to the normative Anabaptist position (Kauffman and Harder, 1975, 135, 149). Mennonite Brethren rate high on the personal moral issues but less so on the Anabaptist distinctive of social ethics or love and non-resistance. This is in keeping with the results of recent research on Canadian Mennonites which show that wholists are more liberal theologically (Driedger *et al.*, 1983, 225-44).

On Making and Enforcing Ethical Decisions

In matters of ethics, Mennonite Brethren do not maintain a consistent position. In keeping with the high response to orthodoxy, evangelicalism, and Anabaptism, they have been shown to be the most restrictive in personal moral issues. They have indeed been prone to prescribed and proscribed behaviour, and have especially been champions of abstinence from smoking, drinking, and dancing. However, contrary to their high rating in traditional and Anabaptist beliefs, they are usually more lenient than their Anabaptist brethren in the matter of social ethics. This incongruency leads one to examine how Mennonite Brethren make and enforce ethical decisions.

Instances of making ethical decisions. Four specific instances are examined to discover how Canadian Mennonite Brethren have wrestled with and settled some of the ethical issues. The position taken with reference to tobacco suggests that in some issues there is virtually no change. The behavioural response on this question indicated that only 1.1 percent of Canadian Mennonite Brethren currently use tobacco. In 1869 twelve members, influenced in their use of tobacco by the German Baptist J. G. Oncken who was ministering to Baptist and Mennonite Brethren congregations in South Russia, were excommunicated for refusing to renounce their smoking habit (Toews, 1975, 73). The decisive stand of the Mennonite Brethren Church, entered into after considerable discussion, was reaffirmed in Vancouver one hundred years later (*GCYB*, 1969, 18-20).

Table v-5

Measures of Social Ethics

Issues	Percentage Response			
	MC (n=1202)	GC (n=614)	NAMB (n=712)	CMB (n=359)
No part in war or war-promoting activities (strongly agree/agree)	87	66	54	65.0
Owning stock in companies producing war goods (always wrong)	55	39	29	37.0
Active promotion of peace position (agree)	54	64	47	52.4
Vietnam necessary to stop spread of Communism (disagree)	50	44	22	20.2
Response to military draft				
___ regular military	2	8	8	3.4
___ non-combative	3	15	23	21.5
___ alternative service	86	62	48	48.7
___ uncertain	7	13	19	22.3
Equality of races (agree)	69	68	65	68.1
Biblical basis for separation of races (disagree)	44	40	29	30.8
Poverty caused by lack of discipline (disagree)	46	50	39	38.6
Minimum annual income guaranteed (agree)	24	30	29	36.4
Stamp out Communism (disagree)	35	31	19	20.1
Confront Communism with Christian truth (agree)	84	72	65	73.4
Church member should not join labour union (agree)	25	10	11	11.8
Capital punishment necessary (disagree)	46	50	17	15.2

Source: Church Member Profile, 1972.

On the question of the use and ownership of television, the Canadian Mennonite Brethren have shown their capability of changing their stance on an ethical issue. Influenced by the long-standing proscription (which is now considerably relaxed) on movies and theatres, the Mennonite Brethren Church was quick to respond to the first impact of television. In 1954, after listing eight dangers of the television, the Conference prohibited the sale and purchase of television sets and requested the Christian Press to publish a tract of this proposal for distribution in the churches (YB, 1954, 84-86). The 1958 Conference reaffirmed the position taken in 1954. A major change was made through a resolution by the Committee of Reference and Counsel in 1963. After acknowledging the need for timely warnings in previous conferences, the Committee proposed the following concession:

In view of the fact that there are more acceptable programs . . . we believe that the purchase and use of TV will have to be determined by the conscience of the individual and especially Christian parents in the light of circumstances in the individual homes. Nevertheless, let us not close our eyes to the destructive effects of uncontrolled and indiscriminate viewing of programs.

May the Lord grant us grace to maintain a tender conscience about the advisability of purchasing a TV set and about the type of programs we permit to be viewed in our homes . . . (YB, 1963, 118).

Guidance, however, on the Christian's discriminate use of television continued. Reflecting on such change in Conference thinking, columnist John Redekop remarked, "TV is what we make of it, or what we permit it to make of ourselves; nothing more and nothing less" (Redekop, 1968, 2).

A third instance, the attitude to war, indicates on a behavioural level only partial compliance to a doctrine or ethical position to which the church has continuously given lip service. The first decade after 1925 represents a time of adjustment for the largely immigrant denomination. Looking for political and religious freedom, along with economic opportunity, the Canadian Mennonite Brethren needed to be reassured that they held such a non-resistant view and, in the event of war, would be granted military exemption. The *Mennonitische Rundschau* became a suitable vehicle to accomplish such socialization. The next decade provided the occasion to test the non-resistant stance. In the years before World War II, B. B. Janz in particular appealed to the Canadian Conference annually to alert the church to the possibility of war and to propose ways to avoid participation (*YB*, 1934, 76-77). With such indoctrination and provision for non-combatant alternative service, some 4,425 Mennonite men (including other than Mennonite Brethren) avoided the draft (Toews, 1959, 99). Moreover, a small number was involved in non-combatant military service (the medical corps) following an order-in-council in September 1943 (*YB*, 1944, 64-65). Yet a number of Mennonite Brethren chose to join the military service, a fact regretted by the Committee of Reference and Counsel and resulting in another appeal to teach the doctrine more thoroughly (*YB*, 1945, 144). No other single aspect of Mennonite Brethren belief received such attention in the years after the war. There seemed to be a fear that a time of peace would result in an erosion of this distinctive. Year after year the Conference expressed concerns over the failure in teaching the doctrine, and a resolution was passed in 1946 requiring baptismal candidates to assent to the teaching (*YB*, 1946, 163). In the last decades peace literature and peace conferences have, on the one hand, rigorously objected to the involvement in Vietnam and, on the other hand, have interpreted the peace witness to apply to the injustices of society. Throughout the past fifty years, and in the last quarter century particularly, Canadian Mennonite Brethren emphasized this distinctive doctrine; yet a segment of the membership has consistently refused to take a separatist stand, and increasingly as Mennonite Brethren are assimilated into Canadian society and become more aggressively evangelistic, this ethical distinctive becomes more difficult to enforce.

A fourth ethical issue suggests a doctrine over which there is considerable diversity of opinion and in which the church assumes an openness. Most Mennonite Brethren apparently support capital punishment despite their non-resistant stance. Only 15.2 percent disagree that capital punishment is necessary to deter crime. The discussion on this issue has surfaced only in recent years, and as yet the Conference has taken no official stand. Influential leaders, however, have addressed themselves to this issue. In 1966 J. H. Redekop presented his five reasons for opposing capital punishment, among which is the fact that it is inconsistent with the non-resistance position (Redekop, 1966, 2). More recently yet, Dr. F. C. Peters admitted his former ambivalence and declared his unapologetic stand in opposition to capital punishment, in view of his non-resistant interpretation of the New Testament (Peters, 1976, 17). In a series of ten letters to the editor, which Dr. Peter's declaration generated, only two favoured capital punishment. Thus, while the majority of members may still side with capital punishment, the leadership is strongly influencing the membership to the contrary. As yet the Mennonite Brethren Church has not taken an official stand.

How the decisions were made and enforced.   At least several, and in some instances all, of the following means are employed to make and enforce ethical decisions. First, and most important, is the role of systematic and authoritative teaching. As chapter eight indicates, socialization occurs from childhood at several levels—in the home, in private schools, and in the church. Adults meet for regular Sunday worship, delegates attend annual provincial and national conferences, and pastors and lay persons interact at occasional study conferences. The publication of D. Ewert's presentation, "An Approach to Problems of Christian Ethics," first given at a Faith and Ethics Conference of Mennonite Brethren at Winnipeg on February 15 and 16, 1967, was widely circulated as a pamphlet insert in the *Mennonite Brethren Herald*. Ewert outlines ten principles to guide one in solving ethical problems (Ewert, 1967). In a similar, popular vein, Dr. F. C. Peters published a series of articles on ethical subjects under the broader title, "The Christian in the World" (Peters, 1965, 7). An evaluation of situation ethics was given at the Canadian Conference in Clearbrook in 1968 by Victor Adrian, in which he maintains that Christian ethics repudiates legalism, subjectivism, and relativism, and submits itself to the norms and principles of Scriptures (*YB*, 1968, 81-94). Such thorough-going, Bible-based teaching has been the greatest single factor in deciding and enforcing ethical issues.

A second means of enforcing ethical decisions has been exemplary leadership. In addition to teaching, preaching, and writing, the example of prominent ministers, teachers, and Conference leaders has been instrumental in shaping the life-style of Canadian Mennonite Brethren, especially until recent times. This role of charisma cannot be elaborated upon in this chapter, except to provide the illustration of such an effect. When Dr. F. C. Peters, former pastor and Bible College professor, more recently moderator of the Canadian Mennonite Brethren Churches and President of Wilfrid Laurier University, openly indicated in the *Mennonite Brethren Herald*, "Moderator's Corner," that he had abandoned an ambivalent position and fully opposed capital punishment, such example, for the many who have not independently thought through the issue, is bound to have an effect. Unfortunately, the measure of impact of such a single example cannot be determined.

A third and more concrete means has been the debating of controversial issues until consensus is reached on local, provincial, or Canadian Conference levels. The Mennonite Brethren Church has repeatedly sought to avoid an individualistic approach to ethics and to strive for consensus. In F. C. Peters' presentation at the Study Conference at Reedley, California, "Consensus and Change in our Brotherhood," he explains that group consensus is not ultimate authority, and that "the value lies more in the process than in the product" (Peters, 1968). Examples of wrestling with such issues occurred at the same conference when a measure of consensus was reached on the subjects of the divorced and of planned parenthood (Quiring, 1968).

A fourth means of effecting an ethical decision is through the behavioural requirements of a local church. Dean Kelley has observed that Anabaptists and Wesleyans traditionally conserved social strength by the "power of the gate," not being in haste to take anyone into membership, demanding attitudinal and behavioural tests for membership, and requiring continuing faithfulness (Kelley, 1972, 125-29). This, in fact, characterized the Mennonite Brethren Church until recent times. Marvin Hein, one-time moderator of the General Conference, has argued that ideally the church needs no rules, but because of human frailty, it has them; however, he maintains, "Church rules can hardly be called requirements for membership" (Hein, 1968). This is in keeping with the more ameliorative approach of a once legalistic moralism, as also the resolution on "The Individual Member and Guidelines of the Church" indicates, "that we will consider such guidelines, not as conditions for membership in our church, but rather as ideals, the attainment of which remains the constant goal and desire of each member" (*GCYB*, 1969, 13). Whether this weakening of the "power of the gate" will enable the church to maintain a separatist stance or further facilitate accommodation still needs to be tested.

Finally, the church exercises discipline to implement its ethical stance. Admittedly, excommunication is the ultimate step in exercising discipline, yet a comparison of membership, baptisms, and number of excommunications suggests a general relaxation in the same. If one compares the number of excommunications with the membership and baptisms in four separate decades, the early 1920s offer a significant difference from the time after the Russian immigration. The early 1930s and mid-1950s indicate excommunications roughly at the rate of 10 percent of the number of baptized, which in early 1970s is less than 5 percent. The percentage of excommunicated compared to membership suggests a similar decline in recent times. Changes in recent times can be attributed to increased secularization, but also to renewed understanding of discipline. Considerable effort has been made to teach church discipline. Despite such teaching, recent years have witnessed a decline in excommunication. Rather than reflecting secularization alone, this decline may well be because of the new understanding of discipline. Typical of this redemptive approach to discipline is Herbert Giesbrecht's plea for a covenanted code of ethics in which one distinguishes between principle and prescription. He explains: "A brotherhood of believers can be spared much needless perplexity and pain if it understands from the outset that while ethical principles are fixed and enduring, specific ethical prescriptions may require periodic amendment or may even be altogether discarded without spiritual loss to the church in a given situation" (Giesbrecht, 1976, 4). Church discipline is not thereby discarded but reinterpreted in a less legalistic spirit. Unquestionably, Mennonite Brethren ethics have helped delineate boundaries and thereby perpetuate the religious group. J. Howard Kauffman similarly concludes that boundary maintenance is positively associated with adherence to Mennonite norms (Kauffman, 1977, 237).

Summary

The Canadian Mennonite Brethren Church has successfully confronted change and accommodation during the past half century by consciously delineating boundaries with its beliefs and ethics. The resulting continuity in its sectarian beliefs is evident in the high measure of orthodoxy, evangelicalism, and Anabaptist distinctives, separating itself significantly from the Mennonite church from which it seceded. In analysing the *modus operandi*, which might explain such retention of conservative beliefs, at least four contributing perspectives reoccur in its official proceedings, principal spokesmen, and denominational periodicals. First, Mennonite Brethren have continued to look back at the pattern of Menno and the first-century church. This is not simply equivalent to saying it is biblical in orientation. It is biblical in an Anabaptist sense, that is, even as the sixteenth-century Anabaptists did, it seeks to take the New Testament as final and the model of Christ as determinative. Secondly, the church has demonstrated a rigorously biblicist position, repeatedly appealing to the Scriptures for its final authority, not through arbitrary proof-texting but through diligent study and application. Thirdly, the beliefs of church members are those of believers who have consciously experienced Christ and voluntarily submitted themselves to the norms of the group, including the possibility of exclusion from the group. Fourthly, the group sees itself in constant conflict with society which is non-Christian, not simply withdrawing from society, but confronting the societal value system in terms of its own value system.

In personal, moral issues Mennonite Brethren hold a rather conservative position, similar to the Mennonite Church, but significantly more restrictive than the General Conference Mennonites. In social ethics Mennonite Brethren are more lenient than other Mennonite groups, except for capital punishment. Instances of ethical decision-making show that Mennonite Brethren refuse to change in some issues, such as smoking; change their stance in some issues, such as owning and selling television; partially comply to one of the distinctives of the faith, as in non-resistance; and indicate an openness in such a matter as capital punishment. In order to teach and enforce an ethical position, Mennonite Brethren follow one or more of the following: systematic instruction, exemplary leadership, reaching consensus, behavioural requirements, and the exercise of discipline, the ultimate form of which is excommunication.

It would appear that by delineating cognitive and normative boundaries, Canadian Mennonite Brethren have successfully sacralized their identity and facilitated the persistence of sectarianism. Indeed, it appears that the reports of God's demise have been exaggerated.

VI

Enhancing Cohesion

A religious movement may be held together by other than strictly cognitive and normative parameters. Group cohesiveness may also be the product of simple biological and cultural continuity. In his study of Manitoba Mennonites, sociologist E. K. Francis attributes Mennonite group solidarity to region, church, and family (Francis, 1955, 277). While the latter two surely apply to Canadian Mennonite Brethren, settling in close geographic proximity, as the conservative Mennonite groups did in their emigration to the East and West Reserve of Manitoba in the 1870s, can hardly be applied in the same way to Mennonite Brethren. And yet, since the mid-1940s many an isolated Mennonite Brethren family moved to a larger Mennonite community, St. Catharines, Winnipeg, Saskatoon, or the Fraser Valley. To a degree, no doubt, all three of Francis' perspectives apply to Canadian Mennonite Brethren.

This chapter analyses two factors—family solidarity and ethnic seclusion—which contributed to cohesiveness and, thereby, enhanced sectarian continuity. The chapter will test the hypothesis that "the more compact an immigrant group is and the fewer its contacts with the host society the stronger the transplanted church will be and the more it will reinforce the cohesion of the group" (Mol, 1961, 75). It will also indicate that with the disruptive influences upon family life and with the loss of ethnicity, the sectarian group will need to rely more and more for its continuity on such transcultural factors as ideology. The preeminence of such theological identity is the thrust of Redekop's critique:

To the extent that we have exhibited a theological identity in the past few generations it has rested largely on social, ethnic and geographic separatism. That age is past. Unless we manage to teach younger generations the distinctive qualities of our orientation our future is not particularly bright. We may well become little more than a recruiting ground for both narrow fundamentalism or easy-going, "cheap grace," common denominator, evangelicalism (Redekop, 1966, 2).

This chapter examines the past with its social, ethnic, and geographic separatism to determine how, sociologically speaking, group structure enhances the maintenance of religious values.

1. Mennonite Brethren Family Solidarity

In examining the extent to which the Canadian Mennonite Brethren family contributes to group cohesiveness, one does well to begin with the biblical understanding of the family, then note the empirical evidence of its solidarity, review its role in counteracting the disruptions wrought through migration and confrontation with a secular society, and finally note its rigorous attempts to retain solidarity in the face of the threats of erosion.

The Biblical Understanding of the Family

It is not the intent of this study to explore the usually acknowledged contributions of the family to society, such as reproduction of the young, physical maintenance of family members, social placement of the child, socialization, and social control (Goode, 1964, 5). It is the added dimension which a religious group contributes to the meaning of a family that is of interest here. In keeping with their biblicism, Mennonite Brethren anchor marriage theologically as an institution ordained of God. It follows that marriage is monogamous and indissoluble, and, because of its sanctity, believers are advised to marry believers only. Until 1975, marriage of believers and unbelievers meant automatic excommunication (*YB*, 1975, 10). Emphasis is also placed upon the sanctity of courtship and engagements, and weddings are meant to have a distinctly Christian quality. Children are viewed as gifts of God, and abortion is generally opposed. When asked by the editor of the *Mennonite Brethren Herald* "What have been the strengths of the Mennonite Brethren home?" twelve Mennonite Brethren replied: simple biblicism, spontaneous fellowship, dignity of work, respect for authority, family altar, healthy economic struggle, Bible discussions, sanctity of marriage, father as priest of the family, authority of God's Word, church doctrines stressed, and genuine conversion experience (*Mennonite Brethren Herald*, hereafter *MBH*, Dec. 2, 1966, 4-8). The collective thrust of these subjective evaluations underscores the impression that for Canadian Mennonite Brethren family solidarity is rooted in more than just a sociological understanding of the family, for it is understood biblically.

A Look at the Data

Is there empirical evidence to support the facts implied by the above impressions? In the Church Member Profile, 88.0 percent (n=316) of

Canadian Mennonite Brethren view marriage as a lifelong commitment broken only by death, and another 11.1 percent (n=40) view it as a
lifetime commitment as well, but which may be broken if every attempt
to reconcile disharmony has failed. On a behavioural level, the 1975
Year Book lists a total of 494 marriages contracted, over against 17
separations or divorces for Mennonite Brethren families (the previous
year 7 divorces occurred) (*YB*, 1975, 113). Table vi-1 summarizes those
facts, indicating the types of marriage unions, which could be gleaned
from yearly statistical reports to the Canadian Conference. The percentage of mixed marriages (that is, where only one party is a believer)
remains roughly the same from 1955 to 1975, with a fluctuation of
about .01 percent. While the number of marriages of unbelievers seems
to have increased rather sharply, statistically this does not affect the
marriages of church members, since neither party belongs to the
church. However, the number of divorced members remarrying is
significantly increasing, and 53.8 percent (n=189) believe that divorced members who have confessed their wrong and made all possible
restitution can also be readmitted to church membership.

Table VI-1

Types of Marriage Unions

	Churches			Marriages					
Year	No.	Members	Total	Between Believers	Mixed No.	Mixed %	Between Unbelievers	Civil	Of Divorcé/e
1948	79	8,921	152	120	14	.157	18	0	0
1955	79	12,437	260	219	12	.096	1	27	1
1960	82	13,573	241	215	13	.096	12	1	–
1965	110	15,315	240	206	13	.085	19	2	–
1970	124	17,056	319	263	16	.094	32	6	2
1975	130	19,051	494	393	18	.094	70	4	9

Source: Canadian Conference Year Books.

The solidarity of the marriage union is further confirmed by the
largely endogamous marriages. The Church Member Profile showed
that at the time of marriage 80.8 percent (n=214) belonged to the same
denomination as the spouse, the percentage increasing by the time of
the survey to 96.3 percent (n=258). Moreover, 73.9 percent (n=260)
have no other denominational affiliation in any member of the immediate family, and for 79.3 percent (n=284) of the respondents both
mother and father were of the same denomination.[1] Thus, there is

---

1 Using a national sample of Mennonites (in a survey conducted by Currie, Driedger,
  and Linden in 1977), Driedger, Vogt, and Reimer report that 48 percent of Canadian

considerable denominational homogeneity. A quick survey of the family names of the largest Mennonite Brethren Church in Winnipeg shows that of 376 families (with a church membership of 736) nine family names account for one-third of the church families. Other factors reflecting on the solidarity of the family can similarly be gleaned from the Church Member Profile: 90.5 percent (n=340) say grace before every meal, and another 4.5 percent (n=16) before most meals; 69.3 percent (n=242) have family worship other than grace at meals; 95.8 percent (n=338) believe that premarital sexual intercourse is always wrong; 86.5 percent (n=300) believe that extramarital sexual intercouse is always wrong; 86.6 percent (n=284) believe that a legal abortion is wrong if one does not want a baby; 73.4 percent (n=254) allow it only if it endangers the mother's health. Finally, the fact that 87.7 percent (n=314) of Canadian Mennonite Brethren own a home (with 9.8 percent renting and 2.5 percent living in a home which is rent free) may also reflect upon the solidarity of the family.

The Sociological Function of the Family

Fifty years after the major immigration of Mennonites into Canada, the Mennonite Brethren family still occupies essentially the same pivotal place in the whole social structure, for it has acted as a buffer for individuals both in their adjustments as immigrants and in their encounters with a secular society. The mediating function of the family within the larger society is especially apparent among immigrants. While retarding social integration, the family served as a shock-breaker for those who felt alienated and thus enhanced personal integration for the first generation particularly. The dependence upon the immediate family and the desire to locate relatives in the newly adopted host society is especially evident in the letters and reports that Mennonites sent to *Die Mennonitische Rundschau*.

What the family provided by way of personal security for first generation immigrants in the face of their strange environment, it also does for the third and fourth generation sectarians for whom the church is a haven in an uncertain and secular world. This haven must have a Christ-centred atmosphere, according to F. C. Peters. Having depicted the influences upon the family by secular society, he concludes in his article, "Families in a Secular Society," by posing a question and supplying the answer:

What then makes a home Christian? A home is not Christian by default. In our society, it's not Christian simply because it is nothing else. It's not Christian

---

Mennonites have no marriage to non-Mennonites within their family (Driedger *et al.*, 1983, 137). However, this statistic does not include intermarriage between various Mennonites, while the above statistic does.

because the parents belong to the Church. It's not Christian in the deeper sense simply because the parents are saved or the Bible is read. The home is Christian because of an atmosphere—an atmosphere that permeates everything which happens in that home—in which Christ is truly centre and a philosophy of living grows up which honors him (Peters, 1969, 6-7).

Peter and Brigitte Berger have suggested that "the family is a refuge from the macro-world; it is a place to which they can retreat from the latter's tensions, frustrations and anxieties . . . the locale of highly significant expectations for self-fulfilment and emotional satisfaction" (Berger, 1975, 86). For Mennonite Brethren, the family provides both this sociological dimension and the added Christian atmosphere.

The Threat of Erosion

Despite the ongoing sociological functions of the family and the Mennonite Brethren consciousness of the unique dimension of the Christian home, the data suggest that Mennonite family solidarity is no longer to be taken for granted. Increasingly the crises of society at large impinge upon the church-related family. And yet, it is not a recent phenomenon to lament the crises that the families face.

Already in the 1920s there were threats to Mennonite family solidarity. Immigrants suddenly suffer anomie when the security of belonging to a closely knit group with similar norms and habits is removed. The result may not only be loneliness and nostalgia, but also disappointment and hopelessness. No doubt, such nostalgia and pessimism added to the adjustment strains of the immigrant.

By mid-century, the threat of erosion was certainly more real and accurately defined and scientifically measured. Mennonite sociologists commented on the Mennonite family in the United States. Because of the close parallel to the Canadian Mennonite Brethren, these studies are a helpful commentary on the Canadian scene for the 1950s. J. Winfield Fretz drew attention to seven long-time trends which were affecting the family: first, the family in the home is ceasing to be a production unit and is almost totally a consumption unit; second, increasing impermanence of location; third, decreasing family size; fourth, changing morality; fifth, decline of masculine dominance and emergence of the democratic family; sixth, changing roles in modern marriage; seventh, gradual acquisition of new family functions (Fretz, 1957, 131-35). Pooling the joint response of 150 students, Dr. Fretz reports the following forces pulling apart the family at mid-century: over-activity, individual independence, failure to adjust to technological change, mobility, competition between individuals within a family and between families in a community, materialism, working mothers, urbanization, and conflicting time schedules (Fretz, 1957, 136-37).

More recently, George Konrad, a Mennonite Brethren professor of Christian education and a Canadian, viewed the societal influences of mobility, changing roles, neglect in child training, and depersonalization as leading to deterioration of the family, seen in the loss of stability, loss of faith, and loss of function (including reproduction, protection and care of children, economic production of family goods and services, socialization of children, recreation and giving affection) (Konrad, 1971, 12-20). The erosive forces at work upon the Canadian Mennonite Brethren family are keenly felt by perceptive analysts, and hence the concern to nurture its solidarity.

The Nurture of Family Solidarity

Because of the firm belief in the supra-societal components both in the very foundation of marriage and in the ongoing life of the institutional family, and because of their awareness of the erosive forces of society at large, Canadian Mennonite Brethren have consciously and increasingly sought to nurture family solidarity. Such nurture, in turn, has facilitated the persistence of the religious movement. The nurture has transpired at two levels at least. On a general and more theoretical plane, the socialization has involved academic discussion among Conference leaders, pastors, and Christian educators. On a more specific and practical plane, the nurture thrust actually reached the family members. A closer examination of how this nurture has occurred will enable one more readily to understand its enduring impact despite the continuing erosive forces.

Examples of the first level of socialization include the publication of articles in Conference academic journals which reach its schools, pastors, and interested individuals who choose to subscribe. As will be seen below, this focus on the family just after mid-century was continued by the denominational weekly periodicals, *Mennonite Observer* (1956-1961) and *Mennonite Brethren Herald* (1962 to the present). The preservation of the Christian family has also become the subject for position papers at study conferences. In a like manner, for one decade (1954-1963), almost annually one of the devotional sermons at the Conference was centred on the family. The concern with the family at the Conference level has thus been especially prominent in the past twenty-five years. This is in keeping with the counsel of Driedger, Vogt, and Reimer, who suggest that Mennonites will increasingly need to work at family and religious network strengthening to retain their endogamy patterns (Driedger *et al.*, 1983, 143).

On a more practical plane, various ways and means have been used to reach the family itself. On a social level, Mennonites are known for family reunions. Some of these even receive news coverage in the denominational weekly. They assemble particularly on festive days—Christmas, Easter, Thanksgiving, and Mother's Day—and for numerous less auspicious occasions—birthdays, anniversaries, and routine visits. Family camps have become a special attraction, every province having one or more camp sites.

More specifically geared to occur in the church setting are weddings and funerals, for which whole families assemble, and Mother's Days. Increasingly, Mennonite Brethren attend special family seminars or clinics. At a recent interdemoninational family conference in Hamilton, 1,754 adults attended. Of these 410 were Mennonite Brethren from the Ontario churches. Moreover, ministers preach sermons specifically focusing on family needs.

Reaching the family in its homes are the denominational periodicals, one German (*Mennonitische Rundschau*) or one English (*Mennonite Brethren Herald*) automatically being sent to each home. The *Mennonitische Rundschau* served as an inter-Mennonite paper from its inception in 1877 in United States, through its move to Canada in 1923, and increasingly became denominational in coverage as it was gradually acquired from private ownership from 1945 to 1960. It continues to serve the elderly, German-speaking church community today. The *Konferenz-Jugendblatt* (1946-1957) became the official, bilingual organ designed for youth, initially 80 percent German in content and concluding its thirteen years of publication of sixty-nine issues almost wholly English. From 1955 to 1961 the *Mennonite Observer*, a private English weekly published by the Christian Press, served a somewhat broader Mennonite constituency. In 1962, the *Mennonite Brethren Herald*, in coverage and content very similar to *Mennonite Observer*, became the official successor to *Konferenz-Jugendblatt*. Produced in English only, its focus was on the family. To achieve this purpose, the first editor, Rudy Wiebe, included a family section (*YB*, 1962, 203). Subsequently, beginning January 8, 1965, a daily devotional guide was included, since "mid-Twentieth Century families have a harder time staying a cohesive unit than did their forebears two or three decades ago" (Jantz, 1965, 2). The devotional guide was discontinued when a special family worship booklet, *Worship Together*, was published in 1966, followed by an inter-Mennonite family devotional quarterly, *Rejoice*, in 1972, sent to all who subscribe through their local church. Thus, through an aggressive effort to nurture family solidarity, Canadian Mennonite Brethren have enhanced that cohesiveness which sacralizes their identity and thereby facilitates the continuity of the movement.

2. Mennonite Brethren Ethnicity

Ethnicity denotes a social group which, within a larger cultural and social system, claims or is accorded a special status in terms of traits it exhibits or is believed to exhibit, prominent among which are traits of linguistic and religious character. Shortly after their immigration, Mennonites did not hesitate to admit such ethnicity. However, assimilation for one-half a century has considerably changed both facts and attitudes.

Interpreting Ethnicity

It is the sociologists who recognize what ethnicity does to retain both the cohesiveness of a group and, thereby, the continuity of a religious movement. John Ross found that ethnic differences helped maintain denominational pluralism and that each wave of immigration brings a new church into being (Ross, 1973, 24). Sociologist E. K. Francis, who studied Mennonites in Manitoba, grasped the ambiguous meaning of the word "Mennonite," a notion of a distinct religious affiliation in one case, but something quite different in another (Francis, 1955, 2). However, his study showed that "ethnic communities perform a valuable function in adjusting immigrants to the ways of their adoptive country, and in maintaining social controls during the crucial period of transition following immigration" (Francis, 1955, 6). In other words, ethnicity enhances group cohesion, which, in turn, enables a religious group to remain viable while adjusting to society. In addition, true integration also occurs within the absorbing society, for there is an "interactional process of mutual change and adjustment between immigrants and receiving groups" (Francis, 1955, 7). Mennonite Brethren critics of ethnicity, impatient with the adjustment process, possibly fail to recognize that, sociologically viewed, precisely the ethnic aspects contributed strongly to the preservation of the church.

Intimations of Ethnicity

Is there empirical evidence of continuing ethnicity of the Canadian Mennonite Brethren, or are they completely assimilated? Several studies by Mennonite sociologists reflect such ethnicity. Mennonite Brethren sociologist L. Roy Just, former president of Columbia Bible Institute, discovered in his research of social distance that, of the three largest Mennonite bodies, Mennonite Brethren had the least social "nearness" (that is, being tolerant and sympathetic in understanding). Yet, he found that generally among Mennonites "separation from the world" was not positively correlated with "farness" (Just, 1953, 73-77). Although Just's findings reflect the American scene in the early 1950s, they do support two of the above observations about contemporary Canadian Mennonite Brethren: that their attitudes do in fact reflect ethnicity, and that holding a separatist religious stand does not necessarily militate against social adaptation. In 1971 two Manitoba sociologists, Leo Driedger and Jacob Peters, compared ethnic identity among Mennonite and other German university students. Using factors of parochial education, language, religion, endogamy, friends, and voluntary organizations, they discovered that a greater percentage of Mennonite university students in Manitoba hold positive attitudes towards their in-group (Driedger and Peters, 1973, 225-44). And John W. Friesen, in his recent study of Mennonite identity in Southern Alberta (including Mennonite Brethren, General Conference, Old Mennonite, and Holdeman), concluded that a Mennonite culture exists, for "the ways, manners and customs of Mennonites differ significantly from those of other Canadians, so that they are easily distinguished by non-Mennonite as well. Language is ranked as a second factor" (Friesen, 1971, 25-41).

The data from the Church Member Profile show that of the 359 Canadian Mennonite Brethren respondents, all but one are white racially, 63.0 percent (n=218) were born in Canada, 30.6 percent (n=106) in Russia, 2.9 percent (n=10) in South America, the remaining mostly in European countries. The fact that in excess of one-third of the sample population is foreign-born would in itself indicate the likelihood of a high degree of ethnicity. Nonetheless, on the basis of Leo Driedger's factors of ethnicity, devised by factor analysis in his search for cultural identity factors (Driedger, 1975, 150-62), the following table (vi-2) has been constructed and summarizes the responses to similar questions posed by Kauffman and Harder in the Church Member Profile. Driedger's third factor, language, representing 8 percent variance, is not included because the survey questionnaire did not include questions about language.

Ethnicity factors relating to religion (accounting for 27.9 percent of the variance in Driedger's factor analysis), more exhaustively treated in chapter five, indicate an attitude similar to other groups for the general question of feeling the presence of God, although it is high compared to Congregationals (25 percent) and Roman Catholics (43 percent) (Stark and Glock, 1968, 131). However, in such more specific, separatistic items as a sense of being saved by Christ or in weekly church attendance or degree of voluntarism in church participation, Mennonite Brethren rank significantly higher, in the latter two items Canadian Mennonite Brethren ranking higher than their American brethren—no doubt, because of their more recent immigration.

Endogamy factors (accounting for 9 percent of the variance in Driedger's analysis) indicate Mennonite Brethren to be higher than the General Conference and much like the Mennonite Church, the Canadian being significantly more endogamous than their American counterparts, again, no doubt, on account of the more recent immigrant influx. In all instances, spouses seem to join the same denomination after marriage, suggesting that Mennonites prefer denominational homogeneity.

Table VI-2
Factors of Mennonite Brethren Ethnicity

Ethnicity Factors	Percentage Distribution			
	MC (n=1202)	GC (n=614)	NAMB (n=712)	CMB (n=359)
Religion				
Feeling the presence of God	72	69	74	75.2
Sense of being saved by Christ	80	70	92	91.5
Weekly church attendance (or more)	71	58	80	82.7
Voluntary participation in church	70	69	76	80.5
Endogamy				
Same denomination as spouse at marriage	82	65	75	80.8
Same denomination as spouse now	94	94	96	96.3
Important to marry member of own denomination	56	49	55	59.9
Both parents now of same church	82	77	75	79.3
Organizations				
Youth groups (church organizations included)	--	--	30	33.6
Church organizations (percentage belonging to one or more)	--	--	15	14.9
Should continue to publish two or more publications (rather than join U.S.)	--	--	55	60.1
Parochial Education				
Attended Mennonite school	--	--	53	59.1
Should attend at least one year in Mennonite post-high school	--	--	60	73.6
Social dancing not permitted in church college	--	--	85	92.4
Required chapel attendance at church college	--	--	82	86.1
Admit more students from minority groups	--	--	61	68.6
Friends				
Three or more closest friends in local church	43	48	52	58.1
Four or five closest friends in same denomination	48	47	51	61.2
Miscellaneous				
Most satisfaction in being Mennonite	13	17	16	14.0
Fit fairly well or very well with people of church congregation	--	--	85	76.3

Source: Church Member Profile, 1972.

The questions relating to church organizations (over 6 percent of variance for Driedger) show that about one-half the members are involved in one or more church-related organizations and more than one-half feel strongly about publishing their own denominational paper, rather than jointly with the United States Mennonite Brethren. Again the Canadian Mennonite Brethren response appears somewhat more parochial than the American.

The parochial education factors (only 5 percent of variance for Driedger's analysis) uniformly show a higher response for Canadian than for American Mennonite Brethren, and the friends factor (only 4 percent variance) shows Mennonite Brethren to be more communal than other Mennonites, with Canadian Mennonite Brethren being more restrictive to their own church than the Americans. Finally, in several miscellaneous factors, not included in Driedger's analysis, Canadian Mennonite Brethren appear less smug about satisfaction with their own denomination or fitness within their own local church. On the basis of the earlier data, one would have expected them to rank higher than their American counterparts. Perhaps these last questions reflect a measure of anomie in which the more recent immigrant still has not as fully been assimilated.

With fifty or fewer years in Canada, most Canadian Mennonite Brethren still indicate ethnic overtones. Although such conspicuous factors as clothes, houses, modes of transportation, occupational involvement, or foods do not set aside Canadian Mennonite Brethren as ethnics, other more subtle factors relating to religious separation, endogamy, parochial organizations, education, and their choice of friends do intimate ethnicity.

The Pertinacity of Ethnicity

To examine the impact of the survival remnants of ethnicity is not to vouch for their rightness nor wrongness, but rather simply to analyse those factors which have contributed to the persistence of a religious movement. It does not mean that the process of assimilation has not rigorously been at work, as will be seen in chapter ten, nor does it mean that entrenchment in excessive ethnicity may not lead to petrifaction and loss of religious vitality. The present discussion is meant, simply, to view historically those factors which have contributed to the present remnants of ethnicity and to discover what impression these factors have made on Canadian Mennonite Brethren.

Immigration. The upheaval of transplanting a church from one culture to another naturally brings a new cohesiveness to the group. Three separate waves of immigration brought a new consciousness of ethnicity to the slowly assimilating *Kanadier* already resident. But none of the waves was as forceful as the immigration of 1923 to 1930, during which time 20,201 Mennonite immigrants came from Russia (of these approximately 25 percent were Mennonite Brethren) (Toews, 1975, 282). No doubt, many of the earlier immigrants came because of economic and cultural reasons, but increasingly the pressure was political and religious. This transplantation of people severed families and villages in Russia, but formed new bonds among immigrants as they retold their individual experiences, travelled together, had their names published in immigrant lists, and were grouped in new settlements scattered across the prairies. The relatively few names,[2] both Christian and surnames, suggest the ethnic bond of these immigrant communities (Neufeld, 1925, 5, 8). Such ethnic ties between old and new, and among those who together experienced transplantation, are not readily forgotten nor abandoned.

More recent waves of Mennonite immigrants represent similar reasons, the post-World War II immigration of refugees seeking political asylum, religious freedom, and economic opportunity. The Mennonite immigrants from South America (Paraguay, Uruguay, and Brazil) were attracted by better economic conditions and the cultural opportunities among a larger and more affluent Mennonite community. Both immigrations strengthened ethnic ties and revived an interest in the retention of German.

The full saga of the Canadian immigrant settlement needs yet to be told. Vignettes of unexpected hardships and heroic endurance, of courageous ambition and humbling despair, of bumper crops and crop failures, of inflation and depression have been attempted in novels, in poetry, in autobiography, history, and personal recollections—all by Mennonite Brethren authors (Hamm, 1978, 217).

It was the common experience of wrestling with the exigencies of pioneer life that welded together new cohesive communities of the scattered and potentially fragmented immigrants. The account of one such immigrant could well have been the story of many. Five problems are treated as uppermost in his concerns: the *Reiseschuld* (travel debt), the many who left Russia but were not allowed to enter Canada on account of illness, the sick ones among the new immigrants, those desperately poor, and the need for the many immigrant teachers to learn the language to be able to enter their own profession (*MR*, 1927, 4). The importance of living in proximity with the Christian

---

2 A statistical analysis of the 4,070 immigrants of 1924 indicates that the most prominent 12 Christian names for men and women each constituted 87.4 percent and 72.7 percent, respectively, and of the 152 different family names the 12 most prominent (Dueck, Friesen, Wiens, Thiessen, Neufeld, Penner, Rempel, Enns, Toews, Klassen, Janzen, and Peters—in order) constituted 41.4 percent.

community is likewise recognized. All the immigrants, however, did not adjust to the new conditions and find refuge in an ethnic group. For some immigrants, ethnicity made them marginal to the group and to society, as E. K. Francis so perceptively observed:

While some submit to the painful and slow process of acculturation, many others never lose an attitude of superiority mixed with resentment at having lost their former—real or imaginary—social status. These live and pass away as strangers to both cultures, that of their native, and that of their adopted country—truly marginal men, uprooted, lonely and out of tune with their environment. Usually the isolated of this type has little chance of causing a great stir (Francis, 1955, 212).

Despite such exceptions, most immigrants were forged into a new cohesive unit through migration and settlement itself, and by doing so the ethnicity of the new community enhanced the vitality of the religious movement.

Reiseschuld.   Not only the experience of migration itself, but the debt incurred in the emigration (*Reiseschuld*) was a reminder to many immigrants of their foreign origins. The cohesive impact of the *Reiseschuld* was not so much in the common experience of having a debt (as it was for two-thirds of them), but in the experience of a common debt, that is, the collective burden of debt was placed upon all the immigrants, for the C.P.R. had assumed a debt of $1,924,727 on behalf of the Mennonite community (Epp, 1962, 281-95). On account of the depression, almost one-half was still unpaid by 1939; and in the meantime, some debtors had died, and others refused to pay. Since the original contract with the C.P.R. had required full payment in two years, interest at 6 percent mounted. It was the struggle of the Canadian Mennonite Board of Colonization, representing members of both the General Conference and Mennonite Brethren churches, to have the churches assume jointly the debt (less the interest of over one million dollars which was cancelled by the C.P.R.) which helped forge the immigrant community once again. In the end it was the church community that collected the total remaining debt, which was paid in full by November 1946. The burdensome *Reiseschuld* had not only helped weld together the Mennonite Brethren in their common dilemma, but also brought together the larger Mennonite community of Mennonite Brethren and General Conference.

Muttersprache.   The retention of the German language constituted another, sometimes dubious legacy of ethnicity. The longer the immigrant community resisted change and social integration, the more secure it remained in its ethnic seclusion, but the surer the day of a radical transition. To prevent serious conflict and loss of community, the change required the passing of a generation, for the *Muttersprache* had an aura of sanctity which sacralized the identity of its bearers.

Several distinct phases marked the total transition. Until 1939, the immigrants were comfortable with the German language, and numerous almost jingoistic pieces of literature resounded their glory in the *Muttersprache*. The *Kanadier* had similarly held tenaciously to the German. German was to be preserved not only for its cultural worth, but for the preservation of youth and for its religious value for the future of the church. German and religion were thought to be inseparable.

During World War II, Mennonites learned to be more cautious about their use of the *Muttersprache* to which they clung so fondly. Moreover, increasingly they acknowledge the need to be bilingual. The pacifist stance of the Mennonite community during time of war had already elicited considerable criticism and resentment and to insist upon speaking German, the language of the enemy, only aggravated the suspicion of the Anglo-Canadians. The *Muttersprache* facilitated the separatism which was centred in religious belief.

Following World War II, renewed, rigorous effort was made at regaining lost ground in the retention of the *Muttersprache*. Teachers' conferences conducted entirely in the German language were also held. Over against this apparent resurgence was increased cynicism towards such societies. In the face of such possible conflict over language, appeals were made for a "legitimate compromise" to avoid a "break with our elder brethren and sisters whose wise counsel and wider experience is desperately needed in guiding our churches through the crucial times in which we live" (Toews, 1961, 2).

The 1960s became the decade of change with reference to language. For five years (1963-1968), Conference year books were published in two languages. Most local churches were shifting from a predominantly German service to a bilingual or from a bilingual to English. By and large, the transition was, if somewhat slow, amicably achieved. But throughout most of the half-century, language continued to be a prominent factor of ethnicity, and with the retention of the language there was also the pulse-beat of religion, the language of the soul.

Commemorations. Finally, what lingers when assimilation is completed and the *Muttersprache* is abandoned are memories of the ethnic distinctives, hallowed by the religious setting in which they are rehearsed. Mennonites, either for reasons of gratitude or for the social occasion, enjoy commemorations. In 1924 the fiftieth anniversary of the coming of the Mennonites to the United States was celebrated. Recollections of the arrival of immigrants were recorded and published. Immigrants assembled as well to discuss common problems along with the celebration of their having emigrated from Russia. Others would assemble as an alumni gathering of a school or as former residents of a village. The centennial of the 1874 immigration proved to be a special year of commemorations. Even more recently a Canadian Mennonite Historical Society was organized in Winnipeg (December 1975) and a centre for Mennonite Brethren Studies was established in Winnipeg in July 1976, as well as a Mennonite Brethren Historical Society of Canada. Driedger identifies three further benchmarks that emerged in Winnipeg in 1978: the fifty-year celebration of the settlement of Mennonites in North Kildonan, a Heritage Centre built in Tuxedo, and the establishment at the University of Winnipeg of the first Mennonite Chair in Canada (Driedger, 1980a, 122-23). Such deliberate attempts to recollect and rehearse Mennonite ethnicity will only further sacralize their identity and help preserve their separateness.

Summary

The cohesiveness which contributes to sectarian persistence is particularly evident in the family solidarity and, until recently, the ethnicity of Canadian Mennonite Brethren. Because of their biblical understanding of the family, Mennonite Brethren emphasize the sanctity and indissolubility of marriage. Empirical evidence supports this view and practice of marriage and the family. Marriages are largely endogamous, and few separations and divorces occur. At the same time, the common practice of grace before meals and family worship, and the firm belief that premarital and extramarital sex are always wrong, indicate such solidarity, as does the fact that almost all Mennonite Brethren families own their home. The sociological function of the family serves to act as a shock-breaker to the first and second generation immigrants and to withstand the encounter with the secular world for the third and fourth generations. The threat of family erosion has increasingly been perceived by its church leaders, and rigorous attempts have been made to promote family solidarity both at a Conference level, through study sessions and official pronouncements, as well as at the family level by encouraging social functions which tie families together, deliberately structuring local church events to focus on the family, and bringing appropriate literature into the home.

Despite obvious change in the degree of ethnicity and the increased self-criticism which it engendered, ethnicity nonetheless prevails, if not conspicuously, then in rather subtle factors. The large percentage of foreign births and the continuous use, until recently, of the German language have been strong factors in the pertinacious hold of ethnicity. Not so obvious are factors of religious belief and participation, endogamous practices, parochial education and organizations, and the communalism apparent in the choice of friends. Yet, intimations of ethnicity continue to characterize Canadian Mennonite Brethren. The cohesive force of such ethnicity becomes apparent when one notes the common experiences accompanying successive waves of Mennonite immigration, when one appreciates how the collective responsibility of the *Reiseschuld* forged a common community, when one senses the emotional and associational bonds of a common *Muttersprache*, or when one rehearses through commemorative occasions those events which have become part of an ethnic heritage.

The cohesive impact of family bonds and peoplehood have undoubtedly facilitated the sacralization of the Mennonite Brethren identity and to that degree contributed to the persistence of sectarianism.

VII

Consolidating Identities

Crucial to Mennonite Brethren reality is the notion of a believers' church. Both the Anabaptist movement of the sixteenth century and the sectarian emergence of the Mennonite Brethren in the nineteenth century insisted upon a church in which believers voluntarily joined following baptism upon confession of faith. The believers not only witnessed to an experiential faith, begun through a conversion experience, but to an ongoing growth in faith, referred to here as sanctification. The consequence of such an experiential faith was devotionalism, that is, the cultivation of habits of devotion, and evangelism— encouraging others to embrace the same faith. Psychologically and sociologically, such personal transformation resulted in a new identity formation. Old ways were broken up and abandoned and a new self was forged, not only, theologically speaking, through regeneration or conversion, but sociologically speaking, through adopting a new orientation and reordering of priorities and values and by interaction with a new community. Through conversion and its correlatives, thus, a new identity was consolidated on a personal or micro-sociological plane.

But why, in the following discussion, does one associate conversion or religious transformation with charisma or religious leadership? It is because what happens psychologically through conversion and sanctification on a personal level occurs sociologically through charismatic leadership on a group level or macro-sociological plane. As Hans Mol maintains, conversion is to the person what charisma is to the social group (Mol, 1976, 50). In both instances, identities are consolidated— one personal, the other group or denominational. Gifted, influential leaders enable a group to make major adjustments and to forge a new identity so that members of a group evolve a collective awareness of their unity. Both conversion and charisma are in this sense mechanisms to facilitate change and consolidate identities. Such consolidation of identities enabled the Canadian Mennonite Brethren to persist as a religious movement in the twentieth century.

1. Conversion and Spiritual Life

Among the seven distinctives of the Mennonite Brethren Church, listed by J. A. Toews in his recent history, are experiential faith and personal witnessing. Especially these two distinctives come into focus at this time. The overarching purpose in the discussion of these aspects is to show that religious transformations have consolidated identity on a personal level. As a result the identity of Canadian Mennonite Brethren has been sacralized, thus facilitating the continuity of the religious movement.

Empirical Evidence of Identity Change

To incorporate the full scope of the identity change on a personal level, four separate measures are used to indicate the same.

Initial conversion. As in the discussion by Kauffman and Harder, "initial conversion" indicates the first major, subjective encounter with God accompanied by a personal crisis and resulting in a change of allegiance and behaviour (Kauffman and Harder, 1975, 84). Its measure through four separate questions taken from the Church Member Profile is summarized in Table vii-1. Initial conversion was explained to the respondents as a definite decision to become vitally committed to God, an explicit acceptance of Christ as Saviour, or as a time in life when they became aware of making a new start to walk with God. Among the groups measured, Canadian Mennonite Brethren have the highest percentage of conversion experience. The score of 95.3 percent (n=341) for Canadian Mennonite Brethren compares to only 34 percent (n=2174) in a sample measured by E. T. Clark (Clark, 1928, 47-48). Since baptism upon confession of faith is a requirement for membership, such a response is not surprising. In fact, while one would not expect all members to have a particular type of conversion experience, all would be expected to witness to some experience with Christ. It may be that several exceptions simply cannot pinpoint the "initial" part of the experience. What is astonishing is that almost one-half of the respondents had more than one such experience. Perhaps the second or subsequent experience is viewed as renewal of the original commitment. The median age, interestingly, is lower than in other Mennonite groups. While most decisions for Christ (i.e., 48 percent where n=158) are made in public church meetings, Mennonite Brethren, much more so than the other Mennonite, are led to such a decision by personal invitation (19.1 percent where n=63), which indicates that personal evangelism is stressed among Mennonite Brethren.

Sanctification. The ongoing experience of being saved by which the new identity is further consolidated is referred to as sanctification. The

Table VII-1

Initial Conversion Experience

	Percentage Distribution			
Questions and Responses	MC (n=1202)	GC (n=614)	NAMB (n=712)	CMB (n=359)
1. Was there a particular point in your life when you had a conversion experience?				
____ Yes	80	65	93	95.3
____ No	7	19	3	2.2
____ Uncertain	13	16	3	2.2
2. How many such experiences have you had in your life?				
____ One	42	52	57	51.5
____ Two	34	27	26	29.7
____ Three	14	10	12	14.1
____ Four or more	10	10	5	4.7
____ Median number	2.2	2.0	1.9	1.97
3. How old were you at the time of the first such experience?				
____ Median age	13.7	14.9	13.1	12.78
4. Where or how did this first experience occur?				
____ Public church meeting	72	55	56	48.0
____ Personal invitation	10	10	19	19.1
____ Church camp or school	5	12	6	8.5
____ Private experience	7	9	7	8.8
____ Small group	0	4	1	2.4
____ Other	5	10	11	13.1

Source: Church Member Profile, 1972.

understanding is not simply theological in which an instantaneous moral perfection or forensic righteousness is ascribed to the believers; it is also, on a practical level, the awareness that believers encounter experiences of God, especially also the presence of the Holy Spirit in their struggle against a personal devil. Table VII-2 lists the responses which indicate "Yes, I'm sure I have" to a number of such religious experiences in the day-to-day believers' life. Again, these were taken from the Church Member Profile. As the religious factor of ethnicity, so also here Canadian Mennonite Brethren have intense religious experiences, sensing keenly the presence of God and being saved by Christ, as well as the presence and activity of the devil; yet, few feel that personal misfortune was caused by the devil. While 72.8 percent (n=257) feel that God delivered them from danger in a difficult situation, only 26.8 percent (n=92) have experienced healing. Again while most Canadian Mennonite Brethren have experienced the work or filling of the Holy

Spirit, only 0.9 percent (n=3) have had the ecstatic experience of speaking in tongues. It appears that, while believers experience religion intensely, few claim to have the more radical healing by God, the more ecstatic encounters with the Holy Spirit, and the more direct misfortune caused by the devil. Canadian Mennonite Brethren obviously cannot be grouped with the charismatic movements; yet, they do claim to have consciously ongoing and meaningful religious experiences.

Table VII-2

Measures of Sanctification

Religious Experience Response: "Yes, I'm sure I have."	Percentage Distribution			
	MC (n=1202)	GC (n=614)	NAMB (n=712)	CMB (n=359)
A feeling that you were in a holy place	57	58	60	58.1
An awareness that sin and evil were all around you	64	58	68	69.6
A sense of being tempted by the devil	75	58	80	81.9
A feeling that some personal misfortune was caused by the devil	16	11	16	16.4
A feeling that God had delivered you from danger in a difficult situation	65	61	71	72.8
A sense of being loved by Christ	78	70	85	87.9
An experience of being healed by God	32	31	29	26.8
A feeling that the Holy Spirit gave you a special understanding concerning God's truth	45	39	60	60.6
A feeling of being filled by the overwhelming joy and power of the Holy Spirit	45	38	52	54.4
An experience of speaking in tongues	3	1	2	0.9

Source: Church Member Profile, 1972.

Devotionalism.   The religious practices which reflect these experiences are included in such devotional exercises as Bible reading, prayer, and commitment to God in the decisions of life. Table VII-3 indicates five such measures of devotionalism taken from the Church Member Profile. Once again, in all five measures Canadian Mennonite Brethren rank higher than the others measured. Stark and Glock found that 75 percent of Protestants pray once a week (Stark and Glock, 1968, 112); for Canadian Mennonite Brethren this would be about 99 percent (grouping the responses "several times per day," "daily," and "occasionally"). While 83.4 percent of Canadian Mennonite Brethren study their Bible frequently (at least once a week) or daily (49.4 percent study it daily), Stark and Glock noted that only 23 percent of Protestants in America read the Bible at home once a week or more and only 13 percent study it daily (Stark and Glock, 1968, 110). Canadian Mennonite Brethren, thus, observe fairly rigorous devotional habits.

Table VII-3
Measures of Devotionalism

	Percentage Distribution			
Questions and Responses	MC (n=1202)	GC (n=614)	NAMB (n=712)	CMB (n=359)
1. Other than at mealtime, how often do you pray to God privately on the average?				
Daily or more	78	73	82	86.8
2. Do the members of your household have a family or group worship other than grace at meals?				
Yes	41	42	61	67.4
3. How often do you study the Bible privately, seeking to understand it and letting it speak to you?				
Frequently/daily	68	58	77	83.4
4. In general, how close do you describe your present relationship to God?				
Close/very close	54	48	56	58.7
5. When you have decisions to make in your everyday life, how often do you ask yourself what God would want you to do?				
Often/very often	61	55	68	69.7

Source: Church Member Profile, 1972.

Evangelism.   Three questions on the Church Member Profile measure the degree of personal evangelism. Table VII-4 summarizes this information. Canadian Mennonite Brethren tend to be somewhat more bashful about sharing their Christian experience than their American counterparts. No doubt, the high degree of ethnicity accounts for part of this reluctance. And yet, Mennonite Brethren as a whole tend to be somewhat more active in personal witnessing than the two larger Mennonite groups with whom they were compared.

Non-Theological Dimensions of Religious Transformation

For Mennonite Brethren theologians, identity change or religious transformation has uniquely theological or supernatural components not subject to psychological or sociological analysis. Notwithstanding such contention, for a sociological analysis of a religious movement, one needs to analyse other than strictly theological components. And in doing so, one does not deny the preeminence of the theological.

Table VII-4

Measures of Personal Evangelism

Questions and Responses	Percentage Distribution			
	MC (n=1202)	GC (n=614)	NAMB (n=712)	CMB (n=359)
1. How frequently do you take the opportunity to witness orally about the Christian faith to persons at work, in the neighbourhood, or elsewhere?				
Never	32	40	31	30.2
Sometimes	51	44	49	52.9
Often/very often	17	16	20	16.8
2. How frequently have you invited non-Christians to attend your church and/or Sunday school services?				
Never/seldom	59	62	54	56.7
Occasionally	34	34	39	36.8
Frequently	7	4	8	6.5
3. Have you personally ever tried to lead someone to faith in Christ?				
No, never	25	26	13	13.7
Yes, a few times	67	66	74	76.0
Yes, often	8	9	13	10.3

Source: Church Member Profile, 1972.

The insistence upon conversion.   The importance to Mennonite Brethren of the initial conversion experience is apparent not only in the early history of the movement, but also in its continued emphasis to the present. As chapter five indicates, Mennonite Brethren see the very purpose of their denomination to witness to the need of a decisive conversion. Conversion has veritably become one of the rites of passage in the Mennonite Brethren life cycle. To test the accuracy of such an assertion, obituaries were read of two separate times, the last twenty published in the *Mennonitische Rundschau* in 1950 and the last twenty published in the *Mennonite Brethren Herald* in 1975. Of the twenty obituaries published in 1950, fifteen make special mention of conversion, indicating the age or approximate time when it occurred. Three of the five not mentioning conversion (although baptism was mentioned) were members of the General Conference Mennonite Church. All of the other seventeen obituaries were of Mennonite Brethren. Of the twenty obituaries published in 1975—all initially Mennonite

Brethren—all but one specifically indicated the time of conversion. It has become routine for Mennonite Brethren, therefore, to perceive of conversion as a conscious, measurable (in terms of time) experience of the believer, as the 95.3 percent of the respondents in the Church Member Profile indicated.

A closer look at psychological and sociological components of the conversion experience shows, first, that the median age for the initial conversion experience of Mennonite Brethren is just under thirteen. Moreover, such an experience in earlier times was an emotional crisis during which one felt guilt and remorse for sin, after which came acceptance of forgiveness as a gift from God, the transformation being possible only by faith, not through any rite or merit.

To experience initial conversion as a child, youth, or adult does not resolve all struggle with sin in subsequent life. As the Church Member Profile indicates, a number have a second such experience or more. Mennonite Brethren anthropologist Jacob Loewen analyses his own childhood conversion and asks:

Was I converted in stages? Did the change include only those areas of my self-life of which I was conscious at the time of conversion? Was it the recognition of guilt in "new" unregenerate areas in my life that precipitated the need for further experience? Were some of my intermediate conversions basically attempts to discharge guilt that arose from inadequate mastery of the Christian ideal? Were some of the crisis experiences necessitated by inadequate support during the learning or rehearsal of the Christian role?

Our candid answer to all of these questions is a qualified "yes" (Loewen, 1969, 2-6).

Viewed sociologically, such experiences appear to be renewal or re-vitalization crises in which the identity change is further consolidated. Viewed theologically, Mennonite Brethren have a greater problem explaining such repetition of "conversion." Even more problematic to the theologians is the increasingly early experience. Kauffman and Harder, on the basis of the five denominations surveyed in the Church Member Profile, indicate that the median age for conversion for the older generation (50 and over) was 15.2, for the middle generation (30-49) it was 13.8, and for the younger generation (20-29) it was 12.8 (Kauffman and Harder, 1975, 88). The resulting inability of children to match the deeply subjective and radical change in adults (or of pagans) and the failure of the church to provide for adequate nurture of children has led Mennonite Brethren philosopher Delbert Wiens to conclude: "Because we have a theology of conversion appropriate to adults but no adequate theology of Christian nurture, we know what to do with pagans but not what to do with our own children" (Wiens, 1965, 7). However, these unresolved theological problems have not unduly complicated the psychological and sociological understanding of the need for identity change. In fact, when theology fails to provide the needed rationale, some social-psychological explanation accounts for the ongoing necessity for religious transformation. In this instance, socialization has advanced the age where children can grasp the need for religious commitment.

Despite the theological problems, the necessity of conversion continues to be emphasized. This is apparent in the revised draft of the Confession of Faith, which states:

We are saved by the grace of God through faith in Christ. The Holy Spirit, through the Word of God, convicts man of his sin and need for salvation. Those who repent of their sin and trust in Christ as Saviour and Lord receive forgiveness. By the power of the Holy Spirit they are born into the family of God and receive the assurance of salvation. Saving faith involves a surrender of the will to Christ, a complete trust in Him and a joyful obedience to His Word as a faithful disciple (*GCYB*, 1975, 10).

Evidence of the conversion experience continues also to be the primary test of eligibility for baptism and church membership. Moreover, increasingly membership classes, in which conversion is studied theologically, are conducted prior to baptism. In addition, conversion has been taught in Sunday schools, vacation Bible schools, and from the pulpit. Thus, through various means conversion has been kept central in Mennonite Brethren teaching.

The practice of piety. The high response of Canadian Mennonite Brethren to the measures of devotionalism indicates that conversion is but a beginning in the Christian life, not an end in itself. Instruction to new believers was given not simply to prepare them for baptism, but, more importantly, to develop habits of Christian devotion which would foster spiritual growth. While theologically attempting to straddle the Calvinist-Arminian controversy, in practice Mennonite Brethren have been more Arminian, and failure to cultivate devotional habits has suggested a state of being a back-slider.

Enthusiasm to share the faith. Personal witnessing was one of the hallmarks of Mennonite Brethren in their early days. To a lesser degree such spontaneous sharing of the faith characterized new immigrants in the mid-1920s, often legitimately inhibited by their inability to communicate freely with their Anglo-Saxon neighbours. Theoretically, personal evangelism was believed in and preached and taught (especially in the Bible schools), but practised less. The Canadian Mennonite Brethren record of personal evangelism, according to the Church Member Profile data, while somewhat higher than the other Mennonite groups, does not speak of an aggressively conversionist sect. Only 16.8 percent (n=60) witness often or very often, and only 10 percent (n=37) have often tried to lead someone to faith in Christ. However, the relatively inactive second and third generations are likely not indicative of an indefinite decline in evangelism. Increasingly in recent years, such evangelistic agencies as Inter-Varsity Christian Fellowship, Campus Crusade, Navigators, Child Evangelism Fellowship, and various community crusades have stimulated Mennonite Brethren to become more active.

Sporadic renewal through revival. Routinization of charisma results in a loss of religious vitality. Both on a personal and group level, revival provides renewed commitment to the faith and joyous enthusiasm in sharing the same. Such renewal, then, becomes an effective mechanism for the consolidation of personal and group identity. Through the denominational papers, Mennonite Brethren spokespersons have both lamented the formalism of institutionalized religion and lauded the spontaneity of revivalism. Columnist John H. Redekop lamented that "the average Sunday morning service in the average Canadian M.B. church is much too formal. . . . What I miss is the element of spontaneity" (Redekop, 1964, 2). A year later he dispels the notion that education and sophistication make revivalism unnecessary. The head of a political science department in a Canadian university, he opines: "Revivalism is the antidote for sin and lukewarmness in the life of the Christian, not for ignorance and simplicity. The Christian who has a Doctor's degree needs revivalism just as much as does an illiterate garbage collector" (Redekop, 1965, 2). Editor Harold Jantz expressed the same need a year later:

To speak of revival makes us uneasy. . . . It is an admission of waywardness and coldness. . . . It is a word that doesn't fit easily into our social and cultural milieu.

Yet as I look throughout our Canadian M.B. churches, I sense a deeply felt need for a great quickening from above (Jantz, 1968, 3).

These voices from the media are representative of similar appeals from the pulpits.

Repeatedly, though sporadically, revivalism has spread through the Mennonite Brethren churches in the last half century and brought renewal to individual members. Such sporadic renewal, then, revitalized the spiritual fervour of initial conversion and facilitated growth or sanctification of the believer's life. Sociologically viewed, revivalism served as a further mechanism to consolidate a fragmenting religious identity and lend permanency to a movement, but not at the expense of petrifaction. Rarely, however, did revival occur without the catalytic help of a charismatic leader.

2. Charisma and Religious Leadership

What conversion does to identity formation on a personal level, charisma does on a group level. It picks up the loosened pieces of the social fabric, dislodged by the forces of change and secularization, and welds these into a new identity. It anchors change in the emotions of people. Hans Mol sees charismatic leaders more as catalysts for change than as innovators for revolution (Mol, 1976, 46). Called from within the group, they conserve social order, for they must hear what the masses hear. In keeping with their sectarian character, Mennonite Brethren, especially until recently, have been more prone to charismatic leadership than to the bureaucratic or rational type, or to that of traditional authority. As Max Weber states, "It is recognition on the part of those subject to authority which is decisive for the validity of charisma" (Weber, 1964, 359). This fact and the fact that "the corporate group which is subject to charismatic authority is based on an emotional form of communal relationship" (Weber, 1964, 360) explain why charisma, usually thought of as a quality of an individual, is associated with the identity of a group. What then has charisma done for the preservation of the Mennonite Brethren movement?

Some Facts of Canadian Mennonite Brethren Leadership

Is there a discrepancy between the Anabaptist vision of lay participation in the leadership roles of the church and the actual practice? A look at the empirical data reveals the following real facts. The Church Member Profile reflects a substantial involvement in lay or ordained offices. Table vii-5 shows that 58.2 percent (n=206) of Canadian Mennonite Brethren held positions of leadership (as minister, elder, council member, officer, Sunday school teacher, committee chairman, youth group officer, etc.) in the three years prior to the survey. Moreover, of these 10.5 percent (n=37) were ordained as a minister or deacon. In excess of one-half of the membership is thus involved in leadership roles. Compared to this, Fichter reports that only 6 percent of Catholics carry leadership roles in the parish, and Campbell and Fukuyama report that 36 percent of the United Church of Christ members held an office or served on a board or committee in the previous three years (Kauffman and Harder, 1975, 187).

Table vii-6 reflects the degree of professionalism which members desire in the ministry. Although more than one-half of the Canadian Mennonite Brethren sample believed that all members are ministers, about two-thirds agree that a church cannot be complete without an ordained minister. Most Canadian Mennonite Brethren (about 85 percent) still want a pastor with a full-time salary.

Table vii-7 indicates the role of women in church leadership. Canadian Mennonite Brethren are more conservative than either of the other two Mennonite groups measured or their American counterparts. Only one-fifth of the respondents would like larger numbers of qualified women to be elected, and only 5.6 percent (n=20) favour

Table VII-5

Leadership Involvement in Local Churches

	Percentage Responses			
Questions and Responses	MC (n=1202)	GC (n=614)	NAMB (n=712)	CMB (n=359)
1. Do you presently hold, or have held within the past three years, a position of leadership in your local congregation?				
Yes	58	54	56	58.2
2. Were you ever ordained as a minister or deacon?				
Yes	7	11	10	10.5

Source: Church Member Profile, 1972.

Table VII-6

Lay or Professional Church Ministry

	Percentage Response			
Questions and Responses	MC (n=1202)	GC (n=614)	NAMB (n=712)	CMB (n=359)
1. A proper view of congregational organization and leadership is that all members are ministers and should share, as they are able, in the ministerial functions of the congregation.				
Strongly agree/agree	61	55	54	55.0
2. A church congregation cannot be complete unless there is an ordained minister to lead the congregation and perform the ministerial functions.				
Strongly disagree/disagree	26	31	36	34.6
3. How important is it, in your opinion, that the pastor in your congregation be on full-time salary rather than earning all or part of his income through other employment?				
Of little importance/quite important	23	11	12	14.8

Source: Church Member Profile, 1972.

ordination of women to the ministry. While holding to such a dis-
criminating view, they, at the same time, do not feel that women are
discriminated against. Here, there is a decided discrepancy between
Mennonite Brethren belief and their own practice of giving women
considerable leadership responsibility in the overseas missionary work.
It is also not in keeping with the more radical view of the early Anabaptists who allowed for considerable leadership among women.

Table VII-7

Role of Women in the Church

	Percentage Response			
Questions and Responses	MC (n=1202)	GC (n=614)	NAMB (n=712)	CMB (n=359)
1. In the future, should larger numbers of qualified women be elected or appointed to church boards and committees at denominational, district, and congregational levels?				
Yes	29	40	26	20.8
2. Should the policy on ordinations in your denomination be changed to allow for the ordination of women to the Christian ministry?				
Yes	12	30	12	5.6
3. Do you believe that women in Canadian and American societies are being discriminated against and denied certain basic rights?				
Yes	15	20	14	11.9

Source: Church Member Profile, 1972.

Analysis of Leadership Patterns

With some strongly Anabaptist features, which emphasize lay leadership, and with some views discrepant with the Anabaptist vision, Canadian Mennonite Brethren leadership requires closer analysis. Does this
somewhat inconsistent stance reflect change in leadership patterns,
confusion in the role of leaders, or simply a disparity between the vision
and practice? A closer look at the types of leadership, the problems of
leadership, and the emerging patterns in leadership will help answer
these questions.

Types of religious leadership.   If more than one-half of the membership of Canadian Mennonite Brethren are involved in leadership roles
in the local congregation, what types of leaders are these? The forego-

ing data suggest that this is not tantamount to saying that more than one-half the membership are prophets or priests. Neither do these leaders fit Max Weber's two categories of individual bearers of charisma—ethical or exemplary prophets (Weber, 1969, 55). Nor is Joachim Wach's more extensive classification of types of religious authority adequate for explaining Mennonite Brethren leadership (Wach, 1971, 341-68). From the perspective of organizational types, that is, spheres of authority defined by geographic, political, or ecclesiastical boundaries, one may speak of Mennonite Brethren leadership in terms of congregational and conference levels. Congregational leadership has to do with the independent leadership of the local church, since Mennonite Brethren church polity recognizes congregational autonomy. The local congregation, however, is defined not always geographically but in terms of the members of a specific, local church. In a metropolitan area, therefore, the geographic distribution of the members of the different congregations overlaps considerably, since members are free to choose their own local church. Not only is membership within the local church clearly defined, but the sphere of authority of the leadership is restricted to the members of that respective church. Each local church of the 130 Mennonite Brethren churches in Canada has its body of leaders. Typical of such a group in a somewhat larger than average-sized church is that of the River East Mennonite Brethren Church in Winnipeg in which, of some 300 members, 70 are involved in local church boards, not including the many teachers and counsellors in the teaching agencies of the church on a given Sunday or mid-week.

Conference leadership varies with the type of conference—whether international (called General Conference), national, or provincial. While independent Mennonite Brethren conferences exist in numerous countries, there is not an international conference of all the Mennonite Brethren churches, except for the North American General Conference of Mennonite Brethren Churches (including Canada and United States), first constituted in 1879. Leadership on this level is naturally restricted to Canada and United States. The Canadian Mennonite Brethren Conference (known until 1945 as the Northern District Conference of the Mennonite Brethren Church of North America) was separately organized in 1910, and since then has elected its own leaders and conducted its own sessions of business. Provincial conferences, each with its own executive officers and boards of leaders, were organized as follows: Alberta (1927), British Columbia (1936), Manitoba (1929), Ontario (1931), and Saskatchewan (prior to 1910, initially in two districts—Herbert and Rosthern; after 1946 as one conference). The extent of membership involvement, therefore, in conference leadership at the different levels is rather impressive. In

1975, thirty-four Canadians served on the General Conference executive and boards; seventy-seven served on the Canadian Conference executive and boards, and several hundred served in provincial conferences. To fill executive and board or committee positions only in the local churches and conference structures requires widespread involvement of the individual member in such leadership positions of the organizational type.

From the perspective of function, one could view at least three separate types: first, those, as above, who are involved in administrative or policy-making bodies; second, those, more conspicuously, who provide leadership through the use of the pulpit—pastors, Bible expositors, evangelists, and missionaries; and third, those, usually with less personal charisma, who influence membership as scholars, educators, and writers.

Surveying the last half century of Canadian Mennonite Brethren history, one could isolate the following to be among the most influential leaders, for they exercised multiple gifts of leadership at multiple levels—local, provincial, Canadian, and General Conference levels. Presenting the most charismatic vignettes are H. S. Voth, in administrative and pastoral leadership; A. H. Unruh, in preaching, teaching, and writing; B. B. Janz, in church statesmanship, international diplomacy, and preaching; and J. A. Harder in lay pastoral leadership and Conference work. Less charismatic but perhaps more influential because of their educational contributions are such leaders in recent times as J. A. Toews, in teaching, preaching, and writing; J. H. Quiring, in teaching, administration, and pastoral ministries; F. C. Peters, in administration, teaching, and preaching; and D. Ewert, in teaching, preaching, and writing. Such extensive and effective leadership has significantly contributed to welding together the Canadian Mennonite Brethren identity in times of growth and change.

Problems in leadership. Despite the extensive lay participation, as well as strong exercise of professional leadership by gifted individuals, problems in church leadership have been detected and continue to the present. First among these is the tendency towards elitism. The above discussion of types of leadership indicates the extensive possibilities for involvement of members in leadership roles. Nonetheless, as Henry Regehr has shown in an analysis of leaders in both the General Conference (1945-1972) and Canadian Conference (1956-1973), the bulk of offices are held by a relatively small group of individuals (Regehr, 1972, 112-21). Regehr, however, is addressing himself to the first functional type indicated above, that is, Conference leadership. A long-time pastor, former college teacher and president, J. H. Quiring, raised the question, "Do we create an elite among our ministers?" His rhetorical question has the following reply: "If there is an 'elite' of ministers within our brotherhood it has been unconsciously created by a public that is not in the race for the leadership, but that wants to be served well and is willing to give unqualified recognition to those who meet their needs" (Quiring, 1972, 6). Such elitism, then, is innate to the Anabaptist view of the priesthood of all believers, since leadership positions and recognition are not hierarchically determined by a bishop or pope, but, in keeping with Weber's notion, the membership determines the recognition of charisma among the many who exercise leadership. Canadian Mennonite Brethren even today, therefore, continue to be welded together by such charisma.

The second problem relates to the role of the professional pastor among Canadian Mennonite Brethren. This is a recent problem, because until mid-century there were few, if any, full-time, salaried pastors. Most churches had several lay ministers, one of whom was chosen to be "leader." In the last two to three decades, almost all churches have secured salaried pastors. In recent years, several strong reactions have been noted. Waldo Hiebert, long-time Mennonite Brethren pastor in Kansas and California and currently Professor of Practical Theology at the Mennonite Brethren seminary in Fresno, argues that church leadership is in trouble because of its unholy posture of professionalism, its many demands upon the ministry today, and because of what leadership does to the personality of the leader. He explains the first dilemma in this manner:

He is expected to be "just a brother" but is also expected to have "expertise." He is to deny the division between clergy and laity, yet he is to perform the duties of a special class called clergy. We have created this dilemma ourselves. On the one hand we deny the clergy-laity division as being unscriptural (which it is!), and on the other hand we expect our pastors to be trained in a fully accredited graduate seminary!

So the pastor lives with these ambiguities. He is to lead, yet he is to have laymen lead also. He is to minister, yet he is to encourage the people of the church to minister. He is to preach, yet he is also to encourage others to minister the word. What shall he do? He is in trouble. After all, to be a Mennonite Brethren (Anabaptist) pastor is something very different than being a Lutheran "Pfarrer," different than being a Catholic priest, even different than being a Baptist or Presbyterian minister (Hiebert, 1975, 2-3).

Again, the problem arises because of the tension between adapting to an educated, urbanized, increasingly secularized, contemporary church setting, and simultaneously adhering to the charismatic type of leadership of the Anabaptist model. Little wonder that this tension is reflected in the empirical data, where 55 percent believe all members are ministers, yet 65 percent want an ordained minister for the congregation to be complete. Related problems, not elaborated here, are the ambiguity about the meaning of ordination and the shortage of pastors.

A third problem reflected in the empirical data has to do with the role of women in church leadership. For most Mennonite Brethren this has posed no problem, since women were not ordained. Moreover, in the Church Member Profile, only 6 percent wanted a change, and only 21 percent wanted greater representation on church boards and committees at local and conference levels. However, since the turn of the century women have been commissioned to serve in overseas missionary work—admittedly not as pastors or preachers—and have assumed much responsibility as leaders in administrative, teaching, and advisory capacities. Increasingly in recent years, church spokespersons voiced the need for greater involvement of women. In 1974, at the Canadian Conference in Vancouver, New Testament scholar David Ewert presented a moderate view in which he considerably liberalized the traditional Mennonite Brethren stance, while yet not advocating ordination of women (Ewert, 1974, 30-43). The 1975 Conference session responded to this study by taking the following position:

Be it therefore resolved:
1. That the Canadian Conference of M.B. Churches go on record as not favoring the ordination of women for the preaching and pastoral ministry nor their election to Boards and offices whose work is of the nature of eldership, such as the Board of Spiritual and Social Concerns, and the Board of Reference and Counsel or its equivalent.
2. That the Canadian Conference declare women eligible to be elected as delegates to conferences and to church and conference boards and committees other than those referred to in recommendation #1 (YB, 1975, 106).

Carried by a vote of 339 to 20, this resolution indicates a modified, although not completely liberalized, position of the involvement of women in the church. Here is a case where charisma has still not been validated by the group.

Emerging pattern of leadership. In summary form, the pattern of leadership which appears to be emerging is the following:
(1) Congregational or lay involvement in leadership continues to be prominent. There has been growth from a simple organizational structure with a few strong leaders to a complex structure and extensive participation of members in leadership. Organizational bureaucracy has not resulted in hierarchical authority. Charismatic authority has safeguarded the group identity.
(2) Professional pastoral leadership has come to stay. The tension resulting from the shift of lay leadership to the one-pastor system has brought a corrective which insists upon team or multiple leadership. The pastor does not assume unlimited authority, nor is he

alone responsible for the work of ministry; instead, he leads in a team ministry. Charisma continues to be validated by the group, rather than traditional authority assumed by inheritance or bureaucratic authority assigned by an arch-ecclesiastic.

(3) Women are increasingly recognized as equal in the bestowal of gifts and the exercise of the gifts. Ordination of women, however, is not an option. Charismatic leadership by women is limited only because the group has not validated and recognized such charisma.

(4) Regionalism is increasingly becoming dominant. Few individuals on a national level are recognized for their administrative, theological, or pastoral insights. A single individual does not assume a moderating position for long. Mobility in leadership reflects a charisma which is brittle, albeit necessary, for group identity on a regional level.

(5) The first generation of church leaders following the immigration of the mid-1920s has almost wholly passed from the scene. The third generation is entering the ranks. The charisma of the second generation, somewhat clouded at times, resurfaces sufficiently to assure the brotherhood that the Anabaptist vision of charismatic leadership still prevails, however blighted.

In conclusion, then, the church of 1975 is still firmly rooted in the brotherhood concept. Yet, decisive and effective leadership is demanded, while cautiously shared. As in time past, so today group identity is consolidated through charisma, despite the threats which jeopardize the continuity of the group.

Summary

For a religious movement to persist, identities will need to be consolidated both on a personal and social level. In this sense, conversion is to the individual identity what charisma is to the group—both mechanisms leading to identity formation. Canadian Mennonite Brethren consider conversion and personal evangelism among their continuing distinctives. Empirical evidence confirms not only theoretical belief in, but actual experience of, such conversion, the most frequent occasion being the public church meeting or a personal invitation. Measures of growth in spiritual life through sanctification and devotionalism, according to the Church Member Profile, likewise rank the Mennonite Brethren slightly above other Mennonite groups. Less prominent, although still in excess of other Mennonites measured, is their involvement in personal evangelism. To account for such continued vitality, one must note the place of conversion in the Mennonite Brethren church membership requirement, in theology, and in preaching, despite the practical inconsistency of using essentially an adult conversion model, designed for out-group members, and applying it to children of believers. The resulting neglect in nurture is partly compensated for by emphasizing the cultivation of devotional, pious habits. Inhibitions about sharing their Christian experience, on account of the ethnicity of the first and second generation immigrants, have largely been overcome by the present generation, although loss of religious vitality through routinization of charisma still hampers the witness. To overcome such formalism, revivalism is encouraged and sporadically occurs in local churches and communities and almost routinely in Christian high schools. Conversion and its correlatives continue to be most meaningful means of consolidating a fragile identity on a personal level.

On a group level, that is, on a national denominational level, it is charisma which achieves such consolidation of identity. Weber's view that those subject to authority must validate charisma by recognizing it has been shown to be the case among Canadian Mennonite Brethren. Empirical data from the Church Member Profile indicate that there is in excess of 50 percent congregational involvement in leadership, yet there is a continued demand for ordained, salaried pastors. Women, however, are generally not wanted in positions of leadership. A more intensive analysis of leadership patterns shows two distinct types of leaders from an organizational perspective, congregational and conference, the latter being provincial, national, or General Conference. From the functional perspective one can isolate managerial, proclamatory, and scholarly types. Each level has its own unique charisma. The most obvious problems—the tendency towards elitism, the role of the professional pastor, and the role of women—result from societal change and differentiation which impinge upon the Anabaptist notion of the priesthood of all believers. The resulting emerging pattern is one which honours congregational involvement, professional leadership, increased participation of women, and decentralization of authority. Charisma has enabled the brotherhood notion of leadership to prevail, since those subject to authority—the members—recognize that type of leadership which sacralizes their identity.

VIII

Facilitating Socialization

Those who have strong convictions about being Christian and being evangelical Anabaptists and, even more specifically, being Mennonite Brethren, want to ensure the retention of their sectarian stance beyond their own generation. Whether the process of perpetuating their values is inadvertent and informal or deliberate and through formal instruction, it is the process of socialization which accounts for the transmission of their heritage. This learning process of socialization is defined by Talcott Parsons as "the acquisition of the requisite orientations for satisfactory functioning in a role" (Parsons, 1950, 205) and by Peter and Brigitte Berger as "the process through which an individual learns to be a member of society" (Berger and Berger, 1975, 55). Applying the socialization to being Mennonite Brethren, one has in mind those orientations which specifically prepare a younger generation to embrace those beliefs and practices which characterize Mennonite Brethren. As Gertrude Selznick points out, two complementary processes seem to be at work: the transmission of social and cultural heritage and the development of personality (Selznick, 1973, 91).

The following discussion of socialization of Canadian Mennonite Brethren values is particularly concerned with the first of Selznick's two processes: the transmission of a religious heritage (but one aspect of the social and cultural heritage). The aims of such socialization, according to Selznick, include the inculcation of disciplines, the instilling of aspirations (and restriction of the same), the acquisition of identity, the teaching of social roles, and learning of skills (Selznick, 1973, 94-95). No doubt, much of the socialization occurs within the family and through the informal contacts with members of the closely knit group. This chapter, in particular, examines that facilitation of socialization which occurs outside the family setting and through deliberately, although routinely, structured occasions: the weekly participation in church activities and the educational programs in parochial schools.

114

1. Weekly Church Participation

What transpires from week to week in the local church largely determines the permanency of the religious movement. The activities of the average Canadian Mennonite Brethren Church will much resemble those of a typical evangelical sectarian group. Again, it may be well to examine the specifics of such involvement before assessing its meaning for the continuity of the movement.

Measures of Participation

On a given Sunday morning almost any Canadian Mennonite Brethren local church will provide evidence of vitality. The cursory notice of the many cars which fill the parking lots and the full pews inside the building can be substantiated with the following data which provide more accurate measures of participation.

Associationalism. Table VIII-1 indicates measures of associationalism, that is, the frequency of attendance at church meetings and the degree of actual involvement according to the Church Member Profile. Church attendance is simply taken for granted as 98.2 percent (n=293) of the respondents indicate, if one combines the responses "almost every week" and "once a week or more." This high attendance habit exceeds the United States Mennonite Brethren and that of other Mennonite groups measured. Compared to other Canadian denominations, the Mennonite Brethren exceed considerably the larger Protestant churches and even the Roman Catholic. Table VIII-2 supplies this information, the word "regular" suggesting at least twice a month, usually weekly (Mol, 1974, 3). In yet another survey, Stark and Glock reported the following percentage for those who responded "nearly weekly or better" attendance: Sects, 93; Southern Baptists, 84; Roman Catholics, 80; Presbyterian, 58; Episcopalian, 56; and Congregational, 47 (Stark and Glock, 1968, 84). Again, Canadian Mennonite Brethren exceeded the highest of these American figures, which themselves appear so much higher than Mol's findings for Canada. Sunday school attendance for most Sundays or every Sunday possible is likewise high (72.2 percent; n=257), but not as high as the North American Mennonite Brethren response (79 percent). American Mennonite Brethren appear to attend Sunday school more regularly than Canadian. Attendance on days other than Sunday likewise is high (42.5 percent; n=152). Regular participation in Sunday school teaching in excess of one year for the ten-year period prior to the survey was 40.6 percent (n=144), 28.2 percent serving regularly one to five years and 12.4 percent serving regularly for most of the ten years. One is not surprised, then, to note the point earlier made that 58.2 percent (n=206) have held a position of leadership in the local church in the three years prior to the survey. Mennonite Brethren, thus, have exceptionally high responses in the measures of associationalism.

Table VIII-1

Measures of Associationalism

	Percentage Distribution			
Questions and Responses	MC (n=1202)	GC (n=614)	NAMB (n=712)	CMB (n=359)
1. On the average, how often have you attended church worship services (on Sunday morning, evening, and/or other days) during the past two years?				
Less than once a month	2	6	1	0.6
Once or twice a month	4	8	2	1.1
Almost every week	23	28	17	15.5
Once a week or more	71	58	80	82.7
2. How frequently do you attend Sunday school?				
Most Sundays	11	12	12	8.4
Every Sunday possible	76	54	67	63.8
3. How regularly do you attend any youth or adult meetings held on days other than Sunday that are related to your local congregation?				
Never/seldom	36	45	27	25.7
Occasionally	28	26	30	31.8
Regularly	36	28	43	42.5
4. Within the past ten years, how frequently have you served as a Sunday school teacher or department leader?				
Never	-	-	40	38.7
A few times, or as substitute	-	-	13	12.1
Served regularly for less than one year			8	8.5
Served regularly for one to five years			27	28.2
Served regularly for all or most of the past ten years			12	12.4
5. Do you presently hold, or have you held within the past three years, a position of leadership in your local congregation?				
Yes	58	54	56	58.2

Source: Church Member Profile, 1972.

Attitudes to participation. Over against the practice of attending and participating are the measures of attitude depicted in Table VIII-3. Just over two-thirds (n=239) derive very much or quite a lot of inspiration and strength, and another 27.5 percent (n=98) derive some—these two categories suggesting that for 94.6 percent (n=357) of Canadian Mennonite Brethren such attendance has considerable merit. By the same token, almost the opposite responses are elicited to the degree of boredom and disinterest. Similarly, Sunday school shows a high level of interest, 46.7 percent (n=162) not wanting to miss any and 34.9 percent (n=121) having no regrets if occasionally absent. Thus, for 81.6 percent (n=282) it appears to have considerable meaning, even if not as meaningful as the worship service. It would seem that larger numbers, 79.6 percent (n=284), are interested or strongly interested in serving in the home congregation than in fact do participate (cf. Table VIII-1). Either there is a discrepancy between one's stated intent and actual practice or the Canadian Mennonite Brethren Church has failed to mobilize its human resources. Finally, the question on voluntarism suggests that 80.5 percent (n=284) really want to participate and enjoy it. Only 19.3 percent (n=68) felt they ought to participate, although they did not always enjoy it. Canadians demonstrate a higher degree of voluntarism than their American brethren. Only one respondent felt he participated because of pressure or the expectation of it. The overwhelmingly prevalent attitude to church participation, both in attendance and in service, is positive—providing inspiration, enjoyment, and voluntary participation.

Table VIII-2
Church Attendance by Denomination

Response	Percentage Distribution					
	Mennonite Brethren (n=359)	French Catholics (n=619)	English Catholics (n=283)	Presbyterians (n=103)	United Church (n=474)	Anglicans (n=245)
Regular	98.2	87.8	68.9	24.3	22.7	19.2
Irregular	1.7	12.2	13.1	75.7	77.3	80.8

Source: Canadian National Election Study, 1965;   Church Member Profile, 1972.

Meaning of Such Participation

How, then, can one account for the high degree of church participation among Canadian Mennonite Brethren? It is not sufficient simply to reply that one generation is intent upon socializing the next. This also is true, but more immediate and overt is the meaning that such participation provides for the members and their families. Humans need ritual, want religious knowledge, crave fellowship, and must channel their enthusiasm in service. But the meaning is not without its tensions. The validity of the meaning and the redemptive factor of the tension generated in the struggle for meaning contribute towards the continued participation and inadvertently enhance the socialization process. Such participation achieves at least four functions.

Table VIII-3

Measures of Attitude to Church Participation

	Percentage Distribution	
Questions and Responses	NAMB (n=712)	CMB (n=359)
1. How much spiritual inspiration and strengthening do you feel you get from a typical Sunday morning worship service in your congregation?		
Very much/quite a lot	67	67.1
Some	26	27.5
Very little/none at all	7	5.4
2. How much boredom and disinterest do you experience in a typical Sunday morning worship service at your church?		
Very much/quite a lot	8	5.0
Some	27	27.0
Very little/none at all	65	67.9
3. Which statement best expresses your situation and feeling about Sunday school at your church?		
Would not want to miss any	46	46.7
No regrets if occasionally absent	38	34.9
Attend because it is expected or required	5	4.0
Dislike it, and so skip whenever I can	1	1.2
Don't attend	11	13.3
4. To what extent are you interested in serving your home congregation in Sunday school teaching, church project leadership, or other responsibilities for which you have abilities?		
Strongly interested/interested	75	79.6
Some interest	16	11.5
A little interest/no interest	10	9.0
5. Which of the following statements comes closest to your reason for participation in the life of the church?		
I really want to participate and enjoy it	76	80.5
I feel I ought to participate, but do not always enjoy	22	19.3
I feel I have to participate, because expected	2	0.3

Source: Church Member Profile, 1972.

It enables worship.   Religious persons need ritual, for rites articulate and reiterate a system of meaning (Mol, 1976, 233). Among religious rites are the private and informal, such as the devotional exercises referred to in chapter seven, as well as the formal and public. For Mennonite Brethren, the Sunday morning worship service is such a formal, public gathering which becomes a collective reaffirmation of the meaning and sacredness of religion. As Stark and Glock suggest, it helps people *feel* religious (Stark and Glock, 1968, 82). Drawing attention to the sociological and psychological by-products of ritual does not deny the subordinate role of ritual to theology, for it is only in ideology that ritual finds its meaning and legitimation. In practice, however, the sociological and psychological components are important because of the tangible aspects and expressive nature of such ritual.

The worship service for Mennonite Brethren was never meant to be mere ritual. Contrary to the services of the Mennonite church from which the Mennonite Brethren seceded, their public worship was characterized by informality and spontaneity. Despite the rejection of liturgical elements (including the reading of prayers), certain features of public worship reoccurred. Prominent among these were singing, spontaneous prayer, and preaching. From the outset, congregational singing was always a vital part of the worship services, and hymnals helped perpetuate the musical heritage. And so congregational singing has further been memorialized in the Mennonite Brethren Church. Worship has also been facilitated through choirs, musical instruments, and singing by small male, female, or mixed groups. Especially choir singing received the attention of church musicians, as indicated in the annual reports.

More representative of the spontaneous nature of Mennonite Brethren worship services were the public prayers offered by both men and women in the audience. These *Gebetstunden* for many years constituted a regular part of the worship service. Today they are less frequent, but spontaneous prayers may still be offered by way of introduction, for the offertory, or as a separate part of a Sunday morning worship service. Few prayers are written beforehand and read, although this practice is now growing in frequency.

Most prominent, however, in Mennonite Brethren worship is the sermon, as the central place of the pulpit in church architecture indicates. The pulpit was to draw attention not to the preacher, but to the Word. Typical of such preaching during the first half of the century is the collection in 1953 by Dr. G. D. Huebert of 315 sermon outlines by some sixty-two preachers, mostly Canadian Mennonite Brethren (the exceptions are those of American Mennonite Brethren who frequently preached in Canada). Most sermons submitted could be defined as textual (where the development of the sermon is based on the actual text) rather than topical. Some of the outlines are heavily buttressed with additional Scripture texts. Of the 315 sermons, 108 have Old Testament texts, the most prominent being Psalms (28 sermons), Genesis (16), Isaiah (15), Proverbs (6), Exodus (5), and Joshua (5). Of the 207 New Testament texts, the most prominent were John (37), Luke (33), Matthew (32), Hebrews (25), Acts (18), Romans (16), I Corinthians (11), and Revelation (11). The themes which these sermons reflect are a further interesting commentary of Mennonite

Brethren preaching. Of the 315 sermons selected, 60 had to do with conversion and salvation themes, 60 were exhortations on Christian conduct and life-style ("Wandel, Warnung, und Ermahnung"), 56 related to Jesus Christ, 48 concerned the church and the believers, 34 were mission and service oriented, 31 were sermons relating to trials and comfort, 30 focused on God and the Holy Spirit, 24 exhorted to faith and trust, and only 15 spoke of love and grace. Smaller numbers of sermons for special occasions were also included. It may be fair, therefore, to characterize Mennonite preaching until about 1950 as simple, biblical preaching centred on New Testament themes relating to salvation by Jesus Christ, the New Testament church, and the life of the believer. Rather than being profoundly theological, the sermons appear to be more practically oriented. Exceptions to the average Sunday morning sermons were the expository messages by such men as J. W. Reimer and A. H. Unruh, the latter being lauded as "expository preacher without peer." One glimpse from his biographer depicts Unruh's preaching as follows:

Unruh wanted his sermons to build up the congregation; for that reason they had to have content. For him they had to be instructive and informative. But that does not mean his sermons were stuffy, for his interpretations of the Scriptures usually turned into a strong appeal directed at the hearts of his listeners. At times he cut deeply into people's consciences; then again, he would put the balm of Gilead on troubled souls (Ewert, 1975, 122-23).

Whether referring to singing, prayer, or preaching, the tension between routinization and spontaneity is becoming increasingly apparent. In congregational and choir singing, the tension becomes evident in the difficulty of choosing a hymn on the continuum with a gospel song by Sankey at one extreme and an anthem by Bach at the other, or in finding the appropriate accompaniment by guitar, piano, or organ. All forms find their expression in today's Mennonite Brethren Church. Increasingly prayers are read from the Worship Aids of the hymnal or written beforehand by the worship leader. At the same time, conversational prayer (where sentence prayers are alternately uttered) and casual, spontaneous "talk" with God is characteristic of the small Bible study groups and occasional worship service. Sermons, once extemporaneous or memorized, are mostly written out and not infrequently read. With increasing diversity of taste and vocational and educational background, today's church members make demands for both the spontaneous and informal as well as for the liturgical and formal. It appears the most viable worship practice is to attain a balance in which the tension between the casual and the structured is preserved.

It provides instruction. Religious persons also want to be taught, for knowledge legitimates rites and gives substance and meaning to the tenets of faith. Related to belief, religious knowledge does not necessarily produce belief, for belief can exist on the basis of very little knowledge. Nonetheless, knowledge of its history, traditions, and scriptures helps to preserve belief and perpetuate a religious movement. No doubt, the single most effective teaching agency in the Canadian Mennonite Brethren Church has been the Sunday school. To demonstrate the growth of the Sunday schools as well as youth work, Table VIII-4 summarizes the information at five-year intervals. Until 1969 there was continuous increase, the Sunday school enrolment having exceeded the membership. A sharp decline occurred between 1970 and 1972 (the total enrolment dropping from 19,084 to 15,645). No doubt, the smaller families contributed to the decline.

Table VIII-4

Growth of Churches, Sunday Schools, and Youth Programs

Year	Churches	Member-ship (no.)	Sunday School (no.)	Classes (no.)	Total Students	Collection ($)	Youth Groups (no.)	Youth Attending (no.)
1924	22	1,797	20	144	1,637	$ 1,686.58	18	883
1929	32	3,143	32	210	2,320	2,258.53	26	960
1934	54	5,195	54	294	3,895	1,488.82	43	3006
1939	65	6,421	61	414	5,408	2,650.16	52	3852
1944	67	6,866	59	476	5,581	7,283.42	54	3984
1949	82	10,313	59	612[a]	7,905	21,034.00	--	--
1954	79	12,206	79	879	11,371	42,838.81	67	--
1959	82	13,946	82	1297	14,180	70,527.00	56	--
1964	108	15,145	108	1539	16,496	98,562.00	47	--
1969	124	16,660	124	1982	19,986	121,453.00	--	--
1974	115	18,459	115	2281	16,112	--	--	--

Source: Year Book, 1924 to 1974.

[a] Teachers with assistants.

Despite the fluctuation in the total enrolment pattern in recent years, Sunday school by no means belongs to the era of the past for Canadian Mennonite Brethren. Since before 1925, Sunday school statistics and occasional expressions of concern were brought to the attention of the national Conference. Since then annual reports have been submitted to the Conference. With the reorganization of the Conference structure in 1967, the Sunday School Committee was subsumed under the Board of Christian Education, which, in turn, appointed a Sunday School Commission to attend to perennial concerns. In 1964 an executive secretary for Sunday school and youth was appointed on a part-time basis, and in 1967 a full-time executive secretary was appointed to promote Christian education.

Such intensive socialization is not without its tensions. Recurring problems mentioned in annual reports include: the language problem (transition from German to English), inadequate curriculum, lack of trained teachers, and the disparity between knowledge and practice. The last-mentioned problem becomes especially apparent in Kauffman and Harder's Church Member Profile. While Sunday school participation showed a positive correlation with Bible knowledge, spiritual maturity, and morality (Kauffman and Harder, 1975, 207-10), Mennonite Brethren, who ranked highest among the Mennonite groups in variables of faith, ranked among the lowest in variables of ethics (not personal morality, but social ethics). Thus, socialization at the cognitive level appears to be more successful than at the practical level.

It allows for fellowship.   Among the teaching agencies of the local congregation are those which accommodate the socializing penchant along with the socializing function. While their alleged intent is to meet for devotional and instructive purposes, such church groups as ladies' societies, often called mission circles, and youth groups also satisfy the need for fellowship. Table viii-4 indicates the number of youth groups through the years and the average attendance where this figure was submitted in annual statistical reports. In addition, one could include the participation in choirs. For example, in 1959, there were 66 major church choirs with 1,901 singers and an additional 18 youth choirs with 471 singers. And 1974 lists 91 church choirs and 16 youth choirs, in addition to 46 children's, 9 girls', 25 male, and 19 ladies' choirs (*YB*, 1974, 112; *YB*, 1959, 137). How then can one account for such extensive participation of youth in Canadian Mennonite Brethren churches?

Throughout their history, Canadian Mennonite Brethren have organized church activities which include the youth. Until mid-century, the monthly *Jugendverein* involved mainly the youth in sponsoring a worship program (including music, drama, poetry, sermon, and children's features) to which the whole community was invited. More recently, youth meetings with their own adult sponsors have been separately conducted. In recent years, special national youth meetings have been conducted at the Banff School of Fine Arts with a program comprised of devotional, instructional, athletic, and entertainment features. Finally, the sermons, published articles, and booklets specifically directed to youth have been instrumental in retaining the youth in church activities. In the varied activities of the youth in the local church, provincial or national levels, the tension continues between the human need for socializing and the church's prescription for socialization. In the church setting, the balance finds expression in fellowship, and it is this fellowship which contributes to the continuity of the religious movement.

It motivates outreach.   While the socializing agencies are primarily designed to unite and retain the church family, that is, the in-group, several of the agencies incorporate the evangelistic concern of the conversionist sect. Annually, it is the vacation Bible school and camp programs which include this evangelistic concern for the out-group. In 1975, for example, enrolment in vacation Bible schools was 4,544 for the five provinces with a staff of 781 (*YB*, 1975, 110-11).

While the mission Sunday schools have decreased in number, two new teaching and outreach agencies were aggressively incorporated into the socialization program of the church, Pioneer Girls and Christian Service Brigade. Initially simply organized as boys' and girls' clubs, the growth in these programs has been remarkable. The 1975 record indicates 3,095 enrolled in Pioneer Girls with a staff of 709, and 2,389 enrolled in Christian Service Brigade with a staff of 586 (*YB*, 1975, 110-11). This quasi-educational program greatly facilitates the congregation's influence in a given community, mobilizing both youth and adults to staff the program and inviting new recruits for Sunday school and the church program generally. The tension it generates is that between conservation of the in-group children and evangelization of the out-group. Again, both are required for a continued, viable program. Church participation, then, achieves four of the primary goals of any local Christian congregation—worship, teaching, fellowship, and evangelism—all in the deliberate attempt at socialization.

2. Formal Instruction in Educational Institutions

The structured socialization which occurs for longer periods, possibly several months to several years at a time, encompasses four types of private institutions—Bible schools, high schools, Bible college and college of arts, and seminary. Numerous Canadian Mennonite Brethren have attended such private schools of other denominational or interdenominational agencies. The present discussion, however, is limited to the influence of Canadian Mennonite Brethren institutions, although recognition must be given to the substantive contributions of other schools.

The Church Member Profile Data

A look at the present facts will highlight the importance of such parochial training. It is significant that 59.1 percent (n=211) of the Canadian Mennonite Brethren respondents attended a Mennonite school.

This is higher than any of the groups measured in the Church Member Profile data. Table VIII-5 indicates the large proportion of Canadian Mennonite Brethren who have attended Christian high schools (25.8 percent) or Bible schools or institutes (the latter "institutes" being a more recent designation for "Bible school," perhaps somewhat upgraded and with longer terms), which together constitute 39.7 percent (n=142). Kauffman and Harder observe that, taken as a whole, the proportion coming under the influence of one or more of these schools is increasing, since among respondents aged 20-29, 53 percent attended such schools, compared to only 39 percent for those aged 50 or over (Kauffman and Harder, 1975, 230).

Table VIII-5
Percentage Attendance at Mennonite Schools

Type of School	Percentage Distribution			
	MC (n=1202)	GC (n=614)	NAMB (n=712)	CMB (n=359)
Elementary	10	6	7	6.4
Secondary	20	14	19	25.8
Winter bible school	12	6	15	24.6
Bible institute	2	4	10	15.1
College	17	24	16	7.8
Seminary (graduate level)	2	5	2	1.4
Did not attend church school	56	56	48	40.6

Source: Church Member Profile, 1972.

A Brief Survey of Canadian Mennonite Brethren Educational Institutions

In 1925 the Mennonite Brethren of Canada already had begun their own unique program of parochial education. It was not simply a carry-over of what the American Mennonite Brethren church had developed in the previous half century. Two separate influences constituted the most formative forces in the development of the Canadian Mennonite Brethren education. On the one hand, the *Kanadier* had early recognized their own need for religious instruction. On the other hand, the *Russlaender* brought with them the strong tradition of instruction in German and religion as part of their elementary and high school training, since all schools in the Mennonite colonies of Russia (from 1869 to 1920) were under the supervision of the Mennonite

Board of Education in Molotschna. Both the *Kanadier* and *Russ-laender*, thus, contributed to the development of Canadian Mennonite Brethren schools.

The Bible schools. The first Bible school of the Canadian Mennonite Brethren Church (founded in 1913 in Herbert, Saskatchewan) was largely patterned after the school of its early teacher, William Best-vater, who had been trained at Moody Bible Institute. The Winkler Bible School was a model of the Tschongrau, the curriculum of which was patterned on similar subjects taught at the Baptist seminary in Hamburg, where its founder had been trained. In time, twenty-one separate Bible schools were operated by the Canadian Mennonite Brethren, the largest number during 1942 when fifteen were in exis-tence, with an aggregate enrolment of some 400 (Klassen, 1964, 6). By 1975 a number of the schools had been consolidated, so that there were only three Bible schools with an aggregate enrolment of 564 (*MR*, 1974, 9). While facilities have been modernized, teaching faculty has up-graded its credentials, and curriculum has undergone modifica-tions, the objectives of the schools have remained essentially the same. Initially, the intent was to supply churches with members who were thoroughly trained in biblical understanding, from whom the churches could then select its workers. Representative of the continuing purpose of these schools is the terse statement of objective of the Coaldale Bible School in 1955:

1. To teach and instruct young people in the great fundamental doctrines of the Christian faith;
2. To develop Christian character and promote spiritual growth through the study of the Scriptures, devotional exercises, and various Christian ac-tivities;
3. To train and prepare young people for various fields of Christian service. Special consideration is given to Sunday school training (*Konferenz-Jugend-blatt*, hereafter *K-J*, XI, 1955, 15).

Bible knowledge, spiritual growth and commitment, and Christian service continue to characterize the objectives of these schools (Konrad, 1967, 211).

Despite the strength with which they continue, their history has not been without stress and considerable personal sacrifice. Until recently, facilities consisted of bare essentials, teachers were meagerly sup-ported, and students devoted several years to a training which pro-vided no material return, let alone theological degrees. Moreover, for one-half century of history of a small denomination to witness the rise and decline of some eighteen schools appears to suggest colossal in-stitutional experimentation and atrophy. However, viewed develop-mentally, one can see the growth of regional and primitive schools into consolidated and sophisticated institutions. The tensions that have accompanied this development have thus enabled the sound establishment of several widely supported and highly appreciated parochial Bible schools which are attracting increasing numbers of students from other than Mennonite Brethren churches. No doubt, the Bible school movement has contributed greatly to the vitality of the church through this aggressively conspicuous means of socialization.

Christian high schools. That composite vision, which in its early stage embodied a cultural-religious concern in its attempt to preserve both German and religion, eventually found its fulfilment in the Christian high school movement of the Mennonite Brethren. During the first decades of this century, Canadian Mennonite Brethren attended the inter-Mennonite schools at Gretna, Manitoba, and Rosthern, Saskatchewan. The increasing demand for secondary school education and the rapid urbanization immediately following World War II led Mennonite Brethren to establish their own high schools. The Mennonite Educational Institute in Clearbrook, B.C., founded in 1944, has continued to have the largest enrolment, with some 430 students in 1975. In Yarrow, B.C., the Sharon Mennonite Collegiate served the neighbouring community from 1945 to 1970. In Alberta, the Alberta Mennonite High School provided that province with Christian training from 1946 to 1962. In Winnipeg, the Mennonite Brethren Collegiate Institute has continued since 1945 with an enrolment in 1975 of 360. In Ontario, Eden Christian College at Niagara-on-the-Lake was begun in 1945 and in 1975 had an enrolment of 315. As in the case of Bible schools, the high schools not only have improved their physical facilities and up-graded their teaching staff, but have become stable institutions, securing their widespread support from the respective regions.

Typical of the Mennonite Brethren schools established in the 1940s is the following statement of purpose by Eden Christian College, which reflects the conversionist stance of the Mennonite Brethren:

1. direct unsaved students to a conversion experience;
2. train the students in the nurture and admonition of the Lord;
3. lay the foundation for a fruitful life of service in the Kingdom of God;
4. seek to preserve the spiritual heritage with which God has blessed our church;
5. offer a course of studies in which scholarship and academic thoroughness are fostered in a truly Christian atmosphere (*MBH*, 1965, 5).

The Christian high school, then, has become a powerful agency to socialize a younger age group of Mennonite Brethren.

Despite these strong endorsements of the parochial schools, the high schools, especially in the earlier years of their history, were not without their tensions. Building permanent structures, employing qualified teachers, and maintaining the operation without any government grant or tax support have repeatedly required great personal sacrifice of the many contributors. Such tensions, however, have enabled the schools to mature and provide the stability and strength that are apparent today.

Bible College and College of Arts.   While Tabor College in Hillsboro, Kansas, and especially the Bible department, were supported by the Canadian Conference from before 1925 until 1955, such moral and financial support and continuous attendance by some Canadian students did not replace the need for a school of higher theological training in Canada.

The need to establish its own school for higher theological education ("hoehere Bibelschule") was expressed as early as 1939, and in 1943 the national Bible school committee (appointed several years earlier to coordinate Bible school instruction) was asked to investigate the possibility of a higher theological school. At the 1944 Conference specific recommendations were passed to begin the Mennonite Brethren Bible College at Winnipeg (Doerksen, 1948). Established initially as a "hoehere Bibelschule," the college had as its objective "to provide an opportunity for earnest young men and women to prepare adequately for the high calling of Christian service as ministers, teachers, missionaries and workers in other fields of Christian work" (*Calendar*, 1945-46, 1). To achieve this goal adequately, the college soon recognized the need to supplement its undergraduate theological offerings with liberal arts courses, and gradually introduced sufficient courses for the first two years of a three-year B.A. program. A failure to affiliate with the University of Manitoba led to an affiliation with Waterloo Lutheran University (presently Wilfrid Laurier) from 1960 to 1970, at which time an association was entered with the former United College of Winnipeg, now University of Winnipeg. At the same time, to strengthen its theological offerings, the college developed a Bachelor of Divinity program based on a Bachelor of Arts degree as entrance requirement. This program continued from 1962 to 1971.

Once again, the history of the college has not been without its tensions. While the physical plant has never been elaborate and the salaries have been modest, such factors as facilities and finances have not been the most crucial items of concern, for local churches and Conference subsidy have continuously provided a viable, supporting base. The college has been one of the few national institutions—the only educational institution—for the entire Canadian Conference to rally its support.

The seminary.   The story of theological education of the Canadian Mennonite Brethren Church is not complete without reference to its decisions, at the General Conference session in August 1975, to become a joint sponsor of the Mennonite Brethren Biblical Seminary at Fresno, California. The seminary was begun by the United States Area Conference of the Mennonite Brethren Churches in 1955. Prior to this a three-year theological course had been offered at Tabor College since 1945. From 1962 to 1971, Canadians incorporated a seminary program into the Bible College, and only after its discontinuation was the proposal to join United States seriously entertained. By 1975 the seminary had an enrolment of 117 of whom 45 were Mennonite Brethren (U.S.A., 28; Canada, 15; and foreign, 2). Of its 148 graduates during its twenty-year history, 38 were Canadians. For the continued role of the joint seminary in socialization of Canadian Mennonite Brethren, the words of the president, H. Dick, in 1975 may be prophetic, "As goes the seminary, so goes the denomination" (Klassen, 1975, 5).

Summary

Canadian Mennonite Brethren ensure the transmission of their heritage and the retention of their sectarian stance through a deliberate and systematic process of socialization. A major aspect of this socialization is the weekly church participation. Empirical measures of such participation include associationalism, that is, church attendance and a degree of actual involvement, as well as the attitudes which accompany associationalism. Almost all Canadian Mennonite Brethren (98 percent) attend church almost every week or once a week or more, and almost one-half (43 percent) attend a meeting at church on a day other than Sunday. Again, most Canadian Mennonite Brethren (95 percent) feel they can get some or very much or quite a lot from a typical service, and most (91 percent) are somewhat interested or interested or strongly interested in assuming some responsibility of service. Further analysis suggests that such participation is meaningful to the believer because it provides occasion for worship. Mennonite Brethren have preserved a rich heritage of hymns which facilitate the worship, stress spontaneous prayer, and particularly centre their worship on biblical preaching. The Sunday schools provide the strongest weekly instructional avenue. In addition, ladies' societies and youth groups add a dimension of fellowship along with the instruction and worship, while vacation Bible schools, Bible camps, and, more recently, boys' and girls' clubs have given outreach opportunities along with the socialization. Tensions accompanying such socialization means have resulted from the dialectic between the yen for spontaneity and the bent of routinization, the ease of socialization at a cognitive level and the difficulty of practical application, the penchant for socializing and the passion for socialization, and desire for conservation and the duty of evangelization.

The formal socialization through parochial, educational institutions has become a reality for more than one-half of Canadian Mennonite Brethren. Among the schools, the Christian high schools and Bible schools are most frequently attended, about one-fourth of all Canadian Mennonite Brethren having attended each of these schools. Moreover, most Candian Mennonite Brethren not only recommend attending a parochial school beyond high school, but are also prepared to support the same. From the beginning in 1911 Canadian Mennonite Brethren have been concerned with private schools. The Bible schools were begun first, and while twenty-one schools have existed in all, three large Bible schools have reached a degree of stability in program and student enrolment, with an aggregate of some 500 to 600 students. Christian high schools were begun after World War II, and three large schools with more than 1,000 students optimistically continue their parochial education. In addition, a Bible college and college of arts, begun in 1944, serves the entire Canadian brotherhood and attracts other denominational groups as well. A graduate seminary, jointly sponsored with the American Mennonite Brethren, is a recent addition to ensure denominational preservation in times of change. Thus, church participation—through worship, teaching, fellowship, and evangelism—and formal instruction—through Bible schools, high schools, college, and seminary—have significantly facilitated the socialization process and thereby contributed to the continuity of the Canadian Mennonite Brethren.

IX

Reinforcing Integration

This is the fifth and last chapter which tests the hypothesis that the synthetic process of sacralization accounts for the continuity of sectarianism. It remains to be discovered whether or not the structural network, which binds the conference of Canadian Mennonite Brethren Churches and, thereby, enables the joint participation in service and recruiting agencies, has a strongly integrating effect and serves, as well, in providing continuity to the religious movement.

The underlying model which allows for delineating boundaries, enhancing cohesion, consolidating identities, facilitating socialization, and reinforcing integration is a functionalist one. It allows for the emphasis upon consensus rather than conflict, without however precluding conflict. This model is particularly apt in explaining the role of structural networks. Less apparent is its connection with service agencies. Yet, two concerns of any viable movement, of retaining the old and recruiting new members, are linked to the organizational aspect of the sect. On the one hand, organization provides the centripetal force of binding and preserving; on the other hand, it allows for the centrifugal force of disbanding and proliferating while simultaneously ensuring the former. Although sociologically resembling organizational types, the conference structures of Canadian Mennonite Brethren fit Charles H. Cooley's primary groups more closely because of the primary relationships they permit: involving a variety of roles and interests of each participant, involving the total personality of each individual, allowing free and extensive communication, but not easily transferring the relationship to another person (Popenoe, 1974, 162). How then does the organizational structure of Canadian Mennonite Brethren allow for both centripetal and centrifugal forces simultaneously to be operative? While the forces may simultaneously be operative, for purposes of analysis they will have to be treated separately.

130

1. The Centripetal Impact of Conference Organization

If the conference organization of the Mennonite Brethren provided the centripetal force of binding and preserving, such structure did not come accidentally as the by-product of bureaucratization or institutionalization. While ambiguity in the name of the organization and inadequacy in the nature of the organization sometimes prevailed, the structure itself was intentional and has been changed and refined as a result of conscious self-study. To understand the structural dimension, it is helpful to analyse more particularly several aspects.

The Emergence of the Structural Network

Several levels of analysis must be recognized to achieve a more comprehensive view of the development of the structural network of the Canadian Mennonite Brethren.

The General Conference level. As earlier indicated, rapid growth and spread of the movement in Russia led to the first conference organization in 1872. This assembly of three congregations, together with their affiliate groups, was subsequently referred to as the *Bundeskonferenz*, implying a covenant relationship among the member congregations. In Russia this organization remained simple, although centralized. The growth of the comparable *Bundeskonferenz* or General Conference in North America has been depicted in four stages by Mennonite Brethren historian, J. A. Toews (Toews, 1975, 195-215). In its earliest phase (1879-1909), viewed as the period of beginnings and centralization, the General Conference engaged in such common activities as home missions, foreign missions, city missions, and publishing; and expressed its concerns in regard to higher education and Christian ethics. In order to purchase property in its overseas expansion, it was incorporated in 1900. In the next phase, from 1909-1924, the Conference included under its aegis the work of relief and general welfare. The years from 1924 to 1954 witnessed within Canada increased focus upon its own unique interests and problems: the *Reiseschuld*, its own city missions, Bible school education and founding a Bible college, the preservation of the German language, and the acquisition of the Christian Press. This led the Canadian Conference in 1953 to request that higher education, church schools, youth work, and home missions become the responsibility of area conferences (*YB*, 1954, 57-58). The phase of renewed cooperation, from 1954 to the present, has resulted in the following areas of cooperative work: missions and services, Christian literature, Christian education, mass media, seminary training, and reference and counsel. It was the central structure that allowed such coordinated "organization for united action."

Of special importance to Canadian Mennonite Brethren are two developments in the North American General Conference. First, already in 1903 the need was expressed to enlarge the conference to be able to incorporate the expansion of the church into Canada. This was followed by a revised structure in 1909 which included Canada along with a congregation in North Dakota to constitute the Northern District Conference. Second, the large-scale immigration into Canada in the mid-1920s led to such a rapid increase in the membership of the Northern District Conference that by 1951 its membership exceeded that of the other three district conferences. The result was a constitutional crisis, and in 1954 the whole General Conference structure was reorganized to constitute two area conferences, the United States and Canada (*GCYB*, 1954, 16-17). Significant to note in this emergence of the co-equal Canadian area conference within the international General Conference was the manner in which the covenant relationship was honoured. While the impetus for such reorganization came from Canada (*YB*, 1954, 57-58), the authorization came from the *Bundeskonferenz* itself. Although for many years the Northern District, that is, Canada, was disproportionately over-sized among its American counterparts, it sufficiently cherished the cohesive and integrating strength of participating in a General Conference that it deterred any action disruptive to the brotherhood relationship.

The Canadian Conference level. Despite its being inadequately represented on a General Conference level for several decades prior to 1954, the Canadian Conference had since 1910 held its own annual conference sessions on a "district" level and organized its own action in evangelism and education. Only in 1945 was it separately incorporated with a charter.

The structure of the Canadian Conference was significantly changed at the annual conference in 1967 (*YB*, 1967, 23-24). To divide the responsibilities assumed by the Conference, it established six boards: Reference and Counsel, Management, Christian Education, Higher Education, Evangelism, and Publication. These boards along with the Conference executive would constitute the Council of Boards, which would meet twice annually to act as "Conference in interim." From 1925, when the Northern District had 21 churches in two provinces with a membership of 2,090, the Canadian Conference has grown in 1975 to include 126 churches in six provinces with a total membership of 19,051 (*YB*, 1975, 114-15). After fifty years of carefully defining the Canadian Conference's rights and responsibilities, the conference structure today is a strongly binding network which ensures unity and perpetuates a covenant relationship on a national level in the face of repeated threats of regionalism and disintegration or assimilation into society at large. The joint tasks that the Conference undertakes become the cohesive force to integrate the otherwise fragile structure, for the only answer to jointly assuming such responsibility is to have conference structures.

The provincial level. Conference structures emerged not only on an international and national level, but also on a provincial level. The first Mennonite Brethren churches in Canada were established in Manitoba and Saskatchewan as early as 1888 and 1898, respectively. It was years later that they became separately incorporated as provincial conferences. Records for provincial conference sessions in Manitoba date back to 1929. The conferences occurred semi-annually and reviewed the work of evangelism, Bible teaching, and house visitation on a local level; and youthwork, city missions, and education on a provincial scale. Ordinations of ministers were also reviewed, as were the reports of contributions for home missions. In 1940, the Mennonite Brethren Church of Manitoba was incorporated, and subsequently the sessions were called provincial conferences instead of merely "*Vertreterversammlungen*" (assembly of representatives). The first all-provincial conference for Saskatchewan occurred in 1946, the northern and southern districts having met separately prior to this. Areas of work reviewed at this first conference included Western Children's Mission, city mission, tract mission, choir conductors' conferences, and the matter of incorporation, which was revised in 1952. Churches in Alberta were first organized in 1927, and conference sessions apparently began the same year. The Alberta Provincial Conference was incorporated as recently as 1957. Ontario had its first convention in 1931, was incorporated in 1932, joined the General Conference in 1939, and the Canadian Conference as recently as 1946. British Columbia, with only one congregation in 1929, organized into a provincial conference in the 1930s, burgeoned in growth during the 1940s, so that by 1975 it had thirty-six churches with about one-third of Canada's Mennonite Brethren membership. The independent churches of Quebec as yet did not constitute a separate provincial conference, although belonging to the Canadian Conference. Thus, what unity in action through conference structure was facilitated on an international and national level was made even more effective on a provincial level, since the conference concerns were even more closely related to the life of the local congregation. While helping to bind the local churches together in a centripetal manner, the structures did not stifle the initiative of the individual nor of the local church, because of the underlying polity.

Mennonite Brethren Church Polity

There has not always been clarity as to the polity that did in fact, and should, prevail. On the one hand, there is the association of churches which is banded together in voluntary interdependence. A local church does not have to join the provincial conference. However, by remaining separate from the conference, the church would lose out on the benefits that accrue, since a group of churches has greater strength to carry out larger projects of action than does one congregation. At the same time, the local church retains its autonomy in local affairs. The General Conference constitution, for example, stipulates the following autonomy for the local church:

In the administration of local affairs each individual church handles its own matters without Conference intervention. Churches respect the autonomy in relation to each other. But when a church is engaged in activities or is confronted with problems which it is unable to solve alone, it shall solicit the aid of the Conference (*General Conference Constitution*, 1963, 20).

Its obligations with reference to Conference decisions are also stated:

Inasmuch as the Conference is one brotherhood, the local churches consider Conference decisions as morally binding and seek to support Conference activities, to recognize and abide by all Conference resolutions, and to carry them out to the best of their ability (*General Conference Constitution*, 1963, 21).

The constitution of the Canadian Conference includes a similar statement covering the above dual relationship of autonomy and obligation.

Each member church is autonomous in the structuring and management of its own local affairs. However, member churches accept as binding the decisions made by the Conference according to provisions of its constitutions (*Canadian Constitution*, 1970, 11).

In addition, the Canadian Conference subordinates itself to the decisions of the General Conference: "The Conference is an area Conference of the General Conference of Mennonite Brethren Churches and is subordinate to its decisions." And it further adds, "The provincial conferences are functionally united with the Canadian Conference and are subordinate to it" (*Canadian Constitution*, 1970, 124). So also a provincial conference constitution, as for example in Alberta, disallows the Conference "to interfere with the local affairs of a church," but when it is "battling unsuccessfully against dangers," it shall be "the right and duty of the Committee of Reference and Counsel to inquire of said church in a brotherly spirit whether any outside assistance would be acceptable" (*Alberta Constitution*, 1957, 8). The polity, then, is one which balances local autonomy with external control, holds in tension the individualism of democracy with the interdependence of brotherhood (Toews, 1955, 13-16), and mediates between regionalism and centralization (or federalism) (Peters, 1959, 17-21).

The Functions and Dysfunctions of Conferences

Having traced the emergence of the separate conference structures and reviewed the ecclesiastical polity which is implicit, one is further interested to discover how the individual member responds to such structural networks which appear to have been imposed from without. Do these structures in fact reinforce integration, or are they merely binding in that they inhibit vitality and lead to rigidity. The reply to this question is both positive and negative, and refers both to the structure of the conference itself and to the process of assembling for conference sessions (mainly the latter). Once again the reply comes from the editors of periodicals and the scholarly persons who reflect on these matters, but they do present the viewpoints of diverse individuals. What then are the functions and dysfunctions of a conference structure or assembly?

Positively, the spokespersons view the experience of attending a conference as serving the following functions.

It enables fellowship. Particularly in earlier times when travel was infrequent, the scattered, lonely immigrant settlers used the conference session as an occasion to meet old friends and make new acquaintances. Even prior to the large-scale immigration of the 1920s, the assembly at a conference session was viewed as a "foretaste of heaven" (*YB*, 1913, 13). It was customary to receive and extend official greetings from fraternal Mennonite and Mennonite Brethren churches or from prominent members of the conference who were absent for reasons of health or service abroad. Fellowship, the social dimension of attending conferences, has remained a prominent feature throughout the history of the Canadian Mennonite Brethren churches.

It fosters brotherhood. The conference session has prompted columnists and editors of church periodicals to reflect on the meaning of brotherhood. Interim editor of *Mennonite Brethren Herald*, Peter Klassen, in 1964 defined brotherhood as implying "a high regard for each other, a warm fellowship, a spiritual intimacy, a concern for the physical and moral welfare of other members of the group . . . more than a democratic social order where behavior is regulated in such a way that the majority is served at best. Besides having a spiritual orientation, the brotherhood principle involves sharing and concern on a personal level" (Klassen, 1964, 3). The added dimension of brotherhood over another social group, according to columnist Redekop, is that "a brotherhood consists of people who are interested in and accept each other as total people. . . . Each member of the brotherhood has its own function to perform but the work of the individual is always part of a larger total thrust. . . . Each esteems the other more than himself" (Redekop, 1965, 2). Conference sessions not only stimulated such theoretical articulation of brotherhood, but provided opportunities for its practical application, as the following further aspects indicate.

It cultivates sensitivity.   Part of the brotherhood experience is to be sensitive to the needs and feelings of the minority. An example of such brotherhood sensitivity was evident in the very first Canadian conference session in 1910. When fifteen members abstained from voting for the increase of the salary of evangelists, the moderator at a later session of the same conference reopened the discussion to allow for dissent, lest there be offence. At the conclusion of the conference, the moderator wanted to be reassured that there were no hurt feelings and that unity and harmony prevailed (*YB*, 1910, 15). Each conferernce session similarly gives opportunity to listen to the voice of the minority. Allowing them to speak helps prevent alienation.

It facilitates reconciliation.   When differences in belief and practice become apparent, the conference sessions facilitate reconciliation. It may be a controversial issue, such as one's assessment of a private school, which evokes a clash of opinion. When in 1941 such a sharp debate ensued, the Conference subsequently expressed its regret and gave opportunity for public apologies (*YB*, 1941, 56-57). More subtle than an unkind remark of a single person is the economically superior attitude of a particular group, thus displaying provincialism. When the Canadian Conference assembled in British Columbia in 1949, such an attitude was confessed by the host province and an apology was requested (*YB*, 1949, 6). Such a formal reconciliation melds a brotherhood together—indeed an integrating effect of conference sessions.

It expresses unity.   Numerous spokesmen have repeatedly stated that church conferences unite a brotherhood. Peter Klassen in 1963 explained:

In order to work effectively on a conference level the members must *feel* that the conference does in fact exist—i.e., that churches are in fact working together to achieve common spiritual goals.
   To get this necessary feeling (conference spirit) the members must have some *physical* entity in mind, since our membership is not made up of "souls" only. The personal contact with actual people and the working together at specific tasks in the service of God gives us the impression that a "real" Conference exists, and that the Conference is not some nebulous entity that other people talk about but we know little of (Klassen, 1963, 3).

The physical bond, however, is only one aspect of the unity. Editor Harold Jantz points to the underlying common aspirations and goals which draw the members together.

What holds this conference of churches together? Yes, it is first of all the Christ whom we trust and love. . . .

Yet there is more that binds us together. I'm overwhelmed every time I attend a convention of our churches at the remarkable interest in one another that one senses. I agree, we have our differences . . . yet the level of common aspirations and goals is far greater than anything which might fragment us. I'm always impressed by the degree of closeness in our theological stance when we get together to confer with one another (Jantz, 1973, 11).

A conference thus gives visible expression to a unity pertaining to invisible aspirations and beliefs.

It strengthens commitment. Attending a conference already indicates a degree of commitment. Such commitment, however, is intensified, as the comment on the first "Faith and Life" Conference held on a Canadian Conference level in 1968 suggests. Columnist J. H. Redekop asks about the involvement of young people.

Were the young people present? Indeed, they were, by the hundreds, and many were delegates. . . . Surely a church has a potentially strong future when at the height of the "busy season," and on a beautiful summer evening, a large congregation of young people assemble after a regular service to share Christian concerns. . . . All in all, the convention helped to raise the spiritual barometer of our churches. It revealed clearly that we have come to the point where we are willing to consider radically different responses to crucial questions of the day in a spirit of acceptance and brotherly love. For these reasons I believe that the convention was rewarding and valuable (Redekop, 1968, 3).

It motivates service. Attending conferences, finally, broadens horizons and thus motivates for service. J. A. Toews argued in 1955 that attending conferences would provide new incentives for service (Toews, 1955, 9-11), and Leslie Stobbe, first editor of *Mennonite Observer*, argued about attending conventions and conferences generally that "if you come with a right attitude you will go away a richer man in experience and knowledge. Your horizon will be much wider and work of the conference will have taken on a new significance. With new zeal you will support church and conference projects" (Stobbe, 1957, 2). It is not difficult, then, to isolate the functions that attending conferences serve.

There are also dysfunctions in conference organizations and conference sessions. While commentary on this aspect is less frequent, it comes as a caveat of concern by both critics and leaders and reflects a persistent reality.

There is the tendency to stifle initiative. The first editor of the *Mennonite Brethren Herald*, Rudy Wiebe, warned that the danger was not in the organization itself, nor in the officers who are elected to it, but "there is a good deal of danger in the attitude individual church members can gain toward the Conference as such," for "the Conference never actually does anything except as it acts through dedicated individuals" (Wiebe, 1963, 3). He cautions one not to count on the Conference to initiate things. Relying on a structure can thus lead to the loss of personal initiative.

There is the tendency to send the same people as delegates.   Again, Wiebe laments that "extremely few laymen in the 20-40 year age group attend even provincial conferences unless they are directly appointed to conference or church work. ... It is not that they are too apprehensive about younger brethren's views to send them to conferences. The problems usually center around the men directly involved: many do not want to go to conferences, even if they are named" (Wiebe, 1962, 4). His caution may well be in place, for the gifted, experienced, and highly motivated persons will naturally be elected as delegates.

There is the danger of elitism.   If the more prominent church members are sent as delegates, these are the ones who assume offices on a Conference level, and some repeatedly. Reflecting on one conference session, political science professor and columnist Redekop asked "whether we are actually a brotherhood or a hierarchy, or perhaps a hierarchical brotherhood." He continued:

I suspect that a casual visitor at the sessions would have gotten the impression that while we all claim to be brethren, some are more brethren than others. Many of us seem to be reluctant to see ministers and pastors (especially of big churches) as equal brethren and tend to be embarrassed when we force ourselves to refer to medical doctors simply as brethren. Apparently we feel compelled to point out who these people REALLY are. There is clearly a time when deference and degree are in place, but I suggest there is also a time when they should be left out entirely (Redekop, 1965, 2).

The conference structure itself requires a measure of hierarchy, and becoming involved in conference sessions fosters the dysfunction of elitism.

There is the danger of bureaucratization.   Not only social critics, but leaders who have served as educators, pastors, and moderators recognize the institutionalization of the church, a church which took a sectarian stance precisely because of the shift from a believers' church to a parish church prior to 1860. One such leader, after rehearsing the merits of attending conferences, wrote: "But now the danger exists that in view of the great, one forgets the small; that in view of the many, one neglects the individuals; that in view of the Conference, the churches and the individual members are disregarded. The means becomes the end" (Quiring, 1957, 7-9). He then concludes that the Canadian Mennonite Brethren Church could well afford to have fewer conferences, fewer constitutions, fewer committees, and fewer resolutions. He keenly sensed the process of institutionalization and, therefore, warned against the dysfunctions of conferences.

Despite the dysfunctions implicit in conference forms and assemblies, the overarching impact of these is predominantly functional. Maintaining a viable, rationally oriented conference structure demands considerable effort and necessitates the centripetal force with the attention focused upon the conference entity. At the same time, this centripetal force generates a momentum which not only is integrating and enduring, but also leads to an extension of the movement, as the further analysis indicates.

2. The Centrifugal Impact of Conference Organization

A further force which is channeled through conference structures and has enabled the movement to persist is centrifugal in direction. Although rooted in the organization, the focus in this instance is directed away from the conference structure, for it expresses itself in service and outreach. Earlier chapters have already illustrated other action-based expressions of faith, such as overt behavioural modes, group-oriented associations, decision-based commitments, and institutions of socialization. It is the evangelistic and service-oriented agencies of the conference which are used to illustrate the centrifugal impact of the structural base of this religious movement.

The Empirical Data

The evangelism and service agencies, loosely referred to as mission structures, represent collectively the Anabaptist understanding of mission—presenting the total gospel to the total person. Yet, Mennonite Brethren have chosen usually to separate the sphere of activity as evangelism and service, as the differing structures used to achieve this goal indicate.

Evangelistic agencies.   Traditionally, Mennonite Brethren in Canada spoke in terms of "home" missions (*Innere Mission*) and "foreign" missions (*Aeusere Mission*)—the former the domain of the provincial and Canadian conferences, the latter the concern of the General Conference. For this analysis, the distinction will simply be evangelism *in* Canada and *beyond* Canada.

Even a brief survey of Mennonite Brethren evangelistic efforts *in* Canada must include the concerns prominent prior to 1925. From its first session in 1910 until well into the 1930s, the annual sessions of the Northern District Conference dealt almost exclusively with evangelism and missions, and were interspersed with numerous inspirational sermons relating to missions. The reports on "home missions" systematically reviewed the work of individual lay evangelists and Bible colporteurs for each of the participating districts. The work of "city missions," initially a General Conference concern, and especially "foreign" missions also highlighted these reports. Accordingly, the budget was largely devoted to evangelism and missions. With the massive immigration of Mennonite Brethren in the mid-1920s and the need for involvement in relief, colonization, and *Reiseschuld*, the evangelism and missions reports gradually receded in prominence, and by 1945 the Canadian Inland Mission was organized to coordinate the separate "home mission" efforts of the different provinces. At the same time, new forms of evangelism were employed. In 1947 a tract mission was begun. Increasingly short-term ministries in evangelism occupied Bible school teachers during summer months (Toews, 1975, 316). Already in 1953 the need for a conference evangelist was expressed, and in 1959 the conference accepted in principle the appointment of the same. With the formation of a Committee on Evangelism in 1958, new inspiration for evangelism was stimulated and new techniques employed. Radio programs were sponsored provincially, none perhaps as prominently as the Gospel Light Hour, begun by a group of students at Mennonite Brethren Bible College in 1946. Since the reorganization of the Canadian Conference in 1967, the Board of Evangelism has aggressively furthered the work in Quebec and extended itself into Nova Scotia. Evangelism seminars in which laity are trained and campaigns employing professional evangelists have characterized the 1960s and 1970s. In addition, on a provincial scale, a systematic church extension program has been promoted in recent years (Penner, 1957, 43-113).

Through the deliberate lay involvement from its earliest times, Canadian Mennonite Brethren churches extended their outreach by colportage and visitation evangelism, mission Sunday schools and summer vacation Bible schools, summer camps and radio ministries, and evangelistic campaigns and seminars. The result was an outreach into such ethnic communities as the Russians in Saskatchewan, the Doukhobors in British Columbia, the Old Colony Mennonites in Manitoba, the Jews in Winnipeg and Toronto, and the French Canadians in Quebec. Moreover, the church extended itself into such Anglo-Saxon communities as Prince George and Terrace in British Columbia, Pincher Creek and Medicine Hat in Alberta, The Pas and Leaf Rapids in Manitoba, Orillia and London in Ontario, and Dartmouth in Nova Scotia.

While the numerical results of evangelistic efforts within Canada are difficult to ascertain because of the assimilation of Mennonites into the mainstream of Canadian society and the simultaneous loss of members to other than Mennonite Brethren churches, the churches in Canada have grown through other than merely biological or internal growth. Beyond Canada such growth is more readily measurable. Already in Russia, Mennonite Brethren sent financial contributions to German mission societies and eventually their own missionaries under Baptist sponsorship (Peters, 1952, 55-60). The earliest conference sessions of the North American Mennonite Brethren churches were primarily missions festivals, with interest centred on "home missions." In 1885 a "foreign missions" committee was elected to administer mission funds and to support missionaries under other organizations. In 1898 the General Conference chose to send its own missionaries to India which was the first and only "foreign" field until 1919, when the Conference assumed the responsibility for an independent Mennonite Brethren work in China (Peters, 152, 73-94). From its very outset the Canadian Conference in 1910 included "foreign missions" in its annual conferences. Not only were missionaries on furlough invited for the inspirational sessions, but a major segment of the conference was devoted to reporting on foreign missions, including a financial report. However, triennially the Canadian Conference participated in the General Conference sessions where foreign missions throughout the years has received greater attention than other conference issues. Especially significant to Canada was the decision of the General Conference in 1943 to assume the sponsorship for the Africa Mission Society, an independent society of Mennonite Brethren in Canada which had its own missionaries and field in Bololo, northern Congo, since 1932. Thereupon an increased representation in the Board of Missions was requested by Canada (*YB*, 1945, 143). Of importance in shaping the further work of missions and service was the General Conference decision in 1966 to merge the Board of Missions and Board of Welfare which then became the present Board of Missions and Services (*GCYB*, 1966, 22-23).

The impact of this outreach in missions beyond Canada can be measured in terms of resources invested, as well as the growth of the church in other lands. One significant component of these resources is that of finances. The following facts gleaned from conference year books and missions pamphlets indicate a growth in commitment of Canadian Mennonite Brethren:

(1) In 1925, when Canadian membership was about one-fourth that of the United States, contributions to missions were considerably less, about one-twentieth of the total income.

(2) By the end of the depression in 1940, when Canadian membership became almost equal to the U.S.A., giving to missions was still considerably less in proportion, although the disparity was not as pronounced as in 1925. However, one must remember that Cana-

dian Mennonite Brethren were also supporting Africa Mission Society which had still not been accepted by the General Conference Board of Missions.

(3) By 1950, when Canadian membership had exceeded American, Canadian contributions to missions were still only about one-half of the American.

(4) The 1950s was a decade of enlargement for Mennonite Brethren contributions to missions. While Canadian membership continued to lead the U.S.A. through 1960, giving to missions had also proportionately exceeded the U.S.A. giving per member, with Canada giving $25.52 per member annually and the U.S.A. $21.41.

(5) Since 1960, the growth of Canadian church membership increased at approximately the same rate as the U.S.A., yet the giving to missions has continued to spiral, so much so that by 1975 the Canadians were almost doubling the per member giving of the Americans, with Canadians giving $58.25 per member and Americans $36.96 per member (Hamm, 1978, 349-51).

In as much as voluntary financial contributions to a cause are a measure of commitment, Canadian Mennonite Brethren have increasingly shown this commitment since 1925 and in this sense have consciously facilitated the formation of an enduring denominational legacy in areas beyond Canada.

A second significant component of the investment of resources is that of personnel. Gleaning additional facts from the General Conference year books, one can make the following statements about involvement of Mennonite Brethren personnel in missions beyond Canada:

(1) The total number of Canadian Mennonite Brethren has gradually increased from only two in 1925 to seventy-two in 1972, when Canadians constituted just in excess of one-half of North American Mennonite Brethren missionaries.

(2) The total number of missionaries was at an all-time high in 1967, with 243 missionaries.

(3) In addition to the seventy-two Canadians serving under the Mennonite Brethren Board of Missions/Services, an additional eighty-nine Canadian Mennonite Brethren are serving under other mission societies (*MBH*, 1972, 18).

Thus, in 1972 Canadian Mennonite Brethren churches had one missionary for every 105 members (compared to United States with one for every 134 members), certainly an important indicator of Canadian Mennonite Brethren interest in extending its outreach beyond Canada.

Thus, the impact of Canadian Mennonite Brethren beyond Canada has been very significant, as these empirical measures of monies contributed and missionaries sent indicate. The coordination of these efforts to disband such a centrifugal force is rooted in the conference structure, as shown earlier.

Service agencies. The impact emanating from this centrifugal force is not to be measured solely in evangelistic outreach. The other very meaningful dimension is humanitarian service. An overview of the two levels of analysis—within Canada and beyond Canada—indicates a continual growth as well in this humanitarian dimension.

Within Canada opportunity for such service occurred with the large-scale immigration of economically deprived Mennonites from Russia in the mid-1920s. Usually immigrants got their start in Canada through the hospitality of other Canadian Mennonites who provided food and lodging for the initial months while immigrants found jobs, purchased land through the Mennonite Land Settlement Board, and began to pay their *Reiseschuld*. Mennonites in the United States provided large quantities of clothing. It was the Canadian Mennonite Board of Colonization, an inter-Mennonite organization founded in 1922, which coordinated these efforts. Much effort was extended to negotiate and collect the *Reiseschuld* and more recently to assist conscientious objectors to secure alternative service during World War II. Assistance in immigration was also given after World War II both by the Board of Colonization and many individual families. Eventually in 1960 the Canadian Mennonite Board of Colonization merged with the Mennonite Central Relief Committee to form the Canadian Mennonite Relief and Immigration Council, supported by the Canadian Mennonite Brethren and the Conference of Mennonites in Central Canada. This organization became the Mennonite Central Committee (Canada) branch in 1964 and has subsequently expanded its services to other than merely Mennonites, including peace education, rehabilitation of residents from correctional institutions, and ministries to natives of Canada. Also, within Canada, Mennonite Brethren, as well as inter-Mennonite groups, have built and continue to administer with government support mental hospitals and numerous retirement homes. Since 1966, the domestic branch of the General Conference Board of Missions/Services has opened numerous opportunites for short-term "Christian" services within Canada itself.

Humanitarian service beyond Canada has been channeled by the Board of General Welfare and Public Relations or, more frequently, the Mennonite Central Committee, an inter-Mennonite agency. The Board of General Welfare and Public Relations, organized in 1924, channeled relief via Mennonite Central Committee and, in particular, gave assistance to the Mennonite Brethren churches in South America, especially Paraguay where the struggle for survival was the severest

(Toews, 1975, 213). In 1960, a new form of voluntary "Christian Service" was initiated by the Board to attract young people to short-term services at home and abroad. By 1966, when the Board merged with Board of Missions/Services, it reported ninety-three workers in thirty projects, of which eight projects were overseas and in which nineteen Canadians were serving (*GCYB*, 1966, 44-48). In 1975, the Board of Missions/Services listed sixty-seven Christian Service workers, who since 1971 had been involved in an overseas assignment of education, medicine, economic development, carpentry, social service, and maintenance.

Mennonite Central Committee, organized in 1920 to coordinate several relief committees active since the 1890s in both India and Russia, was predominantly non-Canadian and non-Mennonite Brethren in its early stages, yet gradually included participation of Mennonite Brethren in Canada. Beginning as a relief agency, it extended its services overseas to include agricultural development, education, material aid, medical services, child sponsorship; while at home it promoted peace education, voluntary service, mental health services, disaster service, travel service, aid societies, and an indemnity company (Kehler, 1970, 298-315). In a comprehensive study of Mennonite Central Committee personnel from 1920 to 1970, Paul Classen lists a total of 5,241 persons having served one or more assignments in ninety countries. Among these there have been 252 men and 260 women from the Mennonite Brethren Church, of whom 101 men and 183 women were Canadian Mennonite Brethren (Classen, 1970, 324-29). Of the total number of assignments (6,018), of which 595 were by Mennonite Brethren, 290 were in countries other than United States and Canada. With the exception of six persons, all Mennonite Brethren served since 1940. Mennonite Brethren, therefore, have demonstrated themselves to be active not only in evangelism, but perhaps even more so in social service. Empirical data strongly support the centrifugal forces at work, both in evangelization and service agencies and both in Canada and beyond Canada. While rooted in organizational structures held together by covenantal bonds or centripetal forces, the centrifugal thrust of the Canadian Mennonite Brethren has stimulated vitality and strengthened its world-wide impact as a religious movement.

The Integrating Effect

It is quite apparent that Mennonite Brethren have had extensive involvement in agencies of service and outreach. How does such involvement strengthen the bonds with the organizational structure, and why does the extensive interaction with the non-Mennonite Brethren world not become counter-productive by weakening the ties with the structural core?

Whether active at home or abroad in evangelistic outreach or in a service assignment, such activity integrates the individuals involved with the cause with which they identify so overtly.

It legitimates the existence of the movement.   On the one hand, as adherents of the movement explain their involvement in religious recruitment or humanitarian service, the very purpose of the organization is singled out. The sociological or psychological explanation for such involvement proves inadequate. As editor Jantz explains in an editorial regarding a study conference on evangelism and discipleship:

Mennonite Brethren Christians face an intense challenge to demonstrate that what they possess cannot be explained in mere sociological or psychological terms. People have a right to ask whether our motivation, our practices, our goals, our rationale are really any different than that of a concerned person who makes no claim to having Christ resident within him (Jantz, 1968, 3).

Mennonite Brethren would argue that Jesus Christ is the legitimating purpose of their activity. They evangelize to "win them to Christ" and serve "in the name of Jesus." On the other hand, in order to expedite a service assignment with efficiency and allow for a supporting body to whom one appeals for funds and reports the action, an organizational entity is a must.

It channels the interest in mission.   Evangelism and service receive much emphasis from Mennonite Brethren pulpits. Historian J. A. Toews asserts, "No other cause or concern has received such wholehearted and universal support in the Mennonite Brethren Conference as the work of missions and evangelism" (Toews, 1975, 373). For those individuals who then cannot personally be involved, the structures which support the participating personnel allow for such participation by proxy.

It reaffirms commitment.   Involvement strengthens the commitment of participating personnel, not only to the ideological objective, but also to the supporting constituency of the agency. Without the constituency, the agency would be impotent—of money, of worthy goals, of moral support, and of a sounding board to test one's progress in the work. The commitment, hence, is not merely to the brotherhood, but to the organization which furnishes the coordinating structure.

Despite such an integrating effect, the very centrifugal force which sends participating personnel away from the structural base also weakens the ties and threatens possible assimilation with the world it seeks to convert. What, then, prevents such secularization and eventual total assimilation.?

The repeated assessment.   Voluntarism in a religious movement does not foster irresponsibility. Instead, once adherents voluntarily commit themselves to the cause, they become responsible to the brotherhood, giving account of their work, and assessing the degree of their accomplishments. Voluntarism affirms identity with the group, and helps retain the former members. It purges the movement of obsolescent forms and functions.

The new recruits.   The successful evangelistic enterprise results in new recruits, for Mennonite Brethren believe that, where no evangelism occurs, the church will ultimately die. Whereas evangelism results in a loss to the denomination of some of the recruits from the out-group, many more are normally gained than lost. Despite the loss of those whose commitment is half-hearted and who do not feel at home within the brotherhood, others who continue add vitality to the sectarian movement.

The added vitality.   Evangelism requires exposure and confrontation. Through the associations with the out-group, the movement gains new perspectives along with the vitality that the new converts bring to the movement and that the evangelists experience in their faithfulness to, and in the success of, their mission. Despite the risks of such exposure and confrontation, the movement gains not only numerically but in vitality as the new adherents choose to make the sectarian break from the parish church which they have abandoned to the believers' church with which they choose to identify. The overall, revitalizing and integrating effect is greater for the movement, therefore, than the eroding consequences which its adherents perceive by identifying with the host society.

Sectarianism persists, therefore, because the integrating reinforcement of structural networks and service and outreach agencies have further sacralized the movement. Despite some loss and obvious fragility, Canadian Mennonite Brethren have grown in strength and number and have witnessed the erosive force of secularization implicit in a pluralistic world. The next chapters trace this process of secularization.

Summary

When the dynamic force of sectarian religiosity is given structural form, the vitality of the force is not only properly channeled to give persistence to the religious movement, but also more capably harnessed to produce action. Conference structures, thus, help to retain its old members and to recruit new ones. Implying a covenant relationship among a number of congregations, such conference structures appear on three levels among Canadian Mennonite Brethren, every congregation usually being a member at each of these levels. Most local in nature is the provincial conference in Canada (or district conference in the United States) with its own charter and constitution and its annual or semi-annual sessions. On the Canadian national level is the Canadian Conference (until 1954 referred to as the Northern District Conference). Although separately incorporated with its own charter and constitution since 1945, it has held its annual sessions since 1910. Most inclusive is the General Conference of the Mennonite Brethren Churches of North America, of which the Canadian churches constitute one equal area conference. First formed in Russia as a *Bundeskonferenz* in 1872, it organized in the United States in 1879 and soon extended itself to include Canada. At each conference level, specific common tasks unite the action of the participating churches. The polity of these structures emphasizes the autonomy of the local church in matters of local interest, but conference decisions become morally binding upon all churches participating in a given conference, the provincial conferences subject to the Canadian, and the Canadian subordinate to the General Conference. Attending conference sessions has generally been found to be a positive experience—enabling fellowship, fostering brotherhood, giving ear to minority views, facilitating reconciliation, expressing unity, strengthening commitment, and motivating for service. At the same time, relying upon conference structures stifles personal initiative, limits universal representation in decision-making, promotes elitism, and invites bureaucratization.

While the centripetal impact of conference structures helps to retain its members and preserve the movement, the centrifugal impact of conference agencies facilitates recruitment of new members despite the implicit hazards of such a conversionist stance. Canadian Mennonite Brethren have been active in both evangelistic and service-oriented agencies. Evangelism within Canada has expressed itself in many types of outreach—Bible colportage, city missions, tract missions, summer vacation Bible schools and camp ministries, radio programs, home visitations, and evangelistic campaigns. More successful numerically, both in terms of financial and personnel resources employed as well as church membership experienced, is the evangelistic outreach beyond Canada in such countries as India, China, Japan, Zaire, Colombia, Mexico, Paraguay, Peru, Brazil, Uruguay, Germany, and Austria. Likewise, involvement in humanitarian service has been prominent both within and beyond Canada. Mutual aid was extended by Mennonites to their own brotherhood both to fellow immigrants within Canada as well as to those settling in Paraguay. Assistance was given to many handicapped and deprived groups outside of their denomination as well. Particularly effective have been the efforts through the Christian service branch of the denominational mission board and through the inter-Mennonite agency of Mennonite Central Committee. The impact of these outreach and service efforts has been integrating, despite the centrifugal tug, because such involvement has legitimated the movement for its adherents, has channeled the momentum of their motivation, and has involuntarily reaffirmed their commitment. Conference structures and service agencies have sacralized the sectarian movement and given it tenacity and vitality in the face of a threatening society into which it is increasingly assimilated.

Part Four

SECULARIZATION PROCESS

X

Education and Relativization

The preceding five chapters dealt with factors enhancing the continuity of a religious movement and supported the central hypothesis of this study, namely, that the synthetic process of sacralization contributes to the continuity of sectarianism. Sacralization has been viewed as a process whereby people reinforce and eternalize patterns of religiosity and thereby modify and obstruct or even legitimate change in order to safeguard identity. The sacralizing process is, thus, a response to change, but safeguards the identity of the movement against the dysfunctional and erosive strain of excessive adaptability.

The following cluster of five chapters analyses the components contributing to such religious change and tests the hypothesis that these components of change lead to secularization. As indicated earlier, it would be over-simplifying the processes at work to insist that the factors of sacralization are solely integrative in their effect and the factors of secularization are solely disruptive. Admittedly, a complex dialectic is at work, and these chapters test the overall effect of change. For this reason, both chapters eight and ten are concerned with education, chapter eight occupying itself with the synthesizing process of socialization and chapter ten with the relativizing effects of education.

The sequence of the following chapters is deliberate; not simply do they analyse the usual components of socio-economic status, education, occupation, and wealth, but they trace a larger number of components in a more chronological and causal order, namely, education, urbanization, occupational change, economic ascendance, and assimilation. This order fits more clearly the actual developments among Canadian Mennonite Brethren from 1925 to 1975. Because of the fuzzy boundaries which characterize such concepts as change, secularization, and dialectic, a further note on social and religious change and its relation to secularization is in order at this time.

1. Religious Change and Secularization

Each of the chapters in the cluster begins with one aspect of social change, but attempts also to indicate the religious implications of such

150

change. It is important, however, to note that social change and religious change are not to be confused; nor are they to be viewed as totally separable. What, then, is the relationship between these modes of change?

Simply to assert the occurrence of social change is to engage in one of the most obvious of platitudes. Not only is social change normal and ubiquitous for the contemporary world, but some kinds of change have been universal throughout human history. It is probably the rapidity of social change which is unique to the present age. Because of the reverberating implications of such change, religion must necessarily be affected and, indeed, religious change becomes a concomitant of social change. One cannot, therefore, analyse religious change in isolation, without reference to other components of social change. For this reason, chapters ten through fourteen analyse aspects of social change with their resulting impact on religion.

To explain the interaction between social change and religious change, one might use the categories of Pitirim Sorokin—the ideational, idealistic, and sensate—without implying that the twentieth century is on the verge of a catastrophic sensate collapse, to be followed by a reassertion of more spiritual values (Sorokin, 1957, 8-19, 28-36, 53-66). While the latter may indeed be the case, the typology of Sorokin is more useful in understanding the dialectic which is at work between the sensate mentality which stresses volatility and flux (being more hedonistic with the emphasis upon things readily available to the senses) and the ideational which stresses eternity and stability (being more ascetic with the emphasis upon things readily available to the spirit). The resulting dialectic is described by the idealistic state, representing a rich mixture of the sensate and ideational extremes (Zollschan and Hirsch, 1964, 375-86). There seems to be a close parallel, therefore, between the dialectic of the sensate and the ideational and the dialectic of social change and religious change, or, more precisely, between the secular and the sacred, or even between society and religion.

How, then, is secularization related to religious change or to change itself? As earlier indicated, change is not to be equated with secularization. Change, a more neutral concept, suggests differentiation or transformation of any type and need not be valuative. Secularization, as it is used in this study, suggests religious decline and loss of faith or conformity to the world, or, as Bryan Wilson defines it, "the process whereby religious thinking, practice, and institutions lose social significance" (Wilson, 1966, xiv). Certain forms of social change have secularizing effects, for they result in religious decline or conformity to the world (to use the expression popularly employed among members of the Canadian Mennonite Brethren Church). However, this is not to suggest that all religious change is to be interpreted as secularization, for some religious change leads to separation from the world (as the instances of sacralization have suggested) rather than assimilation of the world, as the following chapters will illustrate.

This brief treatment of the nature of social change and its distinction from religious change is intended to introduce the understanding of the process of secularization. Neither the processes of change nor secularization is to be viewed independently of the countervailing forces of continuity and sacralization. Here the dialectic of Marx and Sorokin comes into play. One might say that the sacralization process has within itself the seeds of its own destruction or the eternality of the ideational is tempered by the transitoriness of the sensory realm. Or as Hans Mol suggests:

Change has again and again clumsily trampled underfoot the refined web of sacralizations woven around peoples and societies. To account for change and to check the conservative bias we have adopted a framework of countervailing processes: an inexorable tendency towards conservation and integration being crosscut by a similar inexorable tendency towards change and dif- ferentiation. . . . The dialectic as such seems to be a prerequisite for the viability and survival of personal, group, or social identity (Mol, 1976, 262).

The outcome of the following chapters is not a foregone conclusion. While it is anticipated that the overarching impact of social change will be secularization, there will be evidence of countervailing forces as well. According to the models of Marx and Sorokin, something generates its own opposite. The positive function becomes a negative, and the nega- tive produces a positive. Success brings downfall, and failure produces success. To use Sorokin's language, the "ascetic ideational" turns into the "active ideational" and vice versa. In this dialectical process, there- fore, both sacralization and secularization are at work. Even as in chapters five through nine, where the overarching impact was seen as sacralizing the religious identity (although not without repeated evi- dences of erosive forces of secularization), so in chapters ten through fourteen the simultaneous overarching impact is anticipated to be secularization, yet both occurring within the same sectarian movement during the same fifty-year period under consideration. And it may well be that it is precisely the dialectic that brings vitality to the movement.

Chapter ten assesses the degree to which education, one component of social change, has relativized the Canadian Mennonite Brethren during the past half century.

2. Some Empirical Evidence of the Impact of Education

Before attempting an explanation of the change in attitudes that edu- cation has engendered and before assessing the relativizing impact of the same, a closer look at the "hard" facts of empirical evidence is in place. The Church Member Profile provides data on the educational attainment of the church population, as well as on varying aspects of religiosity.

Table x-1

Educational Attainment of Three Generational Groups

Age Groups		Education Levels (%)			
		Grade[a]	High	College	Grd./Pr.
20-29	(n=42)	2.4	45.2	40.5	11.9
40-49	(n=102)	26.5	43.1	5.9	24.5
60 and over	(n=44)	52.3	31.8	2.3	13.6

Source: Church Member Profile, 1972.

[a]
Grade	= grade eight or less
High	= some high school or trade school, or graduate of school
College	= some college or graduate of college
Grd./Pr.	= some graduate/professional school or graduate

Educational Attainment of Canadian Mennonite Brethren

Since 37 percent of the respondents were themselves immigrants, the striking difference in educational attainment for the varying age groups comes as no surprise. Table x-1 indicates that among church members 60 years or over, 52.3 percent had not gone to school beyond the eighth grade, compared to 26.5 percent of those aged 40 to 49, and only 2.4 percent of those aged 20 to 29. Thus, fifty years ago, most Canadian Mennonite Brethren had but a grade school education. Similarly, among those 60 years or older, 84.1 percent had not gone beyond high school, compared to 69.6 percent of those aged 40 to 49, and 47.6 percent of those aged 20 to 29. The fact that only 2.3 percent of those 60 years or more attended college (but not graduate professional school) and 5.9 percent among those aged 40 to 49, compared to 40.5 percent of those aged 20 to 29, confirms how recent is the trend for college education among Canadian Mennonite Brethren. However, larger numbers among the older generations have taken some graduate or professional training or attained the respective degrees, the percentage being 13.6 among those aged 60 or above, 24.5 among those aged 40 to 49, and only 11.9 among those aged 20 to 29. It would appear that until recently professional training was more popular than a college education by itself. It may well be that professional training is a necessity for occupational purposes. Could it also be a commentary on the value system of Canadian Mennonite Brethren, namely, that a college education per se has relatively little worth, while graduate or professional training has pragmatic worth, since it promotes upward social mobility?

Educational Attainment and Measures of Religiosity

Neither the seven measures of religiosity nor the questions from the survey used to constitute a viable measure of such religiosity are simply the result of arbitrary choice. The first two measures reflect the practice of religion, the next three reflect beliefs or doctrine, and the last two indicate attitudes towards ethics.

Table x-2

Educational Attainment and Devotionalism

Questions	Percentage Response			
	Grade	High	College	Grd./Pr.
Other than at mealtime, how often do you pray to God privately on the average?	(n=75)	(n=151)	(n=35)	(n=49)
Daily/several times per day	86.2	86.3	87.5	90.7
Do the members of your household have a family or group worship, other than grace at meals?	(n=62)	(n=109)	(n=29)	(n=42)
Yes	74.7	63.4	72.5	79.2
How often do you study the Bible privately seeking to understand it and letting it speak to you?	(n=73)	(n=139)	(n=36)	(n=48)
Daily/frequently or weekly?	83.9	79.9	90.0	88.9
In general, how close do you describe your present relationship to God?	(n=57)	(n=92)	(n=23)	(n=36)
Close/very close	67.1	52.6	57.5	67.9
When you have decisions to make in your everyday life, how often do you ask yourself what God would want you to do?	(n=59)	(n=113)	(n=32)	(n=45)
Often/very often	70.2	65.3	82.1	84.9

Source: Church Member Profile, 1972.

Devotionalism.   Table x-2 summarizes the cross-tabulations of indicators of devotionalism with levels of educational attainment. Interestingly, in four out of five questions, the most highly trained (the graduate or professional) have the highest score, and in four out of five cases the high-school-trained score the lower. If a simple scale is prepared in which the lowest for each question is assigned the numeric value of 1 and highest 4, then the following rank order results: graduate or professional, 19; college, 14; grade school, 11; and high school, 6. One might conclude that higher education does not affect religiosity negatively, as expressed in the measure of devotionalism; in fact, the reverse seems to be true. If lack of devotionalism is a true and only measure of secularization, then one might tentatively conclude that education does not result in secularization.

Associationalism. Table x-3 summarizes the cross-tabulation of indicators of associationalism, or participation in religious activities, with levels of educational attainment. Again, in this second measure of the practice of religion, the post-secondary-trained rank the highest in most questions (the exception being for midweek meetings, in which high-school-trained are highest). Those who attained only grade eight have the lowest scores. The scale, according to the above pattern, would give the following rank order: graduate or professional, 13; college, 13; high school, 10; grade school, 4.

Table x-3

Educational Attainment and Associationalism

Questions	Percentage Response			
	Grade	High	College	Grd./Pr.
On the average, how often have you attended church worship services (Sunday morning, evening and/or other days) during the past two years?	(n=64)	(n=147)	(n=35)	(n=47)
Once a week/more than once a week	75.3	84.0	87.5	88.7
How frequently do you attend Sunday school?	(n=45)	(n=116)	(n=28)	(n=37)
Every Sunday possible	51.7	66.3	70.0	69.8
How regularly do you attend any youth or adult meetings held on days other than Sunday that are related to your local congregation?	(n=26)	(n=85)	(n=18)	(n=23)
Regularly	29.9	48.3	45.0	42.6
Do you presently hold, or have held within the past three years, a position of leadership in your local congregation (minister, elder, council member, officer, Sunday school teacher, committee chairman, youth group officer or sponsor, etc.)?	(n=30)	(n=100)	(n=31)	(n=45)
Yes	35.3	57.1	79.5	84.9

Source: Church Member Profile, 1972.

Again, one concludes that the higher the educational attainment, the greater the degree of participation. If lack of devotionalism and associationalism are true measures of secularization, then education does not cause secularization. Thus far, the empirical data consistently point in the same direction.

Table x-4

Educational Attainment and General Orthodoxy

Questions	Percentage Response			
	Grade	High	College	Grd./Pr.
I know God really exists and I have no doubts about His existence.	(n=83)	(n=162)	(n=35)	(n=52)
Comes closest to my belief	97.6	92.0	87.5	96.3
Jesus was not only human but also is the Divine Son of God and I have no doubts about it.	(n=85)	(n=169)	(n=36)	(n=52)
Comes closest to my belief	98.8	96.0	90.0	96.3
I believe the miracles were supernatural acts of God which actually happened just as the Bible says they did.	(n=83)	(n=171)	(n=39)	(n=54)
Comes closest to my belief	96.5	97.7	97.5	96.3
I believe Jesus' physical resurrection was an objective historical fact just as his birth was an historical fact.	(n=83)	(n=169)	(n=39)	(n=54)
Comes closest to my belief	98.8	97.1	97.5	100.0
Jesus will actually return to earth some day.	(n=86)	(n=174)	(n=38)	(n=54)
Definitely	97.7	98.9	95.0	100.0
Satan, as a personal devil, is active in the world today.	(n=88)	(n=174)	(n=38)	(n=53)
Definitely	100.0	98.9	95.0	98.1
There is life beyond death.	(n=86)	(n=172)	(n=39)	(n=53)
Definitely	97.7	98.3	97.5	98.1

Source: Church Member Profile, 1972.

General orthodoxy.   Indicators of the first measure of belief, general orthodoxy, were cross-tabulated with educational attainment as shown in Table x-4. The results show little differentiation, perhaps the only significant loss of belief would be among the college group. A scale, constructed according to the earlier model, would give the following rank order: grade school, 21; graduate or professional, 20; high school, 19; college, 10. As expected, college students lack the measure of assurance in beliefs that those with less education have. Surprisingly, once graduate or professional training occurs, there is a greater degree of commitment. Can it be that while college education has a secularizing effect, graduate or professional schools are too committed to vested interests to let their training liberalize their religious beliefs? Moreover, professional schools tend to be technical rather than philosophically probing.

Fundamentalist orthodoxy. A further, more precise measure of a particular belief is that of fundamentalist orthodoxy.[1] Table x-5 shows the cross-tabulations of indicators of such orthodoxy with educational attainment. As in general orthodoxy, so here the college group decidedly ranks lower than the others. On the question pertaining to creation days, very obviously the higher the attainment of education, the lower the measure of orthodoxy. The rank order according to the above scale is as follows: grade school, 19; high school, 15; graduate or professional, 10; college, 6.

Table x-5
Educational Attainment and Fundamentalist Orthodoxy

Questions	Percentage Response			
	Grade	High	College	Grd./Pr.
I believe the Bible is the divinely inspired and infallible Word of God, the only trustworthy guide for faith and life.	(n=86)	(n=169)	(n=37)	(n=53)
Comes closest to my belief	98.9	96.0	92.5	98.1
Jesus was born of a virgin.	(n=85)	(n=174)	(n=38)	(n=53)
Definitely	98.8	98.9	95.0	98.1
God created the earth and all living things in six 24-hour days.	(n=67)	(n=100)	(n=11)	(n=9)
Definitely	77.9	56.8	27.5	16.7
There was a flood in Noah's day which destroyed all human life except for Noah's family.	(n=85)	(n=166)	(n=34)	(n=48)
Definitely	96.6	94.3	85.0	88.9
All persons who die not having accepted Christ as their redeemer and saviour will spend eternity in a place of punishment and misery.	(n=77)	(n=155)	(n=32)	(n=44)
Definitely	88.5	88.1	80.0	81.5

Source: Church Member Profile, 1972.

---

1 This term was taken from Kauffman and Harder's study and is used to include those distinctive beliefs held by Evangelical Conservatives.

One might conclude that, although those with graduate or professional training are more fundamentalist in outlook than college students, generally the higher the attainment of education the lower the degree of fundamentalism. Again, it appears that while college training relativizes belief, professional training strengthens conservatism.

Table x-6
Educational Attainment and Anabaptism

Questions	Percentage Response			
	Grade	High	College	Grd./Pr.
Jesus expects Christians to follow the pattern which he set in his own life and ministry, including such things as putting evangelism above earning a living, and deeds of mercy above family security.	(n=56)	(n=92)	(n=27)	(n=29)
Agree/strongly agree	65.9	52.6	67.5	53.7
If Christian believers proclaim the Lordship of Christ and truly follow him in all of life they can expect to incur severe criticism and frequent persecution from the large society.	(n=71)	(n=133)	(n=31)	(n=45)
Agree/strongly agree	83.5	76.0	77.5	83.3
Baptism is neither necessary nor proper for infants and small children.	(n=82)	(n=144)	(n=35)	(n=44)
Agree/strongly agree	87.1	85.7	95.0	94.4
The Mennonites' churches should practise a thorough church discipline so that faltering or unfaithful members can be built up and restored or, in exceptional cases, excluded.	(n=82)	(n=144)	(n=35)	(n=47)
Agree/strongly agree	96.5	82.3	87.5	87.0
It is against the will of God for a Christian to swear the oath demanded by the civil government on occasion.	(n=75)	(n=132)	(n=33)	(n=45)
Agree/strongly agree	86.2	75.4	82.5	83.3
The Christian should take no part in war or any war-promoting activity.	(n=63)	(n=105)	(n=28)	(n=39)
Agree/strongly agree	71.6	60.3	70.0	72.2
There are certain offices in our government the tasks of which a true Christian simply could not in clear conscience perform.	(n=66)	(n=120)	(n=27)	(n=37)
Agree/strongly agree	75.0	69.0	67.5	68.5
If Christians have a legitimate claim of property damage against another person, they are justified in bringing a suit in a court of law.	(n=43)	(n=53)	(n=20)	(n=18)
Disagree/strongly disagree	48.9	30.5	51.3	34.0

Source: Church Member Profile, 1972.

Anabaptism. An even more precise measure of a denominational distinctive of belief is that of Anabaptism, as reflected in Table x-6. The cross-tabulation reveals that the least educated have the highest overall record. Yet, the next least educated group, that is, up to high school completion, has the lowest record. Moreover, next to the least educated, the college group ranks the highest. The rank order resulting from this scale is: grade school, 27; college, 22; graduate or professional, 21; high school, 10.

At first glance, such a variable response is confusing. However, several interesting new dimensions seem to be reflected. The high score in Anabaptism by those with a maximum of eight years of schooling is explained, not so much by socialization through education, but by the fact that these represent the older, more conservative generation. The fact that the high school group scores so low might be interpreted as a lack of socialization in the denominational distinctives, rather than secularization resulting from education. So far, however, the results support the earlier trend apparent in the measures of belief, namely, that education leads to lower scores of religiosity. The fact that the college group ranks higher than the high school group speaks of socialization through education and of the possibility of being attracted to these normative ideals of Anabaptism. The somewhat lower graduate or professional group score might suggest that in the crucible of reality the ideals of youth are not as practical. Thus, education leads not only to secularization of orthodox beliefs, but simultaneously to the attraction to idealism, while the practical experience of life tempers with realism the loftiness of youth.

Moral issues. Table x-7 summarizes the cross-tabulation of the indicators of personal ethics with educational attainment. The results are not surprising in that the grade school group, represented by the older generation, is most conservative, followed by those with high school only. The most relativized is the college group, with the graduate or professional somewhat less. The rank order resulting from this scale is as follows: grade school, 28; high school, 16; graduate or professional, 14; college, 12. It appears that education does lead to a relativizing of ethics, but that graduate or professional training places some restraint on the relativization. In their national study of Canadian Mennonites in 1977, Curry, Linden, and Driedger observed the highest correlation between the extent of education and increased drinking precisely among Mennonite Brethren, with 16 percent of those with grade school education drinking compared to 42 percent of those with university education (1977, 277-78).

Social ethics. Table x-8 represents the cross-tabulation of indicators of social ethics with educational attainment. Surprisingly, while the college group ranked lowest on the personal ethics scale, it ranks highest on the social ethics scale. Equally astonishing is the fact that the graduate or professional group ranks lowest on this measure. The resulting rank order is: college, 19; high school, 14; grade school, 14; graduate or professional, 13.

Table x-7
Educational Attainment and Moral Issues

Questions	Grade	High	College	Grd./Pr.
Drinking alcoholic beverages moderately	(n=62)	(n=93)	(n=9)	(n=22)
Always wrong	72.9	53.4	22.5	40.7
Smoking tobacco	(n=78)	(n=138)	(n=29)	(n=38)
Always wrong	92.9	78.9	72.5	70.4
Attending movies rated for adults only	(n=65)	(n=85)	(n=16)	(n=20)
Always wrong	76.5	48.6	40.0	37.0
Premarital sexual intercourse	(n=81)	(n=167)	(n=38)	(n=51)
Always wrong	97.6	94.9	95.0	96.2
Homosexual acts	(n=81)	(n=159)	(n=36)	(n=49)
Always wrong	96.4	91.9	90.0	92.5
Gambling (betting, gambling machines, etc.)	(n=78)	(n=128)	(n=30)	(n=42)
Always wrong	90.7	73.1	75.0	79.2
Social dancing	(n=73)	(n=109)	(n=22)	(n=25)
Always wrong	85.9	62.3	55.0	47.2

Source: Church Member Profile, 1972.

One might conclude that education, as in the Anabaptism measure, leads to socialization among the more idealistic college trained group, and that further graduate or professional training tempers such idealism. In fact, the questions which constitute the measure are possibly more representative of traditional Anabaptism than of traditional Mennonite Brethren understanding of social ethics. The relatively low score among the older generation would suggest this.

Summary of the Empirical Evidence

To summarize the findings in consolidated form, Table x-9 indicates the totals of the scales based on the rank order employed for each of the questions used for the different variables of religiosity. The subtotals for each of the three areas of religiosity are also indicated to enable one to detect particular trends. It appears that the overall trend is ambiguous. One cannot say that education necessarily leads to secularization; it also socializes concurrently in some variables of religiosity. It would appear safe to conclude that education enhances such variables of religiosity which reflect the practice of religion: devotionalism and associationalism. Among the variables of belief, a higher attainment in education generally results in greater relativization or secularization for measures of orthodoxy, but not Anabaptism. Again, in ethical matters, a higher attainment in education relativizes one's personal ethical attitudes, but enhances the more idealistic social ethics. Those with least education (the older generation) have the highest measure of overall religiosity; those with the most education (the professional group) have the next highest rating. Those educated up to high school and college have the overall lowest rating or seem to be most secularized. No doubt, the age factor considerably influences the religiosity of these educational groupings. Education leads to both socialization and secularization.

Table x-8

Educational Attainment and Social Ethics

Questions	Percentage Response			
	Grade	High	College	Grd./Pr.
The Christian should take no part in war or any war-promoting activities.	(n=63)	(n=105)	(n=28)	(n=39)
Agree/strongly agree	71.6	60.3	70.0	72.2
Although there is no essential difference between blacks and whites, it is preferable for them not to mingle socially.	(n=36)	(n=102)	(n=32)	(n=30)
Disagree	41.4	58.3	80.2	55.6
For the most part, people are poor because they lack discipline and don't put forth the effort needed to rise above poverty.	(n=21)	(n=40)	(n=8)	(n=11)
Disagree	38.9	38.1	36.4	30.6
The national government should take every opportunity to stamp out Communism at home and abroad.	(n=8)	(n=21)	(n=18)	(n=24)
Disagree	9.5	12.0	45.0	44.4
A church member should not join a labour union even if getting or holding a job depends on union membership.	(n=25)	(n=13)	(n=4)	(n=0)
Agree	29.1	7.4	10.0	0.0
Capital punishment is a necessary deterrent to crime and should not be abandoned by our national, provincial, or state government.	(n=10)	(n=26)	(n=10)	(n=8)
Disagree	11.6	14.9	25.0	14.8

Source: Church Member Profile, 1972.

Table x-9
Summary of the Scales of the Variables of Religiosity

Variables of Religiosity	Totals of Rank Order/Variables				Direction of Trend[a]
	Grade	High	College	Grd./Pr.	
Practice of Religion					
Devotionalism	11	6	14	19	+
Associationalism	4	10	13	13	+
Subtotal	15	16	27	32	+
Religious Beliefs					
General Orthodoxy	21	19	10	20	-
Fundamentalist Orthodoxy	19	15	6	10	-
Anabaptism	27	10	22	21	?
Subtotal	67	44	38	51	-
Ethics					
Moral Issues	28	16	12	14	-
Social Issues	14	14	19	13	+
Subtotal	42	30	31	27	-
Total	124	90	96	110	?

[a] Plus (+) = more education results in enhanced religiosity
    Minus (-) = less education results in relativization

3. An Analysis of the Church's Attitudes to Change, Secularization, and Education

The Canadian Mennonite Brethren Church has not been oblivious to change and secularization, nor to the impact that education has upon these. To understand how social change has, on the one hand, legitimated the sacralization of religious practices (such as devotionalism and associationalism) and religious distinctives (such as Anabaptism and the uniquely Anabaptist social ethics) and, on the other hand, relativized beliefs and morals, it will be helpful to analyse further the church's attitudes to change, secularization, and education.

Attitudes to Change

For Canadian Mennonite Brethren, the decade of the 1960s, more particularly, 1964 to 1974, was an era of change. This can be seen in its expression of the need for change, the awareness of change, and the response to change.

The need for change.   While occasional references in sermons and articles focus on changing times prior to the 1960s, the last decade of the time span covered by this study was particularly cognizant of change. Interim editor Peter Klassen in 1964 welcomed cultural change.

Change in the area of culture should be made constantly in order that our faith may in fact be communicated. . . . Thus a change from the plow to a profession, from German to English, from country to city, from "Die Stille im Lande" to *The Voice*, from poverty to wealth, from clan to a diaspora, etc.—all these changes are in the secondary area of culture and are naturally subject to change (Klassen, 1964, 3).

In the following year, a pastor, Hugo Jantz, called for radical change. Rather critically, he exposed the church's need for change in these words:

To boil it right down: the church is actually very little more than a lop-sided and tradition-encrusted capsule-like institution, bobbing about with little sense of direction on humanity's troubled sea. And she can do little more than estimate the damage sustained and the cost of repair and rehabilitation necessary after riding out a particular storm or typhoon of change. . . . It is time for drastic change (Jantz, 1965, 9).

These expressions of need for change seemingly elicited numerous responses to change in subsequent years.

The awareness of change.   That the church had suddenly entered an era of momentous change became apparent in both conference and special study sessions in the following years. In 1966, Marvin Hein, pastor of one of the largest Mennonite Brethren churches in United States, addressed the triennial General Conference session at Corn, Oklahoma, on the theme, "The Church in Flux." In this keynote address, he asserted: "There is nothing more certain than change. . . . Like it or not, the Christian Church, too, is changing—much too rapidly for some of us. . . . The Mennonite Brethren Church is no exception" (Hein, 1966, 2). At a study conference, "Issues Concerning Church and Home," F. C. Peters, then moderator of the General Conference, expressed awareness of the threat of change. He begins his study paper noting: "Perhaps nothing has vexed our brotherhood more in the last few decades than the phenomenon of change. Those who have viewed traditional positions in social and personal ethics as normative have been seriously threatened by such rapid change" (Peters, 1967). The 1969 report of the Board of Spiritual and Social Concerns reflected a keen awareness of areas of change to which the board was already reacting or envisaged doing so.

The response to change.   The active response to change became apparent both in conference addresses and study sessions, as well as in actions taken by conferences. At a study conference at Clearbrook in 1974, "The Church, the Word, and the World," Edmund Janzen, now President of Fresno Pacific College (a Mennonite Brethren liberal arts college), argued that "change is not a threatening word, but a releasing word"—and appealed to the assembly of clergy, educators, and other laity that "we the church should be at home with change" (Janzen, 1974). In the brief time of a decade, the Canadian Mennonite Brethren had seemingly traversed the whole panorama of response to change—from the place where the mention of change is done with fear and hesitation to the place where one feels released and at home with change. Change in the Mennonite Brethren Church today is viewed not as an unmitigated evil, but as a potential for both good and bad. However, where change would result in loss of faith, it would be viewed as secularizing.

Attitudes to Secularization

Secularization threatens the essence of sectarianism. Therefore, contrary to the more recent phenomenon of change, secularization has been viewed more consistently as erosive to faith, and throughout its history the Mennonite Brethren Church has warned of its damaging effect. Only rarely has the secularization process been viewed positively. Chapter five drew attention to early expressions of separatism. Assessments of the Canadian Mennonite Brethren Church in the mid-1950s by its most prominent leaders, A. H. Unruh and B. B. Janz, include statements about the effects of secularization. In his appending conclusion to *Die Geschichte der Mennoniten-Bruedergemeinde*, A. H. Unruh observed, "The more the Mennonite Brethren Church exposes itself to the influence of contemporary culture, the more human reason seeks to give direction to the church in doctrine as well as in ethics" (Unruh, 1955, 831). B. B. Janz, in his keynote address to the Canadian Conference in 1954, assessed the Mennonite Brethren Church after ninety-four years of existence. After depicting six positive features, he developed eight negative aspects, the fourth of which is the love for the world ("Weltliebe") to which apparently youth was particularly prone. He illustrates: "Many young people along with Demas forsake Paul, that is, the church, to love the world—the glamorous, frenzy, resonant world. Not that the world first penetrates the church, but much more the members penetrate the world and then bring the world with them into the church" (Janz, 1954, 10-15). In more recent times, such a penetration of the world would have been viewed positively as an occasion for evangelism.

The secularization process has but rarely been viewed positively. John E. Toews questioned that secularization of modern society is a tragedy. He writes:

The secularization of society is not a great tragedy for the church, but rather a great opportunity for it to re-examine itself and experience a renaissance. Stripped of our "religion" do we still have something to say?" ... The sacral society is gone, discredited by its hypocrisy. The secular society gives Christians a chance to prove the holiness of Christ's love in inter-personal relationships. Self-examination, questioning, and ferment are in store for the church in a secular society. A tragedy? As Martin Luther King said recently, "There has never been a better time to be a Christian" (Toews, 1965, 19).

In a similar vein, Edmund Janzen more recently drew attention to Cox's distinction between secularism as a world view and secularization as a process, and suggested a positive interpretation to be "both possible and necessary," since "there is no special sacred order through which God works, for he works in all of life." Janzen concluded:

Thus the process of secularization when understood in terms of the biblical background of our faith may be welcomed instead of feared; for it refers not to a way of life which denies God, but to a process of life which frees man from the rule of a sacral order—frees him to choose God personally, not out of coercion, but out of choice, to serve him in the world (Janzen, 1974).

Both change and secularization can, thus, be viewed positively as well. Once again, a dialectic becomes apparent—a single process having both positive and negative attractions, both sacralizing and secularizing forces. In the same way, the overall effect of education is secularizing in both negative and positive ways.

Attitudes to Education

Before summarizing the secularizing or relativizing effects of education, it will be useful to note the attitudes towards education which Canadian Mennonite Brethren have held during the past half century.

The attitude to education per se. In as much as the Canadian Mennonite Brethren have had an attitude of openness to education, they not only welcomed its positive, liberating effect, but also exposed themselves to the negative effects of secularization. Even before the immigration of the *Russlaender* in the mid-1920s, education was already affirmed.

The coming of the Russian Mennonites encouraged education to an even greater extent. Not only were they of a higher socio-economic group than their Mennonite forerunners to Canada, but they had already adjusted to the Russian society, a number having attended schools for higher education in Europe (Driedger, 1967, 65). The effect of this open attitude to education is further depicted by E. K. Francis:

One of the most striking changes in recent years has occurred in the field of education, mainly under the influence of the Russlaender immigrants.... A

quarter of a century later (since the end of the first World War), a whole
generation had grown up which had never attended a parochial Mennonite
grade school. Day after day, year after year, the secular public school had
taught young Mennonites the same language and the same culture it had been
teaching to the youth of all Anglo-Saxon Canada (Francis, 1955, 264).

In more recent years, Rudy Wiebe, first editor of *Mennonite Brethren
Herald*, reflected on the effect of this openness to education and the
slowness of the church to keep up with the change of its members. He
writes:

Our church has encouraged education; in doing so it has opened to its members wider horizons, both in meeting new people whose practices differ from
those common to us, and in meeting new ideas. . . .

We have not really been prepared for the tremendous upswing in the
educational level of our church members. As a result, much of the preaching
and church activity of today is not suited to meet the intensified needs of our
members (Wiebe, 1963, 3).

The attitude to higher education.   Whereas there was an openness to
education per se, the purpose of such education was usually utilitarian
and thus harmonized with the Mennonite drive for upward social
mobility—the urge to "get ahead." Of the Mennonites in Manitoba
alone, E. K. Francis observed that between 1932 and 1947 the enrolment at the University of Manitoba had increased from nineteen to
eighty-eight (Francis, 1955, 264). A closer analysis of post-secondary
training in Canada revealed the following breakdown in 1964 as indicated in Table x-10. The data were based on a 77 percent return of a
questionnaire to local pastors. The results, representing but a part of
the whole, suggest a strong trend towards professional training.

Higher education for Mennonite Brethren has usually meant the
penetration of the professional world, which had its own secularizing
effect, as chapter twelve will show.

The attitude to liberal arts.   Aside from the crassly utilitarian motive
for higher education, increasingly Canadian Mennonite Brethren have
recognized the worth, as well as the risks, of a liberal arts training.
While few advocates have openly argued for a liberal arts education,
many more have simply exposed themselves to it. It is precisely because
of its secularizing effect that this area of education has been dealt with
so gingerly.

Almost from the outset Mennonite Brethren Bible College required
at least one year of liberal arts "with the view of broadening the
theology student's horizon, and with the hope that such subjects would
equip him better for a ministry in today's world" (Ewert, 1962, 11).
Herb Giesbrecht in 1965 argued for an integrated approach, since the
New Testament does not disparage the world's learning as such and

because Christian humanists have demonstrated that liberal education is possible since such learning is also "part of God's truth" (Giesbrecht, 1965, 4-8). The debate continues to the present.

Table x-10
Canadian Mennonite Brethren Post-Secondary Education in 1964

Field of Study		Provincial Distribution of Students Enrolled				
		ALTA.	B.C.	MAN.	ONT.	SASK.
Medical		3	1	12	5	5
Graduate		4	23	34	21	14
Seminaries		-	4	2	-	1
College	(Conference)	23	56	41	34	15
and	(Non-conference)	4	78	88	28	50
universities						
Nursing		3	16	31	11	9
Trades		3	7	1	-	2
Bible Institutes		38	75	7	16	90
Total		78	260	216	115	186

Source: Peter Penner Survey, MBH, May 22, 1964.

The dilemma in which the Canadian Conference finds itself results from the awareness of the secularizing effects of a liberal arts education and the failure to know how best to cope with the situation. In 1965, John Redekop expressed his alarm as follows:

They [the many observers] point out that the church is not relating itself in any truly effective way to the hundreds of Canadian MB's now on our university campuses. . . . I am sufficiently alarmed by our ever-growing academic casualty lists, in terms of our spiritual warfare, to take seriously any suggestion advanced in good faith (Redekop, 1965, 2).

More recently, Dr. Harry Loewen, former Bible College instructor, frankly admits: "Yes, a liberal arts education is dangerous in that it effects change. A young person who exposes himself to the influence of philosophy, psychology, literature, history and science will at the end of three or four years be different from what he was when he entered the halls of learning" (Loewen, 1973, 11). The dilemma is concisely pinpointed by Dr. Loewen when he states, "We want the best of two worlds, our traditional faith and way of life and an education which will give us the goods and comforts of earthly existence" (Loewen, 1973, 11). At the same time, philosopher Don Wiebe laments not only the dearth of theological and philosophical productivity, but the almost total lack of freedom for critical thought. He contends:

There is here no sensitivity to self-doubt and soul-searching, no room for the quest for new frontiers in Christian faith, no room for liberating ideas that may put in jeopardy past experience and knowledge. The limits to intellectual inquiry are as tight in the twentieth century, it seems, as ever they were in the nineteenth—despite the development of "higher" educational institutions amongst the Mennonite Brethren (Wiebe, 1980, 155).

Even then, Canadian Mennonite Brethren cannot entirely escape the relativizing and secularizing effects of education.

Summary

The foregoing discussion of the attitudes to change, secularization, and education has shown how closely these concepts are intertwined, and yet how differently Canadian Mennonite Brethren have responded to these processes. Initial reluctance to change has given way in the last decade to widespread acceptance of, and adjustment to, change. Persistent resistance to secularization has been tempered by tacit approval of certain forms of exposure to the world. Openness to education in order to reap its benefits of upward social mobility has been offset by hesitancy to risk the truly relativizing effects of the same. The earlier summary of the cross-tabulations of levels of educational attainment with variables of religiosity also indicated that the impact of education was not without ambiguity—sometimes enhancing religiosity, at other times loosening the web of religious beliefs and ethics. To assess the overall effect of education, it will be necessary, then, to distinguish between its impact on change generally and on secularization specifically, as well as to distinguish between the countervailing consequences of each. It is the dialectic of these forces, in the end, that not only provides the movement with the tension of the present but also proffers the vitality of the future.

First, there seems to be no question that education effects change. On the one hand, such change brings about conformity, as the emphasis upon socialization in chapter eight intended to show. On the other hand, such change can also release from the sacralizing encrustations of religious conformity and institutionalization. For Canadian Mennonite Brethren, the socialization impact of education, whether through formal training or religious participation, has been prominent throughout the period under study, yet the relativizing effects of education have made their greatest impact on social change within the last decade, as later chapters on urbanization, occupational change, economic ascendancy, and assimilation will indicate. Change, thus, not only molds and strengthens religious beliefs and thereby fosters continuity of sectarianism, but change also weakens and dislodges set patterns of beliefs and ethics, and hence poses as a threat to continuity.

Next, education has also resulted in a two-fold effect upon secularization. On the one hand, from the outset, Mennonite Brethren have resisted secularization, because to them secularization means conformity to the world and loss of separatism. Some forms of idealistic separatism still prevail, even among the most educated, as the empirical tests of religiosity indicate. Education has, in fact, increased the practice of religion (in participation and associationalism) and strengthened the Anabaptist beliefs and social ethics among those who are college educated. In this respect, education has arrested the secularization process. On the other hand, education has also had a relativizing effect upon religious beliefs and ethics and, in this sense, has enhanced the secularization process. Education leads to increased differentiation in the symbolic system, that is, a proliferation of perspectives and specialized social structures, which offers a plurality of viewpoints. This necessitates a tolerance, to view the perspectives with a measure of objectivity, and results in a broadening of outlook. Such relativization, then, loosens the attachment to one's sacralized commitments and sometimes even embraces new perspectives into one's own symbol system. This relativizing effect is apparent in the loss of belief in orthodoxy and personal ethics, as the empirical evidence indicates, and in the concession to view secularization positively in recent times.

In conclusion, then, it is the interplay of these sacralizing and secularizing forces that keeps the religious movement viable. The impact of education illustrates this curious dialectic. Education, at the same time, strengthens religious belief and practice and also loosens or relativizes the fabric. The relativizing or secularizing effect expresses itself not only negatively in a loss of religious belief or a denial of God, but positively as a freeing process to enable individuals to choose God personally. In this latter sense, secularization supports the Anabaptist notion of voluntarism. Education thus simultaneously builds up religious faith and commitment and breaks down taken-for-granted forms of religiosity. It thereby challenges the religious movement to acquire adaptable forms and functions that the changing world demands.

XI

Urbanization and Fragility Hazards

Perhaps more than any single component of change, education broadens the horizons, loosens the moorings, and relativizes the commitment on the level of the symbolic or the abstract. Urbanization not only affects the mind and attitudes, but exposes the whole person, body and soul, to a new cultural environment, so that people continuously live, and work, and enjoy their leisure in a setting which poses both threats and challenges to their world view. Repeatedly, Mennonite Brethren have asserted that the "Bible and plow" motif no longer characterizes them. Questions naturally follow: When did this urbanization occur, to what extent has it come about, and what are the fragility hazards of their loss of rurality? If Canadian Mennonite Brethren are no longer a rural people, what price did they pay for their urbanity? As in the previous chapter on education, so here with reference to urbanization, the process of change has the two-fold effect of exposing them to hazards as well as confronting them with new opportunities. However, the parameters within which the change occurs are broader in the case of urbanization.

1. The Urbanization Process

To understand the process of urbanization among Canadian Mennonite Brethren, it is essential to examine not only the meaning of urbanization itself and how it contributes to secularization, but also the urban and rural backgrounds of the early Anabaptists and Mennonite Brethren respectively.

Its Meaning and Relation to Secularization

To gain a better understanding of urbanization itself, several related terms will need to be differentiated. Structurally, one needs to distinguish between city and suburb, and city and megalopolis. As Louis Wirth states, a city can simply be viewed as "a relatively large, dense,

170

and permanent settlement of socially heterogeneous individuals" (Wirth, 1938, 1-25). The emphasis on heterogeneity suggests the possibility of change and secularization in such an environment. More comprehensive is Robert E. Park's description of a city as "a state of mind, a body of customs and traditions, and of the organized attitudes and sentiments that inhere in these customs and are transmitted with these traditions" (Peachey, 1963, 14). This latter definition does not confine the notion of urbanism to the walls of a city, but allows the consideration of urbanism as a style of life. The suburb, the setting of urbanization of rural Mennonites, is the smaller community adjacent to and dependent on a central city. According to Mennonite sociologist Paul Peachey, "Here many of the decisive battles of the church will be waged and, it is to be feared, lost" (Peachey, 1963, 37). The megalopolis refers to urban concentration of two or more metropolitan areas that overlap. In the subsequent empirical data on Mennonite Brethren a simple division of small city (containing a population of 2,500 to 24,999) and large city (above 25,000) is observed. Naturally, such an arbitrary division based on size alone does not adequately account for differing life-styles better described by "urbanism."

"Urbanization," as a term, indicates change. On the one hand, it refers to the movement of people from rural to urban or city areas and, on the other hand, to a process or "way of life," or "the product of the interacting processes of rising productivity and increasing division and specialization of labour" (Blumenfeld, 1973, 17). Perhaps the term "urbanism" more clearly refers to the patterns of culture and social structure that are characteristic of cities. With such a dynamic concept of urbanism as a style of life, it is quite conceivable that residents of rural farms and, especially, rural non-farms (those, according to this study, living on a plot smaller than three acres or in a village or town of under 2,500) might have urban qualities, or, conversely, that residents of urban areas lack these qualities because of their rural mentality. Moreover, such an understanding of urbanism comes close to the notion of modernization as secularization. The latter must now be reviewed.

That a dynamic view of urbanism implies secularization can be seen from Stewart Crysdale's view of urbanism.

Urbanism as a style of life means openness to new ideas and readiness to question old norms. It means the growth of rationality in everyday life.... Urbanism implies heterogeneity. We live in close touch with people whose religion, colour, language and customs may be different from our own. It implies pluralism. No longer is the community dominated by white, Anglo-Saxon, Protestant norms or interests (Crysdale, 1965, 10).

Such openness, rationality, and heterogeneity both frees and fragments. If secularization is viewed positively, as the alternative interpretations by Toews and Janzen in chapter ten suggest, then urbanization spells openness to change and a freeing from the rule of the sacral, rural order. It should also free one to choose God personally and, thus, strengthen the Anabaptist view of voluntarism. If, however, secularization is viewed as loss of faith, religious decline, or conformity to the world, then the city likewise creates a rather fragile environment where the individualism and pluralism help to fragment the faith through "psychic overload." Mennonite Brethren were quick to discover the secularizing effects of urbanism, and these were viewed both with doleful alarm and welcome alacrity.

Its Early Development Among Mennonite Brethren

As Mennonite historian Cornelius Krahn states, "Urbanism among the Anabaptists and Mennonites is as old as Anabaptism itself" (Krahn, 1968, 189). Anabaptism had its beginnings in major Swiss, German, Dutch, and French cities. It is persecution that drove them to rural areas, and for some 400 years, Mennonites were largely rural. When the Mennonite Brethren Church was born in 1860 it was entirely rural, and at the time of the great influx of immigrants into Canada in the mid-1920s, the church was still predominantly rural despite the education and wealth that numerous individuals had acquired in Russia. Until 1920 the Mennonite Brethren in North America had two city missions (in Minneapolis and Winnipeg), but no self-supporting, urban congregations. As J. A. Toews assesses, "Cities were places for establishing 'missions,' but not for planting Mennonite Brethren churches" (Toews, 1975, 331).[1] However, Mennonite Brethren soon learned that "not everything that is rural is for that reason Christian" (Peachey, 1955, 76).

Especially the depression of the 1930s brought about the process of urbanization. Sociologist E. K. Francis estimates that "perhaps as many as half of the immigrant settlers (speaking of the *Russlaender*) lost their farms during the Depression. Some of them took over smaller holdings while others drifted to towns and cities" (Francis, 1955, 210). In recounting the experiences of his own family and Mennonite community in Northern Saskatchewan, novelist Rudy Wiebe poignantly explains, "We drove into the district in 1933 with what equipment we had on a rented truck and we left fourteen years later in exactly the same way" (Wiebe, 1964, 153). More important, however, to Francis was the middle-class origin of the immigrants.

---

1 Yet, Driedger, Fretz, and Smucker identify the following adversaries to account for the lack of success of Mennonite missions in Chicago: individualism, industrialism, secularism, urban impersonality, anonymity, competition, specialization, and the struggle for material success and social achievement (Driedger *et al.*, 1978, 298).

The main reason for urbanization among the Russlaender group, however, must be sought in the middle-class origin of many of the refugees, who included a disproportionate number of former estate owners, teachers, physicians, nurses, businessmen, clerks, bankers, and so on. At first the provisions under which they were admitted to Canada compelled all of them to work in agriculture. Yet, in the face of great hardships and difficulties, a majority of these new farmers took up more familiar occupations when opportunities presented themselves after they had become naturalized (Francis, 1955, 210).

It was probably this "middle-class origin" of many of the Mennonite families which provided the incentive to capitalize on the lure of the city, whether an economic lure or a legitimate pursuit of cultural and religious ends.

Table XI-1

Number and Membership of Canadian Mennonite Brethren City Churches, 1951 and 1971

	1951		1971	
	Churches	Membership	Churches	Membership
Ontario	2 (8)[a]	517 (1,529)[a]	7 (14)	1,500 (2,770)
Manitoba	3 (26)	977 (2,819)	10 (27)	2,580 (4,445)
Saskatchewan	3 (25)	195 (2,118)	7 (31)	877 (2,576)
Alberta	0 (9)	-- (1,124)	4 (13)	522 (1,486)
British Columbia	3 (15)	738 (3,667)	12 (37)	2,189 (5,702)
Total	11 (83)	2,427(11,257)	39 (125)[b]	7,637 (17,396)

Source: J. A. Toews, HMBC, p. 333.

[a] The numbers in brackets represent the total number of churches and members for each province. (See Year Book, 1951, pp. 106-19.)

[b] The total figures for 1971 include Quebec with 3 churches and 71 members. (See Year Book, 1971, p. 97.)

The major move to the cities occurred after World War II. Most immigrants to Canada after World War II migrated to cities, for many of them had an urban background in Europe. In 1956, J. A. Toews noted that there were thirteen churches in cities of 5,000 or more, constituting more than one-fourth of Canadian Mennonite Brethren membership (Toews, 1956, 1). The growth of Canadian Mennonite Brethren city churches over a period of twenty years, 1951 to 1971, is indicated in Table XI-1, where "city" refers to an urban population of 10,000 or more. The increase in the percentage of the number of city churches is from 13.3 to 31.2, and the urban membership increase is from 21.6 to 43.9. This is somewhat lower than the Church Member Profile results, based on a random sample, indicate for the following year, 1972. In any case, urbanization of Canadian Mennonite Brethren is still considerably below the national level of 72.4 percent at the 1971 census (Kauffman and Harder, 1975, 54). Even the more conservative percentage of urbanization is, at best, a measure of urban residence, not a measure of urbanism in the cultural sense indicated above. This was well illustrated in 1969 by an interpretative remark by F. C. Peters, Mennonite Brethren psychologist, theologian, and educator, and frequent contributor to the *Mennonite Brethren Herald*. "I think 90% of us still have a basically rural mentality. Though we're living in a city, we've never been trained for city life. But our children have developed an urban mentality" (Peters, 1969, 4). Peters observes the resulting conflict of such urban residence coupled with rural mentality. This dilemma will be further explored after a closer examination of the empirical data that relate to rural-urban residence and religiosity.

2. Empirical Findings on Rural-Urban Residence of Canadian Mennonite Brethren

Numerous Mennonite Brethren spokespersons through sermons, feature articles, and denominational columns refer to the urbanization trend. Few, however, have precise empirical data, if any data at all, to substantiate their claims. The following data not only provided the comparison of rural-urban residence patterns of Canadian Mennonite Brethren with other Mennonite groups, but attempt also to relate urbanization to demographic variables of social change and then, more particularly, indicate the impact of urbanization upon components of religiosity.

The Degree of Rural-Urban Residence

While rural-urban residence has to do with the place where people live, urbanization indicates a process not only of change in residence but of change in style of life, including attitudes and rational processes. To know where people live is, thus, but one measure of their urbanity. To what extent their religious life is affected by such location is to be discovered later. Table XI-2 suggests that North American Mennonite Brethren are the most urban in residence among those Mennonite groups measured, since 56 percent live in small or large cities, proportionately twice as many as members in the (Old) Mennonite Church.[2] However, somewhat fewer Canadian Mennonite Brethren live in small cities and a few more live on rural farms than do their American counterparts. The Mennonite Brethren urban residence compares to 73.5 percent for the American census data of 1970 and 72.4 percent for

2 This compares favourably with the findings of Driedger and Kauffman (1982, 290).

the Canadian census data of 1971. Such extensive urban residence of this sectarian group challenges Gibson Winter's assertion that "a sectarian community can preserve its unique identity only if it insulates itself against the pressures of the surrounding world; such insulation, however, is almost impossible in a metropolitan area" (Winter, 1961, 123). If Mennonite Brethren are indeed sectarian, and if they are in fact maintaining their sectness in an urban setting, then Winter needs to modify his theory.

Table XI-2
Comparative Rural-Urban Residence for Mennonite Denominations

Type of Residence	Percentage Distribution			
	MC (n=1,195)	GC (n=611)	NAMB (n=703)	CMB (n=359)
Rural farm[a]	38	33	25	30.1
Rural non-farm	36	28	19	19.8
Subtotal	74	61	44	49.9
Small city	14	16	20	13.5
Large city	12	23	36	36.7
Subtotal	26	39	56	50.2

Source: Church Member Profile, 1972.

[a] Rural farm = residence on farm of 3 acres or more
Rural non-farm = residence on plot of less than 3 acres outside a village or city, or in a village or town of under 2,500
Small city = residence in a city of 2,500 to 24,999
Large city = residence in a city of 25,000 or more

Effect of Urbanization upon Other Demographic Variables of Social Change

In order to examine the impact of urban residence upon religiosity, it will be helpful to know the effect of urban residence upon such factors of socio-economic status as education, occupation, and income.

Rural-urban residence and education. Table XI-3 confirms the usual assumption that urban areas attract the more educated. Comparing the "rural farm" and "large city" column makes this clear. The higher the level of attainment, the lower the row percentage response of those resident on a rural farm; conversely, the higher the level of educational attainment, the higher the row percentage response of those resident in a large city. The "rural non-farm" and "small city" columns do not indicate this trend so consistently. The table simply confirms that the more educated tend to live in the large cities.

Table XI-3

Rural-Urban Residence and Levels of Educational Attainment

Level of Educational Attainment	Percentage Response			
	Rural Farm	Rural Non-farm	Small City	Large City
Grade School	35.3 (n=30)	22.4 (n=19)	14.1 (n=12)	28.2 (n=24)
High School	34.3 (n=60)	17.7 (n=31)	14.3 (n=25)	33.7 (n=59)
College	22.5 (n=9)	25.0 (n=10)	7.5 (n=3)	45.0 (n=18)
Graduate/Professional School	14.8 (n=8)	16.7 (n=9)	14.8 (n=8)	53.7 (n=29)

Source: Church Member Profile, 1972.

Rural-urban residence and occupation.   Table XI-4 shows the cross-tabulations of the ten occupational categories with the four variables of rural-urban residence. Obviously most farmers live on a farm, although a few have possibly retired in the city. Most managerial, professional, clerical, skilled and service workers live in cities. A higher percentage of housewives and students are rural residents. Perhaps more city housewives are fully employed and have indicated their vocation as other than housewife (according to instructions). It is not obvious why a higher percentage of students are rural. Could this reflect the trend of Canadian Mennonite Brethren of recent decades, namely, to leave the farm for the city and let education be the legitimating instrument? Could it be that city youth, once urbanized, are less attracted to further training?

Rural-urban residence and income.   Table XI-5 shows the cross-tabulations of seven levels of income for 1971 with the four variables of rural-urban residence. The most striking differential in income between rural and urban is apparent in the "Below $3,000" category and again in the "$12,000-14,999" or higher categories in which instances rural farm residence has a predominance of the lowest incomes and the large city a predominance of the highest incomes. Collapsing the categories for both rows and columns, one arrives at the following simple analysis:

Table XI-4
Rural-Urban Residence and Occupational Variation

| Occupations | Percentage Response | | | |
	Rural Farm	Rural Non-farm	Small City	Large City
Farmer	81.8 (n=36)	6.8 (n=3)	4.5 (n=2)	6.8 (n=3)
Manager	5.3 (n=1)	26.3 (n=5)	21.1 (n=4)	47.4 (n=9)
Professional	7.8 (n=4)	23.5 (n=12)	15.7 (n=8)	52.9 (n=27)
Clerical	0.0 (n=0)	15.0 (n=3)	25.0 (n=5)	60.0 (n=12)
Craftsman	22.7 (n=5)	9.1 (n=2)	13.6 (n=3)	54.5 (n=12)
Machine Operator	6.3 (n=1)	25.0 (n=4)	18.8 (n=3)	50.0 (n=8)
Service Worker	0.0 (n=0)	30.0 (n=3)	20.0 (n=2)	50.0 (n=5)
Labourer	25.0 (n=1)	50.0 (n=2)	0.0 (n=0)	25.0 (n=1)
Housewife	35.5 (n=38)	20.6 (n=22)	12.1 (n=13)	31.8 (n=34)
Student	35.8 (n=19)	22.6 (n=12)	11.3 (n=6)	30.2 (n=16)

Source: Church Member Profile, 1972.

Table XI-5

Rural-Urban Residence and Levels of Income for 1971

Annual Combined Net Income for Household (before income tax deductions)	Percentage Response			
	Rural Farm	Rural Non-farm	Small City	Large City
Below $3,000	60.0 (n=18)	23.3 (n=7)	6.7 (n=2)	10.0 (n=3)
$3,000-5,999	32.7 (n=16)	12.2 (n=6)	16.3 (n=8)	38.8 (n=19)
$6,000-8,999	23.7 (n=18)	26.3 (n=20)	15.8 (n=12)	34.2 (n=26)
$9,000-11,999	25.0 (n=16)	23.4 (n=15)	17.2 (n=11)	34.4 (n=22)
$12,000-14,999	13.5 (n=5)	27.0 (n=10)	10.8 (n=4)	48.6 (n=18)
$15,000-19,999	20.8 (n=5)	4.2 (n=1)	12.5 (n=3)	62.5 (n=15)
$20,000 or more	33.3 (n=5)	20.0 (n=3)	6.7 (n=1)	40.0 (n=6)

Source: Church Member Profile, 1972.

Income for 1971	Number of Residents		Total
	Rural	City	
Below $6,000	47	32	79
$6,000-12,000	69	71	140
Above $12,000	29	47	76
Total	145	150	295

Those below $6,000 per annum are predominantly in rural areas (47/79). Those above $12,000 per annum are predominantly in urban areas (47/76). Rural-urban residence does indicate something about those among the lowest and highest incomes. The effect of the affluence upon religious beliefs and life will be further examined in chapter thirteen.

Place of residence does affect socio-economic status as the variables of education, occupation, and income indicate. Either the city attracts those of higher education, skilled, service and professional vocations, and higher income, or the city contributes to the same. Both, no doubt, hold true. In as much as education, occupation, and income have a bearing upon religion, urbanization can likewise be expected to influence religiosity. How this occurs will next be discovered.

The Effect of Urbanization upon Religion

To measure the effect that rural-urban residence has upon religion, three measures of religiosity are chosen, and representative questions are selected from the Church Member Profile to constitute each measure. Each of the main indicators is again subdivided into more precise areas to allow for variation of response. The questions used for the items measuring the variables of religion in the tables that follow are the same questions as those in chapter ten, but they are abbreviated in order to conserve space. Also, as in chapter ten, a simple scale will be devised to compare the overall effect.

Rural-urban residence and the practice of religion. Four questions will provide data for each of two components, devotionalism and associationalism. Table xi-6 shows the cross-tabulations. Although the scores on the practice of religion are high for all groups, especially in associationalism, there is a significant difference between the rural farm and the large city. Church attendance and involvement appears to be a little more extensive in rural areas. In devotionalism, the greatest difference lies between the rural farm and rural non-farm. Does this suggest that the rural non-farm may be distantly located from a church and that members find attendance more difficult or do these residents belong to those sophisticated urbanites who have left the suburbs and their churches to find the isolation of the rural non-farm an excuse not to involve themselves in the activities of the local church?

Rural-urban residence and religious beliefs. Five questions for each of three components of religious beliefs constitute the measures for these beliefs as indicated in Table xi-7. While the responses to general orthodoxy are high throughout, the residents of rural farms are exceptionally high, followed by the residents of the small city. A similar pattern prevails for beliefs of fundamentalist orthodoxy. The rank order of the resulting scale for these two measures of beliefs is: rural farm, 37; small city, 32; rural non-farm, 18; and large city, 14. As in the effects of education, so in rural-urban residence, the Anabaptist beliefs do not provide a consistent pattern with the other beliefs. Here the small city ranks highest, followed by rural farm and large city, and rural non-farm the lowest. As in devotionalism, so in Anabaptist beliefs, the rural non-farm residents score the lowest. Does their possible isolation from rural or city congregations account for their low rating on this denominational distinctive?

Table XI-6

Rural-Urban Residence and Devotionalism/Associationalism

Religious Practices	Percentage Response			
	Rural Farm	Rural Non-farm	Small City	Large City
Devotionalism				
Prayer	88.8 (n=95)	81.2 (n=56)	89.4 (n=42)	86.9 (n=113)
Bible Study	86.0 (n=92)	79.7 (n=55)	83.3 (n=40)	83.7 (n=108)
Closeness to God	63.8 (n=67)	58.8 (n=40)	57.4 (n=27)	55.4 (n=72)
Seeking God's will	74.3 (n=78)	64.3 (n=45)	72.1 (n=31)	73.4 (n=94)
Rank Order Scale	15	6	10	9
Associationalism				
Church attendance	84.9 (n=90)	83.6 (n=56)	83.3 (n=40)	80.6 (n=104)
Sunday school attendance	79.4 (n=85)	58.8 (n=40)	68.1 (n=32)	51.5 (n=67)
Mid-week services	50.0 (n=53)	41.4 (n=29)	39.6 (n=19)	38.5 (n=50)
Leadership part	63.2 (n=67)	58.8 (n=40)	60.4 (n=29)	55.1 (n=70)
Rank Order Scale	16	10	10	4

Source: Church Member Profile, 1972.

Viewing the total effect upon beliefs, one might conclude that small city and rural farm residents tend to be more conservative, while urbanism has its relativizing effects upon those in large cities and the rural non-farm residents. The big city residents appear to be more secularized than the rural farmers, but to draw the line more finely is impossible on the basis of the evidence. In a similar analysis of the Kauffman, Harder data, Driedger and Kauffman conclude generally that urbanization does not appear to be an important factor in the Anabaptist and biblical beliefs that Mennonites hold today (1982, 289).

Table XI-7

Rural-Urban Residence and General Orthodoxy, Fundamentalist Orthodoxy, and Anabaptism

Religious Beliefs	Percentage Response			
	Rural Farm	Rural Non-farm	Small City	Large City
General Orthodoxy				
Deity of Jesus	100.0 (n=107)	94.2 (n=65)	95.7 (n=45)	93.8 (n=122)
Belief in miracles	100.0 (n=107)	95.6 (n=65)	97.9 (n=47)	96.1 (n=124)
Jesus' resurrection	100.0 (n=107)	98.5 (n=67)	93.8 (n=45)	97.6 (n=123)
Jesus' return	99.1 (n=106)	97.1 (n=68)	100.0 (n=48)	97.7 (n=127)
Personal devil	100.0 (n=107)	98.6 (n=69)	100.0 (n=48)	97.7 (n=127)
Rank Order Scale	19	9	15	8
Fundamentalist Orthodoxy				
Inspiration of Bible	99.1 (n=106)	95.7 (n=66)	97.9 (n=47)	95.4 (n=124)
Virgin birth	99.1 (n=106)	97.1 (n=66)	100.0 (n=47)	97.7 (n=124)
Six-day creation	62.3 (n=66)	52.9 (n=37)	58.3 (n=28)	41.9 (n=54)
Universal flood	99.1 (n=106)	92.9 (n=65)	93.8 (n=45)	88.5 (n=115)
Eternal punishment	90.7 (n=97)	87.1 (n=61)	93.8 (n=45)	80.6 (n=104)
Rank Order Scale	18	9	17	6
Anabaptism				
Following Jesus	59.8 (n=64)	55.1 (n=38)	52.1 (n=25)	59.4 (n=76)
Against infant baptism	86.9 (n=93)	85.5 (n=59)	93.8 (n=45)	90.6 (n=116)
Church discipline	86.0 (n=92)	87.0 (n=60)	91.5 (n=43)	87.6 (n=113)
Non-resistance	66.4 (n=71)	62.3 (n=43)	72.9 (n=35)	63.8 (n=83)
Non-swearing of oaths	81.3 (n=87)	76.8 (n=53)	83.3 (n=40)	78.5 (n=102)
Rank Order Scale	13	7	17	13

Source: Church Member Profile, 1972.

Rural-urban residence and personal-social ethics.   Five questions for each of two components of the personal-social ethics are used to measure this aspect of Mennonite Brethren religiosity. Table XI-8 shows that for the personal moral issues, traditionally held in taboo, residents from rural farm areas are more conservative with residents of large cities considerably more flexible. The scores on social ethics, however, are less diverse, the greatest divergence being between rural farm and rural non-farm residents. As in the cross-tabulations with education, the results of the measure of social ethics vary significantly from the results on personal ethics. Urbanization has not brought about a significant relativization.

Table XI-8

Rural-Urban Residence and Personal and Social Ethics

	Percentage Response			
	Rural Farm	Rural Non-farm	Small City	Large City
Moral Issues				
Drinking moderately	66.7 (n=70)	47.1 (n=33)	50.0 (n=24)	44.1 (n=56)
Smoking tobacco	85.8 (n=91)	79.1 (n=53)	83.3 (n=40)	74.4 (n=96)
Adult-rated movies	69.2 (n=74)	54.3 (n=38)	52.1 (n=25)	37.3 (n=47)
Premarital sex	98.1 (n=103)	97.1 (n=67)	95.8 (n=46)	92.9 (n=118)
Social dancing	75.7 (n=81)	69.6 (n=48)	64.6 (n=31)	51.6 (n=65)
Rank Order Scale	20	13	12	5
Social Ethics				
Race relations	61.3 (n=65)	58.0 (n=40)	45.8 (n=22)	56.2 (n=73)
Social welfare	43.4 (n=46)	31.9 (n=22)	34.0 (n=16)	40.8 (n=53)
Anti-Communism	12.5 (n=13)	18.8 (n=13)	25.5 (n=12)	24.6 (n=32)
Labour unions	16.8 (n=18)	8.7 (n=6)	12.5 (n=6)	7.8 (n=10)
Capital punishment	3.8 (n=4)	13.0 (n=9)	25.5 (n=12)	22.5 (n=29)
Rank Order Scale	14	10	14	12

Source: Church Member Profile, 1972.

Summary of Conclusion of Empirical Evidence

Mennonite Brethren are the most urban among Mennonite churches, yet their Canadian rate of 50.2 percent (based on 1972 survey) is considerably below the national average of 72.4 percent (based on 1971 census). Although comparable data for Canadian Mennonite Brethren are not available for the 1920s, the immigration pattern and the location of churches would indicate an almost completely rural pattern. Urbanization has unquestionably taken place.

Residence, moreover, affects socio-economic status, as the cross-tabulations with variables of education, occupation, and income indicate. The more educated tend to live in large cities; those in the skilled, clerical or professional occupations likewise tend to be residents of the large city; while most of those listed as farmers, labourers, housewives, and students are rural in residence. Furthermore, while the largest number with lowest incomes are rural farm residents, the largest number with highest incomes are large city residents.

Table XI-9

A Summary of the Scales of the Effects of Rural-Urban Residence upon Religion

	Percentage Response			
	Rural Farm	Rural Non-farm	Small City	Large City
Practice of Religion				
Devotionalism	15	6	10	9
Associationalism	16	10	10	4
Subtotal	31	16	20	13
Religious Beliefs				
General Orthodoxy	19	9	15	8
Fundamentalist Orthodoxy	18	9	17	6
Anabaptism	13	7	17	13
Subtotal	50	25	49	27
Ethics				
Moral Issues	20	13	12	5
Social Issues	14	10	14	12
Subtotal	34	23	26	17
Total	115	64	95	57

Source: Church Member Profile, 1972.

Urbanization has occurred and with it there are changes in education, occupation, and income. It is not clear which is causal, urbanization or the components of socio-economic status. Such changes, however, do affect religiosity. Mennonite Brethren residents of the large city are somewhat less rigorous in their devotional practice and decidedly less involved in local church activities. Again, especially in the orthodox beliefs and the evangelical doctrines, the residents of the large city are less convinced of the traditional beliefs or possibly more open to alternative viewpoints; this is not so, however, for Anabaptist beliefs. As in the study on effects of education, so also the effects of urbanization have not negatively influenced the denominational distinctives. Finally, in personal moral issues, residents of rural farms are decidedly more conservative; this is not so, however, for social ethics. Here the rural non-farm resident, as in matters of religious practice and beliefs, rates among the lower.

A summary of the scales devised in each measure is shown in Table xi-9. The table simply confirms the divergence of religiosity between residents of rural farm and large city. It also indicates that small city residents are more akin in their religious beliefs and practices to rural farm residents, while rural non-farm residents are closer to large city residents. These empirical data may be more meaningfully interpreted with a better understanding of the church's view of urbanization and its effect upon the church member.

3. The Church's Understanding of Urbanization

How does the church view the phenomenon of urbanization of which it is so conscious? Once again, there is no unilateral response. While it is true that in earlier years there was greater anxiety about the secularizing effects of the city, the city has posed not only a threat but also a challenge to the church.

Viewing the City as a Peril

Mennonites were naturally more conscious of their recent rural background than of the urban origin of their Anabaptist forebears. That the perils of the city loomed large is apparent from an idealization of rural life. The perils were not expressed simply through projected concerns, but also in terms of realized consequences.

Concerns expressed in anticipation of urbanization.   Preaching to the Canadian Conference at Hepburn in 1928, Winnipeg city missionary C. N. Hiebert warned of the perils of the city: its restlessness, its enticements to spend, and its lure to conform (*YB*, 1928, 9). Conformity would be wrong because of the sinfulness of city life-styles. Edmund Janzen graphically depicts the traditional Mennonite Brethren repudiation of the city.

Consider what we in our M.B. circles have always been taught about cities and city life: they throb with sin; they are places where sin is rampant, where it is wholesaled. Cities are associated with Sodom and Gomorrah, scarlet women, crime, and filth. . . . As someone has said, we tend to view urbanized society through anti-urban 3-D spectacles, for we see the city as depraved, deprived, and dirty (Janzen, 1974).

The city was a threat not only because of its blatant appeals to sinful living, but because of its more subtle attacks upon the faith of the Christian, especially the young person. The Board of Spiritual and Social Concerns (*Fuersorgekomitee*) expressed its concern about the loss of faith among the young people in the universities of Canada (*YB*, 1955, 131). Related to this concern was the possibility of losing one's confessional distinctive, as cautioned by J. A. Toews in 1956 (Toews, 1956, 1-4). A further danger, included also by Toews, was the loss of community. This was not an unrealistic concern. In 1973, John Redekop listed six "casualties of urbanization," three of which had to do with community: failure for young people to make the church youth group their most important peer group or social activity; the weakening of ethnic ties among church members; best friends are not Christians or even church attenders (Redekop, 1973, 2). A fourth "casualty" listed by Redekop, mentioned also by Toews, was the weakening of the family ties. These concerns, which indicated both suspicion and fear of the city, were not solely hypothetical, for Mennonite Brethren actually encountered some of these perils.

Consequences encountered in the realization of urbanization. Urbanization has perils that are physical, psychological, social, and ideological in their consequences. Physically, residential mobility demands adjustments not only to new working conditions (the impact of occupational change will be separately treated in chapter twelve), but also to new patterns of worship and styles of association in urban congregations. The extent of such mobility was further suggested by Marvin Hein in his keynote address to the 1966 General Conference. He warned, "We will swallow hard when we learn that we must expect a complete turnover of membership every seven years in an urban congregation" (Hein, 1966, 15). The possible resulting loss of membership becomes apparent in the observation by Friesen and Vogt, who estimated that "up to 80 percent of the membership of several large Alliance and Free Evangelical churches in Winnipeg is made up of persons of Mennonite background" (Friesen and Vogt, 1964, 15). The following chapter will further explore the degree of defection among church members as a result of residential mobility.

Psychologically, the perils of urbanization are experienced in the new anonymity and the resulting anomie which mark many urban residents. Professor Leonard Siemens of the University of Manitoba characterizes such anonymity as part of the "terrifying freedom of the city." Siemens indicates the psychological effects when he adds: "having tasted, some people get feelings of guilt, misery, and anxiety. Others may indeed decide to switch primary reference groups—from the church to the club or whatever it may be. Anonymity, namelessness, then offers a measure of freedom" (Siemens, 1974, 108). Such anonymity enhances the fragile nature of his religious association. Of the youth of the city Delbert Wiens writes: "Nor do they have the same hunger to climb. . . . They are more likely to be left with the uneasy feeling of never having risen to the top of anything" (Wiens, 1974, 117). This is a marked contrast to their parents who moved to the city and made every effort to succeed and climb the mobile ladder.

Socially, upward mobility for Mennonites has meant the mushrooming of churches in suburbia. The perils encountered by a particular Mennonite church in Toronto is well illustrated by two psychologists, who observed that the convergence of group cohesiveness and interaction during the early years was dissipated when closer relationships evolved with one's associates at work or near one's home (Dyck and Sawatsky, 1968, 172-76). Leonard Siemens likewise recognized the peril in the freedom to choose one's *Gemeinschaft* group. "In the city a person is a member, at the same time, of many different groups: family, neighbourhood, church, club, Home and School, work, recreation, etc. But the life style of the individual will conform to the values of the primary or Gemeinschaft groups within which he most desires acceptance and status" (Siemens, 1970, 17). There is a social peril, therefore, in the pluralism offered by the city.

Perhaps even more hazardous to religious commitments are the perils of plurality which affect ideology. In 1958 Peter Penner referred to the complexity of modernization which almost imperceptibly brings ideological sophistication, and this comes with the move to the city.

Our people—young married couples, teachers, single girls with their various careers, single men as students, technicians, labourers, and many middle-aged and even older people—are moving to towns and cities. There, especially in the larger centers, they take on a certain sophistication almost without knowing it. They become part of a complex way of life. . . . This professionalization and urbanization are forcing us to change (Penner, 1958, 8).

In his essay, "From the Village to the City," Delbert Wiens explains that modern youth with its "openness to other sorts of realities . . . are also more open to the spiritual and the occult than were previous generation" (Wiens, 1974, 116). However, the options of pluralism do not present perils alone, they also offer opportunities for good.

Viewing the City as a Frontier

Just as change, secularization, and education have both positive and negative forces which dialectically interact, so in urbanization there is an interplay of the perils and opportunities which make it an exciting frontier for church renewal. In fact, Paul Peachey argues: "If the genius of Anabaptism is the creation and perpetuation of the distinct religious community, and is thus involved in social heterogeneity, then the urban environment provides a more congenial setting for a vital Anabaptism than does the rural" (Peachey, 1955, 82). A fuller understanding of the Mennonite Brethren response to urbanization must include such a view of the city to be a "congenial setting for a vital Anabaptism."

Individual voices articulate the challenge of the city. Amid the numerous expressions of concern over the hazards of urbanism are the prophetic voices of Mennonite Brethren, who, while realizing the perils, also exploit the opportunity of this new frontier. In 1956, J. A. Toews discovered in the city opportunities for more systematic instruction (not having to contend with the roads and the weather of the country), for mission, and for banding together organizationally in joint projects (Toews, 1956, 2, 3). A decade later, Calgary history professor John B. Toews rhetorically asked, "Have we really seen the city?" He particularly pointed to the religious challenge of urbanism.

The rise of urbanism is a sign of what God is doing in our world and so provides a galaxy of new opportunities for the Church of our time. The Church can still be God's instrument if it learns to serve the city....

The city forces the church to diversity of action and structure. There is something for everyone to do and endless ways to do it. This does not mean the rejection of the institutional church, only a recognition of its varied structure (Toews, 1966, 4, 5).

In 1970, Leonard Siemens likewise found "justification for a positive attitude." He viewed the city as a symbol of cultural and technical progress with opportunities for health services, education, employment, cultural enrichment, and religious participation well beyond what is offered in most rural areas and the "best opportunity to demonstrate the love of Christ to the aged, the dispossessed, the dependent, the lonely, the sick, and the needy . . ." (Siemens, 1970, 13). In a similar vein, Delbert Wiens sees future promise in the city.

At first glance, the city seems to be the well-nigh universal solvent, destroying community, dissolving ethics, denying greatness, undercutting the Scriptures and theology, and eradicating the sense of God.... But the city is not only Babel and Babylon. The city is also Jerusalem. Even in the Scriptures the future promise is—a city (Wiens, 1974, 147).

These spokespersons, representative of many others, view the urban opportunity (or "metropolitan remnant") as a "springboard" for new frontiers of action.

The collective thrust of the church in response to the city. In summary, then, viewing the city as a frontier enables one, in a sociological analysis, positively to find opportunity which would otherwise appear to have but pejorative overtones. The heterogeneity and plurality offered by the city means multiple exposure and an infinite variety of choice. While the possibility of over-choice exists, human choice is taken seriously, and, thus, one exercises the Anabaptist notion of voluntarism. Again, mobility, be it residential or upward social mobility, means increased accessibility. This also resembles the early Anabaptist movement with people of many professions penetrating the urban and rural areas in their zeal to witness or in their flight from persecution. Moreover, urbanism might help a tradition-bound, ethnically inhibited church to overcome its staleness and ethnicity. As Paul Peachey maintains, true Anabaptism protests the ethnicizing of Christianity (Peachey, 1955, 81). Finally, urbanization means liberation. The new freedom extends beyond enjoying the physical and socio-economic accoutrements of urban life. It bespeaks a world view and a life-style which does not seek merely to conform to pressures of society. It dares to be radical; it dares to protest the conformity to a pagan society; it dares to be sectarian. It is not surprising that in the empirical observations, urbanization apparently was little threat to Anabaptism. It appears that the urban environment may provide a more congenial setting for vital Anabaptism. However, there is not sufficient empirical evidence to demonstrate that urbanization has in fact achieved such revitalized Anabaptism.[3]

Summary

The foregoing discussion has attempted to show how urbanization has increased the fragility of the religious commitment of Canadian Mennonite Brethren. It becomes apparent that urbanization does contribute to secularization, but it is by no means clear that the urbanization process seriously threatens the continuity of sectarianism, as Gibson Winter would intimate. Why sectarianism still persists becomes evident in a three-fold way.

First, understanding the process of urbanization and its particular occurrence in Mennonite Brethren history helps to explain the persistence of religiosity despite increased threat of erosion in recent times. The heterogeneous structures and dynamic processes implicit to urban residence account for accessibility to change and secularization. The increased freedom to choose and the plurality of life-styles from which

---

3 Driedger, Fretz, and Smucker demonstrate that cities such as Winnipeg, Vancouver, Saskatoon, and Waterloo provide for a community-continuity model in which a symbiotic relationship exists between the city and its hinterland, thus facilitating a successful penetration of the city for church planting (Driedger *et al.*, 1978, 294-311).

to choose results in greater voluntarism and more deliberate commitments. Moreover, the cultural qualities which constitute urbanity are not restricted to urban residence, as the residents of rural non-farms indicate. Whether one understands secularization negatively, as a loss of religious commitment, or positively, as increased freedom, urbanization has contributed to secularization of Canadian Mennonite Brethren, especially since World War II. For example, from 1951 to 1971 the percentage of urban church membership doubled from 22 to 44 and by 1975 was at least 50. Although urban mentality lags behind urban residence, secularization has, no doubt, posed as a threat to an increasingly fragile religious commitment.

Next, the empirical data further disclose both increased secularization in some religious components and stubborn persistence in other variables. As expected, urbanization correlates positively with socioeconomic status—the larger cities attract the more educated, the skilled and professional, and those with highest incomes. The correlation with religious variables is less unambiguous. The practice of religion, as measured by devotionalism and associationalism, is less rigorous in urban than rural residence. Particularly in general orthodoxy and fundamentalist orthodoxy, it is the resident of the large city and the rural non-farm whose beliefs are more relativized. Yet in the Anabaptist belief variable, the city residents are stronger than the rural. In the realm of ethics, it is the personal moral issues which urbanization relativizes, but not so in the social ethics, where urbanization makes no significant differences. Interestingly, the rural farm and small city residents are akin in religious beliefs and practice, even as rural non-farm resembles more the large city resident. Residence in urban areas, therefore, tends towards secularization but is no guarantee of it.

Finally, important to understanding why sectarianism persists despite the secularizing effects of urbanization is a religious movement's self-conscious response to such urbanization. Initial fears and perceived consequences with physical, psychological, social, and ideological implications were counter-balanced by increasing awareness of an urban frontier which offered new freedoms and increased opportunities. Anxiety gave way to confidence, retreat from dangers was replaced with acceptance of the encounter with new challenges, and fragility hazards were viewed as potential sectarian strengths. Urbanization does indeed enhance secularization, but it also provides a stimulus that can reinforce fragile structures and eroding beliefs. Whether it will produce the evidence which will bear out the more positive assertions of recent Canadian Mennonite Brethren leadership remains a question for the future.

XII

Occupational Change and Reorientation

For most Canadian Mennonite Brethren in the second half of this century, the move to the city meant not only the abandonment of the farm residence but the adjustment to a new occupation. With the new urban generation, there was a marked occupational change. The grandparents of the generation now coming of age usually were immigrant farmers of the mid-1920s or the offspring of American settlers of the early decades of this century. Many of these, now elderly people retired in the city, continued to be farmers for the duration of their working days. For some, it meant vocational change, for others it required the reorientation that urban residence brings with it. The parents of this present generation had their moorings in a rural setting, but chose occupations suited to urban residence. For them the rural-urban shift necessitated occupational change in addition to the usual adaptations to urban residence. The effects of occupational change are probably most noticeable among this group of parents, many of whom have acquired the life-style of the "secular city." The new generation is largely urban and has naturally assimilated those qualities of urban living which their parents consciously sought to imbibe. The present chapter focuses on the secularizing impact of such change in occupations which accompanies the shift from rural to urban residence.

The order of these chapters—education, urbanization, occupation—represents a causal relationship. It is conceivable that there first could have been an occupational change (such as from farm to factory), which required the move to the city and which then also offered educational opportunities (by extension or adult education). No doubt, this could be documented. It is also conceivable that the move to the city could come first (on account of immigration or bankruptcy during the depression), which was then followed by either vocational change or education within the city. This chapter assumes the more probable course of history for most Canadian Mennonite Brethren of the mid-century decades: from a rural background, they came to the city to study with possibly a change of occupation requir-

190

ing urban residence. The occupation, thus, follows both eduation and urbanization. All the while, religious people need to respond to the changing life-styles and the plurality of world views to which such education, urbanization, and occupation expose them. Before exploring the consequences of such change and reorientation, it may be well to survey further the background to this change.

1. Some Historical Perspectives

Two perspectives will furnish further background to understand the empirical documentation which then follows and to interpret the degree of secularization. The first is historical, while the second is more psychological and analytical.

Historical Considerations

Canadian Mennonite Brethren have a unique historical background which helps explain the large-scale shift from rural to urban vocations.

Loosening the moorings (pre-1925). For those whose moorings were deeply rural because of their settlement in Manitoba and Saskatchewan in the early decades of the century, the occupational shift came less abruptly. With the immigration in the 1920s, the Canadian Mennonite Brethren membership tripled in number, and the majority, therefore, not only were immigrant in background but had experienced political revolution, socio-economic upheaval, and spiritual renewal. Their agrarian village moorings in Russia had been thoroughly uprooted through these crises. Moreover, their choice of becoming farmers in Canada was determined largely out of economic necessity. Despite their survival of the depression, the payment of their *Reiseschuld*, and their favourable progress in farming, their rural moorings had been loosened and as a people they were readily prepared to opt for a change in the predominant vocation.

Breaking the boundaries (1925-1950). For a few Mennonite Brethren, the break with the rural village took place with immigration in the mid-1920s. A number of families settled in Kitchener and Winnipeg. For others the early years on an isolated farm or homestead in the newly adopted land proved to be too demanding. They too left for the city. The Mennonite Collegiate Institute of Gretna attracted still others, especially those who had been teachers in Russia, and these, after a year of normal school training, became teachers in rural Manitoba. The determination of the few to become teachers is but prophetic of the many in the next generation who chose this profession. During the depression and drought of the 1930s, some farmers abandoned their farms in their struggle for economic survival. World War II proved to be a further event which helped to unsettle Mennonites. Many otherwise farm-bound young men, as conscientious objectors, served in alternative service camps removed from kith and kin. Others joined the non-combatant medical corps or even the army. A goodly number of these conscientious objectors, once released from duties, had acquired occupational goals other than farming. A number of today's ministers, teachers, professors, business administrators, and doctors are former conscientious objectors. Most Mennonite Brethren were still rural in residence by 1950, but numerous families had already settled in larger cities, and many young people had broken their ties with their fathers' farming occupation.

Exploring new horizons (1950-1975).   Evidence supports Cornelius Krahn's observation that "the first acceptable occupation of rural Mennonites was usually the teaching profession, which was followed by nursing, the healing physician and gradually other professions" (Krahn, 1968, 190). Although fragmentary, the documentation for Mennonite Brethren is significant.

Reporting to the Canadian Conference in 1955, Peter Bargen noted that of 619 graduates of Mennonite Brethren private schools (excluding Eden Christian College, for which the data were not available), information about their occuption was supplied for 449 graduates as follows: teachers, 194; nursing, 35; medicine, 19; engineering, 9; farming, 25; business, 45; missions, 4; housewives, 32; studying at university, 32; studying at college, 11; studying in Bible schools, 43 (*YB*, 1955, 11). This study indicated that 44 percent of the graduates became teachers and only 6 percent farmers in the early 1950s. This trend to teaching was further documented in 1969 by the twenty-fifth anniversary publication of Mennonite Brethren Bible College which provided a vocational breakdown for 472 of the 565 graduates as follows: teachers, 257; pastors, 68; missionaries, 55; nurses, 19; housewives, 18; others, 55 (MBBC, 1969, 60).

The occupational shift to other than teaching vocations becomes evident from several further sources. In 1963 the *Mennonite Brethren Herald* featured a series of nine testimonies by laymen on "how to live their faith in their vocation." These testimonies by a research scientist, retail merchant, high school teacher, secretary, musician, educational administrator, medical doctor, nurse, and engineer are indicative of the vocational penetration of Mennonite Brethren into their host society. The extent to which numerous vocations are represented in church leadership becomes apparent from the 1963 delegate breakdown for the Canadian Conference at Herbert, Saskatchewan. Of 358 delegates, 110 were farmers, 68 pastors, 44 public school teachers, 38 businessmen, 22 retired, 19 labourers and clerks, 13 professionals (other than teachers), 10 Bible school teachers, and 34 not indicated (*YB*, 1963, 128). More precisely, analysing the vocations of those in the 66-member Council of Boards (including all boards of Canadian Mennonite Brethren Conference), John H. Redekop found no farmer, but, instead, 24 educators, 19 pastors, 12 businessmen, 2 mission directors, 2 students, and 1 each for lawyer, retired minister, civil servant, public relations, and hospital administrator (Redekop, 1975, 8). Noting the 51 vocations represented among the 400 members of his congregation, F. C. Peters asserted not only that the age of occupational conformity was over, but that such specialization and diversification had created a multiplicity of worlds in which "the secularization process began reaching into the church" (Peters, 1971, 21-23). Similarly observing that modern Mennonites have entered virtually all areas of life, with the exception of military forces, Harry Loewen concludes that they "maintain an uneasy truce with the world" (1980, 95).

Motivation for Vocational Change

It is virtually impossible to document the reasons which motivated Mennonite Brethren to enter the wide variety of vocations. Despite the failure to disclose all the reasons which prompt such change in their vocational life, several educators have speculated on the reasons why many chose to become teachers. These reasons are mainly three-fold.

The economic reason.   There is no doubt that, despite the modest remuneration of teachers in the 1950s, the security provided by a steady income lured many to the profession. Just at the time when hundreds of Mennonite Brethren were entering the teaching profession, educator J. H. Quiring presented the "challenge of the public school" as "a field of service with adequate remuneration." Quiring realized that "if anyone is governed by the profit motive in the choice of his profession, he will most likely not go into teaching. . . . The Christian teacher is not governed by the profit motive but rather by the service motive." At the same time, he recognized that even the teachers "have to provide for themselves and their dependents. A Christian teacher must have a field of service and he must be able to make a living. These two go together" (Quiring, 1952, 15).

The social reason.   A more subtle reason, explicitly stated by only a few, is the possibility that teaching leads to upward social mobility. The educational requirement and the added prestige, together with financial security, provided for many a higher socio-economic status than their parents had enjoyed. Indeed, for many teaching became a stepping-stone to higher education and even further vocational change. For example, William Schroeder remarked to his fellow-teachers, "Many teachers are less missionary-minded than mercenary-minded, and so regard teaching as an easy stepping-stone to another profession" (Schroeder, 1959, 10). Teaching was but the first step in their vertical mobility.

The religious reason.   Most prominent in the stated reasons is the religious factor. J. H. Quiring alluded to several such religious reasons in his five-fold challenge to Christian teachers. The influence they can exercise upon children is of paramount significance. "The public school teacher gets the children when they are still teachable, pliable, and easily influenced" (1952, 15). In addition, teachers provide leadership in the community. Moreover, Quiring argues, it is through their personality that Christians most influence the young lives. It is the role of teachers as a "witness" or "missionary" that ostensibly caused many to choose this vocation. Educator Abe Konrad reported such an expansion of witness in British Columbia through the teaching profession.

These teachers are going to the isolated fishing villages and logging communities along the rugged coastline of the Pacific from Vancouver to Port Simpson. They go to the farming areas and the mining camps in the Kootenay and Okanagan Valleys and among the Cascade Mts., even teaching among the notorious Doukhobors. They go north to the ranch-lands and the grain-growing areas of the Caribou and the Peace River. And they go to the fur-trapping areas of the northern rivers and up to the rim of the Arctic Circle. . . . They declare it is the "inner compulsion" to serve the Lord in a special way that motivates their going (Konrad, 1955, 3).

No doubt, similar reasons have motivated Mennonite Brethren young people to enter other vocations, whether nursing, medicine, business, law, or the service occupations. Mennonite Brethren seemingly had gained a new understanding of Luther's conception of "the calling," that is, "the valuation of the fulfilment of duty in worldly affairs as the highest form which the moral activity of the individual could assume. This it was which inevitably gave every-day worldly activity a religious significance . . ." (Weber, 1958, 80).

2. Empirical Observations on Occupational Distribution and Variables of Religiosity

Numerous specific observations indicate occupational change among Canadian Mennonite Brethren in the last half century; yet, in order to measure the degree of shift from the farming occupations to others, precise, empirical documentation for two or more separate periods of time is lacking. However, the Church Member Profile does provide empirical data for the occupational distribution of Mennonite Breth-

ren in 1972 and enables one, consequently, to establish some tentative
generalizations about the religiosity of different occupational groups.

Table XII-1
Distribution of Church Members by Sex and Occupation

Occupational Categories	Percentage Distribution of Members		Percentage of Total
	Male	Female	
Professional and technical workers[a]	79.2 (n=38)	20.8 (n=10)	14.1 (n=48)
Business owners and managers	100.0 (n=18)	0.0 (n=0)	5.3 (n=18)
Sales and clerical workers	50.0 (n=10)	50.0 (n=10)	5.9 (n=20)
Craftsmen and foremen	100.0 (n=21)	0.0 (n=0)	6.2 (n=21)
Farm owners and managers	100.0 (n=44)	0.0 (n=0)	12.9 (n=44)
Service workers	60.0 (n=6)	40.0 (n=4)	2.9 (n=10)
Machine operators	73.3 (n=11)	26.7 (n=4)	4.4 (n=15)
Labourers (farm and non-farm)	100.0 (n=4)	0.0 (n=0)	1.2 (n=4)
Housewives	0.0 (n=0)	100.0 (n=108)	31.8 (n=108)
Students	40.4 (n=21)	59.6 (n=31)	15.3 (n=52)
Total	50.9 (n=173)	49.1 (n=167)	100.0 (n=340)

Source: Church Member Profile, 1972.

[a] Occupational categories were further elaborated in the questionnaire
as follows: professional or technical worker (minister, physician,
teacher, social worker, engineer, librarian, educator, scientist, etc.);
proprietor, manager, or official (business owner or operator, department
manager, official of public or private business or agency, etc.);
clerical and sales worker (office worker, clerk, salesman, postman, etc.);
craftsman or foreman (carpenter, mechanic, die cutter, tailor, etc.);
service worker (barber, beautician, cook, guard, policeman, restaurant
waiter, fireman, janitor, etc.); machine operator (truck or bus driver,
press operator, welder, seamstress, factory worker, etc.); labourer
(farm labourer, construction work helper, car washer, etc.).

Occupational Variation among Canadian
Mennonite Brethren

While the cross-tabulation of church members by sex and occupation
does not instantly reflect the implications of such variables upon religiosity, the male-female occupational roles become clearer, and this
distribution of roles does have religious implications. For example, a
woman who is employed has more exposure to certain influences of

society, and her dominant role in the household is very likely to change. Table xii-1 indicates the occupational distribution of Canadian Mennonite Brethren. Among the employed, the professional and technical workers are, in fact, the largest single group with about 14 percent of the total membership. Together with the business occupations, they constitute about one-fifth of the total membership. The next largest group among the employed is the farmers with about 13 percent. The sales and clerical workers together with the craftsmen and foremen comprise about 12 percent. Interestingly, service workers, machine operators, and labourers together constitute but 8.5 percent of the total membership. Those not officially employed, such as housewives and students, on the other hand, make up almost half the membership. Total rural residence was earlier shown to be 49.9 percent. Even the strictly rural farm residence of 30.1 percent is still in excess of twice the number of farmers by occupation (twice, in order to include the wives as rural residents). In other words, a number of those in rural residence have other than farming occupations. The traditional male-female roles are still largely observed, however, since none of those listed as business owners or managers, craftsmen, labourers, and farmers are women. Yet, half of the sales and clerical workers, almost half of the service workers, about one-fifth of the professionals, and 60 percent of the students are female. Thus, the sex role among white-collar occupations is in a state of flux. With this change there will likely be a change in religious attitudes and beliefs as well. Such possible change will now be tested.

Occupational Distribution and Measures of Religiosity

To determine the differences in the effect of occupations upon religion, similar measures of religiosity are employed in the present as in the previous two chapters. As in chapter eleven, the questions used for the items measuring the variables of religion are abbreviated to single words or phrases.

Occupational distribution and the practice of religion.   Table xii-2 indicates the cross-tabulations for occupational distribution and measures of devotionalism and associationalism, referred to in this study as the practice of religion. It would appear that in devotionalism, housewives, professionals, and farmers rank the highest—in that order—while craftsmen, businessmen, and labourers rank lowest. In associationalism, professionals, students, housewives, farmers, and businessmen rank highest with labourers, clerical and service personnel the lowest. The cumulative effect in the practice of religion seems to be as follows: professionals and housewives rank highest, followed by farmers and students; and the labourers, clericals, and craftsmen rank

Table XII-2

Occupational Distribution and the Practice of Religion

Percentage Response

	Professional, Technical	Owners, Managers	Sales, Clerical	Craftsmen, Foremen	Farm Owners, Managers	Service Workers	Machine Operators	Labourers	Housewives	Students
Devotionalism										
Prayer	86.3 (n=44)	84.2 (n=16)	81.0 (n=17)	81.8 (n=18)	84.4 (n=38)	70.0 (n=7)	93.8 (n=15)	75.0 (n=3)	91.6 (n=98)	86.8 (n=46)
Bible study	88.2 (n=45)	68.4 (n=13)	85.0 (n=17)	68.2 (n=15)	86.7 (n=39)	80.0 (n=8)	75.0 (n=12)	75.0 (n=3)	89.8 (n=97)	77.4 (n=41)
Closeness to God	60.8 (n=31)	47.4 (n=9)	47.6 (n=10)	45.5 (n=10)	62.8 (n=27)	60.0 (n=6)	62.5 (n=10)	66.7 (n=2)	64.5 (n=69)	50.9 (n=27)
Seeking God's will	80.0 (n=40)	68.4 (n=13)	70.0 (n=14)	61.9 (n=13)	66.7 (n=28)	80.0 (n=8)	62.5 (n=10)	50.0 (n=2)	79.4 (n=85)	60.4 (n=32)
Rank Order Scale	31	15	20	9	27	21	24	16	36	19
Associationalism										
Church attendance	86.3 (n=44)	89.5 (n=17)	66.7 (n=14)	81.8 (n=18)	81.4 (n=75)	77.8 (n=7)	81.3 (n=13)	75.0 (n=3)	83.2 (n=89)	90.6 (n=48)
Sunday school attendance	64.7 (n=33)	57.9 (n=11)	28.6 (n=6)	50.0 (n=11)	66.7 (n=30)	40.0 (n=4)	56.3 (n=9)	25.0 (n=1)	68.9 (n=73)	88.7 (n=47)
Mid-week services	45.1 (n=23)	15.8 (n=3)	23.8 (n=5)	40.9 (n=9)	43.2 (n=19)	30.0 (n=3)	25.0 (n=4)	25.0 (n=1)	41.3 (n=45)	71.7 (n=38)
Leadership post	88.2 (n=45)	73.7 (n=14)	57.1 (n=12)	57.1 (n=12)	53.5 (n=23)	50.0 (n=5)	60.0 (n=9)	25.0 (n=1)	51.9 (n=56)	46.2 (n=24)
Rank Order Scale	34	25	11	22	26	14	20	8	27	32
Total Rank Order Scale	65	40	31	31	53	35	44	24	63	51

Source: Church Member Profile, 1972.

lowest. Such data lead one to generalize about the tendency of different occupations towards secularization. Professionals, possibly, rank highest in the practice of religion because of their leadership skills and prior selectivity of those with commitment, and housewives on account of their greater religious sensitivity or their seclusion from the "secular" world. Farmers appear to be less secularized, and, surprisingly, students are actively involved despite their academic pursuits. Such religious vitality among students augurs well for the religious persistence of the sect. As in other studies, the blue-collar groups rank lower in the practice of religion.

Occupational distribution and religious beliefs.   Table xii-3 summarizes the cross-tabulations for occupational distribution and measures of religious beliefs. In general orthodoxy, the machine operators and labourers are conspicuously the highest, followed by housewives, while students are somewhat lower, followed by business and professionals. Interestingly, in the case of Jesus' resurrection, his personal return, and the reality of a personal devil, there is virtually total belief, the students being the principal group with some lack of certitude. Not surprising, those who rate highest in fundamentalist orthodoxy are machine operators and housewives, followed by farmers and labourers. Those who rate lowest are the professionals and sales and clerical personnel, followed by the business managers. Again, it is astonishing to note how nearly total is the belief in the inspiration of the Bible and in the virgin birth of Jesus, the students again being the major exception. As expected, for the Anabaptism variable there is much greater diversity and less assent. Farmers and machine operators rank highest, followed by professionals. The students, here, rank lowest. Rather ironic is the observation that, while the question on church discipline elicits rather high favourable response (87.0 percent) for the Anabaptism measures, only 57.5 percent of Canadian Mennonite Brethren agree or strongly agree that "Jesus expects Christians today to follow the pattern which he set in his own life and ministry, including such things as putting evangelism above earning a living, and deeds or mercy above family security." Summarizing the above responses to the variables of belief, one notes that machine operators are almost consistently the most conservative in religious beliefs. Does their reliance on well-built machines result in a firm commitment to religious belief, or is it that they are simply not exposed to other viewpoints? Housewives, farmers, and labourers come next. The category of "housewife," of course, includes only about two-thirds of the total number of females who responded (108/167), excluding those in the professions and sales and clerical workers. In beliefs, it is the students who are distinctly lowest, followed by business and clerical occupations. It appears, at this

Table XII-3
Occupational Distribution and Religious Beliefs

Percentage Response

	Professional, Technical	Owners, Managers	Sales, Clerical	Craftsmen, Foremen	Farm Owners, Managers	Service Workers	Machine Operators	Labourers	Housewives	Students
Orthodoxy										
Deity of Jesus	90.2 (n=46)	94.7 (n=18)	95.2 (n=20)	95.5 (n=21)	97.8 (n=44)	100.0 (n=10)	100.0 (n=16)	100.0 (n=10)	98.1 (n=106)	96.2 (n=51)
Belief in miracles	96.1 (n=49)	94.7 (n=18)	100.0 (n=21)	95.5 (n=21)	95.5 (n=42)	90.0 (n=9)	100.0 (n=16)	100.0 (n=10)	99.1 (n=107)	96.2 (n=51)
Jesus' resurrection	98.0 (n=50)	100.0 (n=19)	100.0 (n=21)	100.0 (n=21)	100.0 (n=44)	100.0 (n=10)	100.0 (n=16)	100.0 (n=4)	98.1 (n=105)	92.5 (n=49)
Jesus' return	98.0 (n=50)	94.7 (n=18)	95.2 (n=20)	100.0 (n=22)	97.8 (n=44)	100.0 (n=10)	100.0 (n=16)	100.0 (n=4)	99.1 (n=108)	98.1 (n=52)
Personal devil	98.0 (n=50)	100.0 (n=19)	90.5 (n=19)	100.0 (n=22)	100.0 (n=45)	100.0 (n=10)	100.0 (n=16)	100.0 (n=4)	100.0 (n=109)	96.2 (n=51)
Rank Order Scale	15	13	18	22	20	24	31	31	27	9
Fundamentalism										
Inspiration/Bible	96.1 (n=49)	94.7 (n=18)	81.0 (n=17)	100.0 (n=22)	100.0 (n=45)	100.0 (n=10)	100.0 (n=16)	100.0 (n=4)	99.1 (n=108)	92.5 (n=49)
Virgin birth	96.1 (n=49)	94.7 (n=18)	100.0 (n=21)	100.0 (n=22)	97.7 (n=42)	100.0 (n=10)	100.0 (n=16)	100.0 (n=4)	100.0 (n=109)	96.2 (n=51)
Six-day creation	13.7 (n=7)	47.4 (n=9)	23.8 (n=5)	50.0 (n=11)	68.2 (n=30)	60.0 (n=6)	75.0 (n=12)	100.0 (n=4)	72.2 (n=78)	35.8 (n=19)
Universal flood	84.3 (n=43)	84.2 (n=16)	90.5 (n=19)	95.5 (n=21)	97.8 (n=44)	100.0 (n=10)	100.0 (n=16)	100.0 (n=4)	98.2 (n=107)	84.9 (n=45)
Eternal punishment	80.4 (n=41)	84.2 (n=16)	71.4 (n=15)	81.4 (n=18)	86.7 (n=39)	80.0 (n=8)	87.5 (n=14)	75.0 (n=3)	92.6 (n=100)	86.8 (n=46)
Rank Order Scale	13	15	13	26	30	28	37	31	35	19
Anabaptism										
Following Jesus	62.7 (n=19)	36.8 (n=7)	65.0 (n=13)	50.0 (n=11)	70.5 (n=31)	40.0 (n=4)	53.3 (n=8)	75.0 (n=3)	58.3 (n=63)	47.2 (n=25)
Against infant baptism	96.1 (n=49)	94.7 (n=18)	90.0 (n=18)	77.3 (n=17)	86.7 (n=39)	80.0 (n=8)	87.5 (n=14)	100.0 (n=4)	86.9 (n=93)	86.8 (n=46)
Church discipline	90.2 (n=46)	100.0 (n=19)	70.0 (n=14)	100.0 (n=22)	97.7 (n=42)	90.0 (n=9)	100.0 (n=16)	75.0 (n=3)	88.9 (n=96)	66.0 (n=35)
Non-resistance	74.5 (n=38)	57.9 (n=11)	57.9 (n=11)	63.6 (n=14)	80.0 (n=36)	50.0 (n=5)	75.0 (n=12)	50.0 (n=2)	67.9 (n=74)	49.1 (n=26)
Non-swearing of oaths	84.3 (n=43)	73.7 (n=14)	60.0 (n=12)	90.0 (n=20)	93.2 (n=41)	90.0 (n=9)	93.8 (n=15)	50.0 (n=2)	78.0 (n=85)	73.6 (n=36)
Rank Order Scale	36	25	24	27	38	18	38	25	27	12
Total Rank Order	64	53	55	75	88	70	106	87	89	40

Source: Church Member Profile, 1972.

point, that the blue-collar occupations are the more conservative (less secularized) in religious beliefs despite their lower scores on religious practice.

Occupational distribution and ethics.   Table xii-4 shows the results of cross-tabulating occupations with measures of ethics. Responding to those personal, moral issues traditionally viewed as taboo among Mennonite Brethren, the service occupations were most conservative, followed by machine operators and labourers, again the blue-collar class. The lowest in rank were the students, followed by clerical and professional categories (the white-collared). In social ethics, a high score for which represents a more liberal ethical stance, the students rank highest, followed by a cluster of professional, clerical, service occupations, and machine operators (a mixture of white-collar and blue-collar). The lowest level was noted among business managers, farmers, and housewives. The overall effect of balancing the conservative, personal ethical measure with the more liberal, social ethical measure is the absence of great extremes. Yet, despite the leveling effect, service workers and machine operators tend to be least secularized, while business managers and sales and clerical personnel are most secularized. Again, there appears to be a marked difference between the blue-collar and white-collar occupations.

Summary of Empirical Findings

Table xii-5 summarizes the totals of the scales for each measure of religiosity. If these scales constitute true measures of religiosity, then of the ten occupational groups measured, the machine operator is the most religious, followed by the housewife and the farmer. It may well be that these groups represent those least exposed to the changes in society. If a lack of high rating constitutes secularization, then among the occupational groups, the business owners and managers are the most secular, followed by sales and clerical personnel and student groups. The results, although not unambiguous, do suggest that the white-collared occupations are more secularized. As a result, one concludes that the occupational change from rural to urban areas has enhanced secularization. A closer analysis of this secularization process is, therefore, in place.

3. Reorientation and Secularization

The occupational change that accompanied the shift from rural to urban residence did expose the urbanite to new erosive and secularizing forces. At the same time, urban residents were being fortified to

Table XII-4
Occupational Distribution and Ethics

Percentage Response

	Professional, Technical	Owners, Managers	Sales, Clerical	Craftsmen, Foremen	Farm Owners, Managers	Service Workers	Machine Operators	Labourers	Housewives	Students
Personal										
Drinking moderately	29.4 (n=15)	36.8 (n=7)	28.6 (n=6)	52.4 (n=11)	75.6 (n=34)	90.0 (n=9)	60.0 (n=9)	25.0 (n=1)	66.4 (n=71)	30.8 (n=16)
Smoking tobacco	78.4 (n=40)	73.7 (n=14)	66.7 (n=14)	100.0 (n=22)	86.7 (n=39)	100.0 (n=10)	86.7 (n=13)	75.0 (n=3)	86.7 (n=91)	54.7 (n=29)
Adult-rated movies	28.0 (n=14)	21.1 (n=4)	38.1 (n=8)	68.2 (n=15)	75.6 (n=34)	70.0 (n=7)	86.7 (n=13)	66.7 (n=2)	62.0 (n=67)	30.2 (n=16)
Premarital sex	94.0 (n=47)	100.0 (n=19)	90.5 (n=19)	90.5 (n=19)	97.7 (n=43)	100.0 (n=10)	100.0 (n=16)	100.0 (n=4)	99.1 (n=105)	90.6 (n=48)
Social dancing	44.0 (n=22)	52.6 (n=10)	61.9 (n=13)	59.1 (n=13)	79.5 (n=35)	90.0 (n=9)	86.7 (n=13)	100.0 (n=4)	78.5 (n=84)	35.8 (n=19)
Rank Order Scale	16	19	14	27	36	43	38	28	31	12
Social										
Race relations	58.8 (n=30)	47.4 (n=9)	61.9 (n=13)	52.4 (n=11)	37.8 (n=17)	70.0 (n=7)	73.3 (n=11)	50.0 (n=2)	48.6 (n=53)	84.9 (n=45)
Social welfare	37.3 (n=19)	26.3 (n=5)	33.3 (n=7)	45.5 (n=10)	26.7 (n=12)	44.4 (n=4)	33.3 (n=4)	25.0 (n=1)	40.2 (n=43)	49.1 (n=26)
Anti-Communism	60.8 (n=31)	15.8 (n=3)	14.3 (n=3)	18.4 (n=4)	16.7 (n=7)	0.0 (n=0)	25.0 (n=4)	25.0 (n=1)	3.7 (n=4)	24.5 (n=13)
Labor unions	2.0 (n=1)	5.3 (n=1)	9.5 (n=2)	0.0 (n=0)	22.2 (n=10)	20.0 (n=2)	7.1 (n=1)	25.0 (n=1)	19.4 (n=21)	3.8 (n=2)
Capital punishment	23.5 (n=12)	10.5 (n=2)	38.1 (n=8)	14.3 (n=3)	4.4 (n=2)	11.1 (n=1)	7.1 (n=1)	0.0 (n=0)	6.4 (n=7)	34.0 (n=18)
Rank Order Scale	32	17	30	28	20	31	30	24	22	39
Total Rank Order	48	36	44	55	56	74	68	52	53	51

Source: Church Member Profile, 1972.

Table XII-5

Summary of Scales of Occupational Distribution and
Measures of Religiosity

Variables of Religiosity	Total of Rank Order Ratings									
	Professional, Technical	Owners, Managers	Sales, Clerical	Craftsmen, Foremen	Farm Owners, Managers	Service Workers	Machine Operators	Labourers	Housewives	Students
Practice of Religion										
Devotionalism	31	15	20	9	27	21	24	16	36	19
Associationalism	34	25	11	22	26	14	20	8	27	32
Subtotal	65	40	31	31	53	35	44	24	63	51
Religious Beliefs										
Orthodoxy	15	13	18	22	20	24	31	31	27	9
Fundamentalism	13	15	13	26	30	28	37	31	35	19
Anabaptism	36	25	24	27	38	18	38	25	27	12
Subtotal	64	53	55	75	88	70	106	87	89	40
Ethics										
Moral Issues	16	19	14	27	36	43	38	28	31	12
Social Issues	32	17	30	28	20	31	30	24	22	39
Subtotal	48	36	44	55	56	74	68	52	53	51
Total	177	129	130	161	197	179	218	163	205	142

Source: Church Member Profile, 1972.

resist the secularization and through their new vocations to penetrate society with their Christian witness. The analyst must, therefore, note both the disruptive effects of vocational change as well as the countervailing, synthetic forces which arrest the secularization process.

Secularizing Effects of Occupational Change

If secularization is viewed positively as freeing people from the rule of the sacral order and allowing them to choose God personally, then such freedom also allows other choices. Consequently, the secularizing effects of occupational change which accompanied the move to the city have both positive and negative consequences.

Table XII-6

A Comparison of Transfers-in and Transfers-out for Canadian Mennonite Brethren from 1954 to 1974

	1954	1959	1964	1969	1974
Transfers-out					
to Mennonite Brethren churches	647	769	976	580	735
to non-Mennonite Brethren churches	30	105	136	204	160
to no churches	--	--	--	49	102
Total transfers-out	677	874	1112	833	997
Transfers-in	606	819	772	839	798
Differences in totals	71	55	340	-6	199
Net gain or loss in membership	+234	+302	-76	+465	+215

Source: Year Book, 1954, 1959, 1964, 1969, 1974.

Residential mobility and religious defection. Residential mobility, necessitated by vocational change or promotion, provides church members with new opportunities to improve their lot economically, to enter into new experiences within the religious community, and to influence their new neighbourhood and associates and work. Frequently, however, the residential shift from one location to another has given occasion for religious defection. Table XII-6 compares the annual tranfers-in with the transfers-out for Canadian Mennonite Brethren over a period of twenty years, 1954 to 1974. It appears that the Canadian Mennonite Brethren are very much caught up in the "circulation of the saints" syndrome (Bibby and Brinkerhoff, 1973, 273-82). For example, in 1964 when there was a net loss in membership, the transfers-out exceeded the transfers-in by 340. In 1969, when there was a high net gain in membership, the transfers-out were somewhat fewer than transfers-in. Also, an increasing number are released without joining any church at all (the increase is from 49 in 1969 to 102 in 1974). Defection to other denominations need not be viewed as secularization in a negative sense, but using residential mobility as an occasion to withdraw from participation in a religious community could be interpreted as a loss of faith, which, if not occasioned by mobility, becomes overt at such a time.

Increased leisure and decreased commitment.   It appears that with the change from rural to urban occupations, more leisure time emerges. The Puritan life-style, marked by unremitting toil and disinterest in recreation, changed with the move to the city and the orientation to a new vocation. In fact, as F. C. Peters observed, a strange reversal occurred. "Men of thought are working while men of brawn have leisure" (Peters, 1965, 6). Rigorous guidelines were, hence, provided for the "right use of leisure." More recently, there has been a greater openness to both recreation and the arts. Yet, the possible conflict between the Christian artist and the expectations of the church are keenly felt. Mennonite Brethren writer Katie Funk Wiebe laments:

Faith and art are not always compatible bedfellows. . . .
    The whole process of creativity is still sometimes questionable in the church despite the fact that faith and creativity are closely linked in God's economy. The Christian's duty is to live creatively. Creativity is his natural birthright. . . .
    Yet the church continues to ask whether the artist is justified. Certainly our churches have gotten along without the species for more than a hundred years in America quite well. Our Mennonite heritage is singularly weak in the creative arts; we have too few painters, sculptors, composers, writers and poets. Why the resistance to such a person? (Wiebe, 1974, 2-4, 30).

As more Canadian Mennonite Brethren venture into new horizons of the arts and of recreation, one can expect both a greater understanding of the significance of leisure and also continued caution in view of the erosive potential to religious commitment.

Arresting the Secularization Process

Precisely because of the varied effects of occupational change, whether manifest in residential mobility or in the access to leisure, or in the many other changes in values that accompany such shifts in vocation, deliberate attempts have been made to arrest the erosive effect of secularization and capitalize upon the opportunities which the new vocations presented.

The socialization of youth.   Some two decades ago, Leslie Stobbe, editor of *Mennonite Observer*, observed both the occupational change and the resulting trend to materialism with its secularizing consequences.

No more do the farmer's sons automatically settle on a quarter of land nearby to carry on the traditional way of life. His sons and daughters may be doctors, nurses, teachers, engineers, salesmen, office workers, businessmen, labourers and factory workers. . . .

The adjustment in family and church life is great. Yet the churches have offered but little assistance, except such as can be done in a casual way. If, however, we want to stop the trend to materialism and to a life of ease and comfort in order to increase spiritually, we will have to make a much greater effort. . . .

Unless we take the initiative now in this field we will lose still more ground than has already been lost (Stobbe, 1957, 2).

The ultimate objective of any vocation was viewed as glorifying the name of God and promoting the cause of Christ; the wise choice of vocation would exclude a profession detrimental to the Christian life and would provide occasion for nurturing Christian fellowship and the opportunity to witness; and the high standards of honesty, faithfulness, and usefulness would result in the "plus factor" which Christians bring to their vocation. Such thorough counsel on the purpose of life's calling, the importance of choosing the right vocation, and the standards which constitute Christians' work habits fortified young people and arrested the rampant tide of materialism that accompanied the success in new vocational ventures.

The penetration of society. The secularization process was arrested, however, not merely through defensive fortification. Mennonite Brethren were challenged, as well, to capitalize on the opportunities to witness to their faith which such occupational penetration of society permitted. As earlier indicated, counsel was given to choose those vocations which would allow one to witness in the work itself, as well as in the community where one works. Such counsel led many to choose the teaching profession. The variety of vocational pursuits became a diverse means of penetrating society with a Christian witness. In a lecture series at the University of Winnipeg, economist Roy Vogt made the astute observation that Mennonite professionals use their profession to withdraw from the demeaning aspects of the urban class struggle while at the same time apparently supporting a liberal, pragmatic approach to urban political and industrial problems. Non-professionals, not being able to withdraw from this urban class struggle, become conservative and inner-oriented in their religion and use their Anabaptist principles to thwart those forces in their immediate environs which most threaten them. "The professional withdraws and then pretends he is involved. The non-professional is really involved, but pretends he isn't" (Vogt, 1980, 147). What was initially feared to be secularizing in a negative sense, that is, the erosion of one's religious commitment, becomes secularizing in a positive sense, that is, a liberation to choose deliberately the vocation one desired and then to use it to express one's Christian convictions. The reorientation following the shift from rural to urban vocations was secularizing in its consequences, but such secularization was not an unmitigated evil.

Summary

Living in the city and having penetrated society in a wide variety of occupations, Canadian Mennonite Brethren of recent decades resemble more closely their Anabaptist forebears of the sixteenth century than their grandparents earlier in this century. Initially there were concerns about urban residence and the pursuit of non-rural vocations. Eventually, however, the occupational shift proved to be more of an asset than a liability for their religious vitality. Secularization in the sense of decline and defection occurred, but more significant was the secularization process which led to a freeing from a rural setting and a penetration of all segments of society. Secularization in such a positive sense enhanced religious commitment and stimulated sectarian persistence.

The political, economic, and even religious upheavals of the decade prior to the large immigration of the mid-1920s had seemingly loosened the rural moorings of Mennonite Brethren. In the 1930s and 1940s it was the depression, new educational opportunities, the beginning of the drift to the cities, climaxed by the upheaval of World War II, which ended the predominantly rural vocations. The decades after the mid-century mark a large-scale shift to other than farming occupations, with teaching as the most prominent choice. Important in their choice of teaching were the economic security, the upward mobility, and the witness opportunity that this profession offered.

Empirical data indicate that, among the employed, the white-collar occupations constitute some 25 percent of the total membership, the professional and technical workers being the largest single vocational group. Farm owners and farm managers constitute some 13 percent of the total membership. Service workers, machine operators, and labourers make up but 8.5 percent of the total membership; housewives and students, almost one-half. Cross-tabulations of different occupations with the varying measures of religiosity suggest that the machine operator is the most religious, followed by the housewife and the farmer. Moreover, the business owners and managers are the most secular, followed by sales and clerical workers and then students. It would appear that white-collar occupations are more secularized. Among the white-collar occupations, however, the professionals rated the highest in religiosity (excluding the housewives).

Mennonite Brethren have recognized both the erosive effects as well as the challenge to penetrate society with a Christian witness that such a shift to the non-farming vocations brings. The shift in occupations has resulted in large-scale residential mobility accompanied by defection to other denominations instead of transferring membership to another Mennonite Brethren church. Furthermore, the Puritanical distaste for personal indulgence, characterizing the Mennonite Brethren background, changed to an appreciation for recreation and the arts which the leisure of the new occupations permitted. A wholesale defection and secularization has been arrested through the conscious attempt at socialization of youth to understand the significance of the calling. Not only were the young people fortified for the urban vocations, but they were encouraged actively to penetrate a variety of vocations and disperse to diverse geographical locations. The potential defection and disinterest in religion has, thus, been sublimated to sectarian loyalty and missionary energy. Once again, the dialectic of sacralizing and secularizing forces produces a religious vitality that, despite some loss, results in sectarian persistence.

XIII

Economic Ascendancy and Vertical Mobility

The caricature of Mennonite Brethren immigrants of the 1920s and that of typical Canadian Mennonite Brethren today constitutes a marked contrast. Known for their few earthly possessions and frequently sizable *Reiseschuld*, average Mennonite Brethren were among the economically deprived and, because their immigrant status compelled them to be farmers, they were cast into a lower-class structure and belonged to a religious movement with an introverted sectarian stance which had little appeal to the outsider. Fifty years later, average Mennonite Brethren have gained an impressive record of respectability. They live in their own houses in the city and, educated beyond the level of average fellow citizens, they are successful in prestigious vocations and belong to a church known for its extensive educational institutions, its sophisticated international relief and mission programs, and which can boast of numerous millionaires. There is no question that with the rapid economic ascendancy, there has been an accompanying upward social mobility. No doubt, such economic prosperity and vertical mobility have affected the sectarian stance of the Canadian Mennonite Brethren. Chapter thirteen examines the degree to which such environmental change has secularized the movement.

1. Background Factors to a Study of Religion and Economics

The rise to economic prosperity of Canadian Mennonite Brethren is not unique to the history of sectarian movements. Social analysts invariably include the economic factor in their analysis of a religious movement.

Precursors in the Study of Sectarian Religiosity and Economics

The impact of such environmental change upon religion and, in turn, the influence of religion in shaping the economy has been a frequent

208

subject of analysis among sociologists. Most popular is Max Weber's *The Protestant Ethic and the Spirit of Capitalism* in which, to counteract the economic determinists of his day, Weber called attention to the spirit of dedication and commitment to work which marked Protestantism generally and Calvinism and Puritanism in particular. The asceticism of the sixteenth-century Anabaptists—their refusal to bear arms and accept office in the service of the state, their antagonism to an aristocratic way of life, their conduct in worldly callings, and their practice of church discipline—characterized the avoidance mentality of the sectarian Mennonite Brethren in Canada in the mid-1920s. Prominent in Weber's analysis is the importance of the influence of ideas (in this case, religion) upon behaviour (in this instance, economic activity). Varying interpretations of Weber have shown that the connection need not be causal.

While Weber dealt with the influence of religion upon economics, Richard Niebuhr in his classic, *The Social Sources of Denominationalism*, treated the change that environment places upon a religious movement. He maintained that a pure sect-type religion is always transient, part of the change occurring because of the upward social mobility to which sectarianism contributes and the resulting loss of hostility to the world. This chapter will test Niebuhr's hypothesis that upward mobility causes loss of sectarianism and conformity to the church-type denomination from which the sect once separated.

Bryan Wilson has shown that only some sects, especially conversionist sects, are susceptible to the denominationalizing process because of their accommodation to urban and industrial populations for the purpose of recruitment (Wilson, 1967, 30-42). Other sects have, in fact, successfully withstood the denominationalizing process despite their upward mobility. This chapter will show that, despite Will Herberg's thesis that Protestantism is a sanction for the American values of individualism, activism, efficiency, and self-improvement (Herberg, 1960, 99-135), Mennonite Brethren have cherished both these values and their religious separateness. The findings of this study are more in agreement with Gerhard Lenski's thesis:

when men who have been trained from early childhood in different social systems and have internalized differing sets of values are exposed to common stimuli, the result does not have to be convergence in attitudes, values, or behavior. Apparently the stimuli may activate tendencies which previously lay dormant, and thus produce larger, instead of smaller, differences in behavior (Lenski, 1963, 114).

Thus, the environmentalist position which explains economic behaviour solely in terms of the social situation of the individual and the group is seen to be untenable. Chapter thirteen suggests that in spite of the economic ascendancy and vertical mobility, and the accompanying secularization, Mennonite Brethren have retained their vitality as a sectarian group.

Factors Giving Rise to Economic Ascendancy

If the contrast depicted above is in fact true, then the context in which such radical change occurred needs further explanation. Several factors have contributed to the rise of the economic well-being among Canadian Mennonite Brethren.

The frontier spirit.   It is an indisputable fact that the base for the attitudes to economics among Canadian Mennonite Brethren was established by the settlers prior to the big immigration of the mid-1920s. On the one hand, a minority from among the early settlers of the West Reserve in Manitoba joined the Mennonite Brethren at the turn of the century. Yet these Mennonite Brethren had never assumed a rigorous stance against modernity. Instead, Mennonite Brethren became the urbanizers in the Winkler area and were forerunners in establishing an outpost in Winnipeg. On the other hand, American Mennonite Brethren settled in Saskatchewan early in this century. No doubt, the frontier spirit, characterized by freedom, egalitarianism, individualism, and selectivity helped to shape the economic attitudes of these settlers. For example, already in 1915 the Conference was alerted to the need to reserve suitable land for Mennonite settlements in view of the immigrants anticipated after the war (*YB*, 1915, 24). Immigrants in the mid-1920s did not enter a state of economic vacuity. A significant base had already been established.

The immigrant influx.   The economic motive was certainly prominent among the immigrants who settled in Canada in the 1920s. Unlike the Mennonite migrations of 1874 to 1878, this migration did not consist of wholesale transfers of compact colonies, but immigrants came from many settlements and walks of life and required mutual assistance and radical adjustment among themselves in order to survive economically. The qualities they possessed would be reflected in their economic aspirations. While for many immigrants the initial social status meant a degradation from the status held in Russia, the economic opportunities provided the incentive for rapid upward mobility. The depression, however, provided a severe test for many of the Russian immigrants, and their failure to achieve their economic goal added to the stress of their social integration. Nonetheless, from the outset, the industry, honesty, and dependability of these immigrants were lauded. Thus, the immigration of the mid-1920s added significantly to the economic incentive for all Canadian Mennonite Brethren. The immigration of post-World War II from Europe and more recently from South America has witnessed a similar industry and ability to become economically prosperous.

The work ethic.   The Protestant ethic which characterized Mennonites in their settlement in Prussia continued to mark their business acumen to the present. The stereotype of hard work and dependability has characterized both the offspring of the early settlers who emigrated from Russia to Kansas and the more recent waves of immigrants. Such an ethic is not necessarily innate to Mennonites. It is, in fact, taught and fostered through the unique circumstances of migrations which Mennonites have repeatedly undergone. The systematic socialization of such an ethic was apparent until recent times. On the one hand, there has been the constant incentive to be faithful in the tedious tasks of life which receive little, if any, acknowledgement. On the fiftieth anniversary of the founding of one of the most successful businesses among Canadian Mennonite Brethren, William DeFehr, son of the founder, acknowledged: "Honest, hard toil does pay off in the long run. Laying groundwork in a business takes time, not instant success. Integrity and fair play have combined to establish a business fairly well insulated against the ups and downs of the economy" (*Mennonite Mirror*, 1975, 13). A biblical understanding of work has been called for. F. C. Peters explained to the readers of the *Mennonite Brethren Herald*:

Our secular occupations are to be regarded not as ends in themselves but as means to the service of the Kingdom. They have Christian value only in so far as they can be made means to the end of the gospel. It is in this way that a Christian man, having regard to the challenge of his divine vocation, must consider his position as lawyer, mechanic, or surgeon.

Perhaps we have elevated certain occupations too much. We have made them ends in themselves and people have begun to take a sacramental view of work (Peters, 1965, 8).

Socialization includes emphasis not only upon the importance of work, but also upon the limitations of work. Already in 1963, Rudy Wiebe perceived that work in itself would not bring prosperity. "In the brief span of one generation we have prospered in Canada. We have been able to build fine churches, schools, homes, and support great mission efforts. . . . This is due to God's blessing upon us. We have worked hard, but we would be foolish to forget that the very essence of Canada and her resources have been the means of this blessing" (Wiebe, 1963, 3). In 1967, Charles Hostetter stressed the need for temperance in work when he observed that "we generally despise the lazy person and honor the one who works excessively hard," and lamented, "We deplore every other type of addict, but we promote the work addict" (Hostetter, 1967, 5-6). Despite this attempt to balance doing with being and to recognize the limitations of work, the work ethic has been constantly upheld.

The cult of acquisitiveness.   The independence and freedom nurtured by frontier settlement, the economic deprivation encountered by immigrant refugees, and the persistent industry fostered among a God-fearing people—all contributed to a cult of acquisitiveness for which Canadian Mennonite Brethren have become known. Few were satisfied with renting farms or houses; they bought their own. Few became factory workers or labourers; they preferred to establish their own businesses. In recent years, many who began as carpenters or labourers have developed their own construction firms and entered development and real estate enterprises. Others demonstrated the acquisitive spirit by acquiring professional and graduate training. Their ambition (*Strebsamkeit*) coupled with industry has led to a materialism and affluence quite contrary to their sixteenth-century Anabaptist ancestors or their twentieth-century forbears. In a research study of value judgments and attitudes of Mennonite young people, Frank C. Peters discovered that among the three large Mennonite denominations, Mennonite Brethren young people manifested a greater appreciation for material possessions and values (Peters, 1963, 7). The cult of acquisitiveness, while not totally unchecked, has significantly enhanced Mennonite Brethren economic ascendancy. What effect this has had upon their religiosity needs to be examined.

2. The Findings of Empirical Studies

Before ascertaining whether or not affluence results in decreased religiosity, it may be useful to associate levels of income of Canadian Mennonite Brethren with other variables of social change. How are the more affluent to be identified in terms of residence, education, and occupation?

Associating Levels of Income with Non-Religious Variables of Social Change

It was earlier shown that rural-urban residence does indicate something about those who have the lowest and highest incomes: those below $6,000 per annum in 1971 being predominantly rural (47/79), and those above $12,000 per annum being predominantly urban (47/76). Table XIII-1 indicates the distribution of church membership by education and income. About 88 percent of those who have a maximum of grade school education are in the lower two levels, while about 54 percent of those who have partly or fully completed high school are in the middle range of income (with those below and above the middle range equally distributed). Moreover, while those who have only partly or fully completed college are almost equally distributed in the three income levels (although the highest percentage is under $6,000), those who have graduate or professional training are decidedly in the middle or upper category of income. There is an obvious contrast in income between those with only grade school education and those with graduate or professional training.

Table XIII-1

Distribution of Church Membership by Education and Income

Educational Levels	Percentage for Levels of Income for 1971		
	Below $6,000	$6,000-$11,999	Above $12,000
Grade school	41.1 (n=30)	46.6 (n=34)	12.3 (n=9)
High school	22.8 (n=31)	53.7 (n=73)	23.5 (n=32)
College	37.8 (n=14)	29.7 (n=11)	32.4 (n=12)
Graduate/professional	13.7 (n=7)	41.2 (n=21)	45.1 (n=23)

Source: Church Member Profile, 1972.

Table XIII-2 provides the distribution of church membership by occupation and income. White-collar occupations tend to be in the higher income brackets. While about 47 percent of professionals are in the middle range of income, 43 percent are in the upper levels of income. Similarly, about 47 percent of those in business and management positions are in the middle range, with some fewer (37 percent) in the upper levels. A somewhat larger percentage of sales and clerical workers (53 percent) falls into the middle income range, with fewer (18 percent) falling into the upper levels. Most craftsmen (73 percent) are in the middle range, with some 18 percent in the upper range. Most farmers (55 percent) come into the lowest income group, yet with a few (11 percent) among the highest. Service workers, machine operators, and labourers usually fall into the lower or middle ranges of income, with a few machine operators ranked among the higher levels. Surprisingly, the largest number of housewives (47 percent) ranked themselves in the middle range of income, with 25 percent below the middle range and 28 percent above. Likewise, students demonstrated a surprisingly high level of income, with 28 percent in the highest levels, 36 percent in the middle range, and 36 percent in the lower levels.

The most affluent among Canadian Mennonite Brethren seem to be those resident in cities, having received graduate or professional training, and being in the professional or business occupations. The least affluent or economically deprived tend to be those with no more than a grade school education, and occupationally ranked as labourers or service workers. It will be interesting, then, to discover whether or not economic deprivation can be positively correlated with greater religiosity, or if affluence results in loss of religious vitality.

Table XIII-2

Distribution of Membership by Occupation and Income

	Percentage for Levels of Income for 1971						
	Below $3,000	$3,000-5,999	$6,000-8,999	$9,000-11,999	$12,000-14,999	$15,000-19,999	$20,000-or more
Occupation							
Professionals	0.0 (n=0)	10.2 (n=5)	22.4 (n=11)	24.5 (n=12)	20.4 (n=10)	18.4 (n=9)	4.1 (n=2)
Business	0.0 (n=0)	15.8 (n=3)	26.3 (n=5)	21.2 (n=4)	26.3 (n=5)	5.3 (n=1)	5.3 (n=1)
Clerical	5.9 (n=1)	23.5 (n=4)	17.6 (n=3)	35.3 (n=6)	5.9 (n=1)	11.8 (n=2)	0.0 (n=0)
Craftsmen	0.0 (n=0)	9.1 (n=2)	45.5 (n=10)	27.3 (n=6)	9.1 (n=2)	4.5 (n=1)	4.5 (n=1)
Farmers	29.5 (n=13)	25.0 (n=11)	20.5 (n=9)	13.6 (n=6)	2.3 (n=1)	2.3 (n=1)	6.8 (n=3)
Service workers	0.0 (n=0)	37.5 (n=3)	50.0 (n=4)	12.5 (n=1)	0.0 (n=0)	0.0 (n=0)	0.0 (n=0)
Machine operators	6.3 (n=1)	12.5 (n=2)	37.5 (n=6)	18.8 (n=3)	18.8 (n=3)	0.0 (n=0)	6.3 (n=1)
Labourers	25.0 (n=1)	25.0 (n=1)	25.0 (n=1)	25.0 (n=1)	0.0 (n=0)	0.0 (n=0)	0.0 (n=0)
Housewives	10.5 (n=9)	15.1 (n=13)	25.6 (n=22)	20.9 (n=18)	14.0 (n=12)	8.1 (n=7)	5.8 (n=5)
Students	12.0 (n=3)	24.0 (n=6)	16.0 (n=4)	20.0 (n=5)	12.0 (n=3)	8.0 (n=2)	8.0 (n=2)

Source: Church Member Profile, 1972.

Associating Levels of Income with Variables of Religion

To determine whether or not affluence results in a loss of religious vitality, the same measures of religiosity are used as in the preceding chapters. As in chapters eleven and twelve, the questions used to measure the components of religiosity are abbreviated to single words or phrases.

Levels of income and the practice of religion.   Table XIII-3 shows the cross-tabulations for the primary levels of income and measures of devotionalism and associationalism, referred to here as the practice of religion. The differences in percentage response for various levels of income are minimal in items measuring devotionalism, the greatest differences between the low and high levels of income appearing in "closeness to God" and "seeking God's will," where the affluent rate lower. The differences would suggest that the affluent tend to rank lower in terms of devotionalism. However, in the measures of associationalism, the affluent rank higher in three of the four items, particularly in "church attendance" and in "leadership." Applying the simple rank order scale used in the previous chapters one observes that the two groups of measures balance each other out. Looking at the measures separately, one would conclude that the economically deprived are the more religious in devotionalism, while the affluent appear more religious in associationalism. It may, however, be argued that emphasis upon administrative status and activism associated with religious participation is really a secular use of religion.

Table XIII-3
Levels of Income and the Practice of Religion

	Percentage Response		
	Below $6,000	$6,000-11,999	Above $12,000
Devotionalism			
Prayer	88.9 (n=72)	82.9 (n=116)	85.3 (n=64)
Bible study	83.8 (n=67)	82.1 (n=115)	81.3 (n=61)
Closeness to God	68.8 (n=55)	55.8 (n=77)	52.0 (n=39)
Seeking God's will	72.7 (n=56)	73.2 (n=101)	66.7 (n=50)
Subtotal of Rank Orders	10	8	5
Associationalism			
Church attendance	78.5 (n=67)	82.0 (n=114)	82.7 (n=62)
Sunday school attendance	63.4 (n=52)	62.6 (n=87)	61.8 (n=47)
Mid-week services	39.0 (n=32)	38.1 (n=53)	42.1 (n=32)
Leadership post	53.8 (n=44)	65.2 (n=90)	67.6 (n=50)
Subtotal of Rank Orders	7	7	10
Total of Rank Orders	17	15	15

Source: Church Member Profile, 1972.

Levels of income and religious beliefs.   Table XIII-4 indicates the cross-tabulations for levels of income and measures of religious beliefs. In the items measuring general orthodoxy, the differences are too minimal to be significant. What differences occur would suggest that the middle range income group is the most orthodox, with the affluent possibly a little more so than the less affluent. In the items measuring fundamentalist orthodoxy, there is a similar response with the middle range income group as the most orthodox, but with the affluent a little less orthodox, especially in the view on "six-day creation." In Anabaptism, the differences are more significant, with the highest levels of income responding most positively and the middle income group responding least favourably. As in the practice of religion, so also in the religious belief the overall rank order scales balance each other out. One would simply have to affirm that in orthodox beliefs, the middle income group ranks a little higher, while in Anabaptism the most affluent rank a little higher.

Table XIII-4

Levels of Income and Religious Beliefs

	Percentage Response		
	Below $6,000	$6,000-11,999	Above $12,000
Orthodoxy			
Deity of Jesus	96.3 (n=78)	96.4 (n=135)	94.7 (n=72)
Belief in miracles	96.3 (n=77)	96.4 (n=134)	97.4 (n=74)
Jesus' resurrection	96.3 (n=77)	98.5 (n=135)	98.7 (n=75)
Jesus' personal return	97.6 (n=80)	98.6 (n=138)	97.4 (n=74)
Personal devil	96.3 (n=79)	100.0 (n=140)	97.4 (n=74)
Subtotal of Rank Orders	7	13	10
Fundamentalism			
Inspiration of the Bible	95.1 (n=77)	97.9 (n=137)	96.1 (n=73)
Virgin birth of Jesus	98.8 (n=79)	97.1 (n=136)	98.7 (n=75)
Six-day creation	61.0 (n=50)	52.5 (n=73)	42.1 (n=32)
Universal flood	92.7 (n=76)	94.3 (n=132)	88.2 (n=67)
Eternal punishment	84.1 (n=69)	87.1 (n=122)	85.5 (n=65)
Subtotal of Rank Orders	10	12	8
Anabaptism			
Following Jesus	67.9 (n=55)	46.4 (n=64)	68.4 (n=52)
Against infant baptism	88.8 (n=71)	86.4 (n=121)	94.7 (n=72)
Church discipline	91.3 (n=73)	89.2 (n=124)	89.5 (n=68)
Non-resistance	67.9 (n=55)	64.0 (n=89)	69.7 (n=53)
Non-swearing of oaths	79.0 (n=64)	79.1 (n=110)	85.5 (n=65)
Subtotal of Rank Orders	10	6	14
Totals of Rank Order Scales	27	31	32

Source: Church Member Profile, 1972.

Levels of income and ethics. Table XIII-5 shows the cross-tabulations for levels of income and measures of personal moral issues and social ethics. In the questions pertaining to those personal, moral issues traditionally held as taboo, those with highest levels of income were decidedly less rigorous. Yet in the social ethics, those with least income rated the lowest. The net result in the rank order scale was that the middle group rank highest. This table, however, does suggest the influence of wealth in shaping both personal and social ethics. Wealth tends to liberalize one's stand in personal, moral issues (hence, the lower response), as well as to make one more open to social issues (as indicated in the higher response), as long as individual enterprise and reward are not challenged.

Table XIII-5
Levels of Income and Ethics

	Percentage Response		
	Below $6,000	$6,000-11,999	Above $12,000
Personal Moral Issues			
Drinking moderately	61.7 (n=50)	53.6 (n=74)	42.1 (n=32)
Smoking tobacco	79.3 (n=65)	86.3 (n=120)	71.6 (n=53)
Adult-rated movies	56.1 (n=46)	58.4 (n=80)	40.8 (n=31)
Premarital sex	95.0 (n=76)	95.7 (n=133)	94.7 (n=71)
Social dancing	84.0 (n=68)	64.5 (n=89)	49.3 (n=37)
Subtotal of Scales	12	13	5
Social Ethics			
Race relations	47.6 (n=39)	56.8 (n=79)	57.3 (n=43)
Social welfare	35.4 (n=29)	45.0 (n=50)	42.1 (n=32)
Anti-Communism	19.8 (n=16)	20.4 (n=28)	26.3 (n=20)
Labour unions	18.3 (n=15)	7.2 (n=10)	10.7 (n=8)
Capital punishment	9.8 (n=8)	17.5 (n=24)	13.3 (n=10)
Subtotal of Scales	7	11	12
Total of Scales	19	24	17

Source: Church Member Profile, 1972.

Summary of Empirical Findings

The analysis of Canadian Mennonite Brethren church membership in terms of income reveals that those with highest incomes tend to live in cities, have likely received professional or graduate training, and probably belong to professional or business occupations. Table XIII-6 suggests that one cannot readily generalize about the religiosity of different income groups. At best, one can isolate the lower response of the more affluent in devotionalism, fundamentalist orthodoxy, and personal moral issues (that is, one measure in each of the three groups). In this respect they tend to be more secularized. At the same time, in associationalism, in Anabaptism, and in social ethics, they indicate the highest responses and consequently appear to be more religious. Economic ascendancy does not necessarily mean increased secularization. Niebuhr's hypothesis that upward mobility brings a loss of sectarianism cannot be upheld. Nor does economic depravity necessarily vouch for greater religiosity. More, obviously, needs to be said about the consequences of Mennonite Brethren economic ascendancy.

Table XIII-6
A Summary of the Scales of Levels of Income and Measures of Religiosity

	Totals of Rank Order Ratings		
	Below $6,000	$6,000-11,999	Above $12,000
Practice of Religion			
Devotionalism	10	8	5
Associationalism	7	7	10
Subtotal	17	15	15
Religious Beliefs			
General Orthodoxy	7	13	10
Fundamentalist Orthodoxy	10	12	8
Anabaptism	10	6	14
Subtotal	27	31	32
Ethics			
Moral Issues	12	13	5
Social Ethics	7	11	12
Subtotal	19	24	17
Total	63	70	64

Source: Church Member Profile, 1972.

3. Some Further Consequences of Economic Ascendancy

The empirical data based on the Church Member Profile help to provide a synchronic analysis of the effects of economic prosperity. The consequences of such prosperity viewed diachronically, that is, over a longer period of time, allow one to analyse change which occurs gradually and which cannot be measured through a single question-naire. The following further analysis, more diachronic in nature, in-cludes both the consequences which have a direct bearing upon sec-ularization, because of the upward mobility, as well as those which have arrested the secularization trend through the utilization of economic strength for religious purposes.

Effects of Economic Prosperity upon Social Class

The comparison of Canadian Mennonite Brethren of the first quarter of this century with those of recent times shows a significant climb in educational attainment, a radical shift from rural to urban occupations, and a marked increase in income, affecting thus the three usual com-ponents of socio-economic status—education, occupation, and in-come. The result has been a gradual change in social class. This upward mobility has been of two types, mainly of individuals who achieved these desirables, but also of the sect as a whole. Regardless of their status in the old country, immigrants are usually forced to start on the lowest rung of the social ladder (Mol, 1961, 32). Where this class background is of a higher status, immigrants will be especially astute in changing their status through attainment of several or all of the above components. In the meantime, however, the low-status sect has pro-vided the appropriate environment for their unprivileged position. This explains the loss to the sect of some members who attain a higher status before the sect as a whole has changed. In such instances, the advancement of individuals simply exceeds that of the social institu-tion. Besides the tendencies of individuals to rise in status, there is also the gradual acquisition of enhanced status by the whole movement. Not only does a whole movement enhance its social class as the majority of its members become wealthier and participate in the cultural pur-suits of society in general, but more specifically, as Liston Pope ob-served in Gaston County, as a few members of a sect prosper and become its leaders, the sect loses the members of the lower economic class replacing them with members from a higher strata (Pope, 1942, 119-20). Vertical mobility occurs, hence, both on an individual as well as on a group level, the former preceding the latter.

The consequences of such upward social mobility among Canadian Mennonite Brethren are worthy of note. First, it appears that there is an increase in class cleavage. The existence of a class distinction be-tween Mennonites in Russia and their Russian neighbours is an ac-knowledged fact. Such distinctions continued even in Canada, despite their own lower class identity as an immigrant people. John Redekop lamented the unwholesome increase in class distinctions.

Increasingly we seem to be accepting a basically Marxist view of class cleavages if not of class antagonisms.... As the income, occupational, educational, and general status differentiation grows in our brotherhood, some basically un-christian attitudes and behavior patterns are growing as well.

The wealthy tend to isolate themselves.... Those whom we might describe as financially poor tend to avoid socializing with Christians who are more well-to-do.... The broad middle classes mix quite freely among themselves although even here vocational grouping and exclusiveness is common.... From a purely sociological perspective, that makes sense....

And thus the barriers grow (Redekop, 1975, 12).

A second consequence of such vertical mobility, related to the first, is that the integrity of the group suffers. In his plea for "Christian class consciousness," Redekop lamented the loss of homogeneity. "The traditional pattern of general social homogeneity which I recall from my childhood in a Mennonite Brethren setting seems to be dissipating rapidly" (Redekop, 1975, 12). E. K. Francis makes a similar observation concerning the Mennonites of Manitoba, namely, they were "more successful in advancing economically than in preserving their social institutions" (Francis, 1955, 110). The result has been a considerable defection in membership.

A third consequence of such upward mobility is the accentuated value placed on worldly success. Paul Erb, editor of the (Old) Mennonite *Gospel Herald*, berated the Mennonite community in a guest editorial in the *Mennonite Observer* for selfish "status seeking." "It is all pretty silly, and sad, and un-Christian. Jeremiah tells us not to seek great things for ourselves" (Erb, 1959, 2). As Susan Budd notes, "The saved make good workmen, if not good entrepreneurs" (Budd, 1973, 106). No doubt, it could also be argued conversely that the value placed on worldly success results in upward mobility.

A final consequence is the loss of what Weber called "inner-worldly asceticism" (*innerweltliche Askese*) (Weber, 1958, 139-94). No longer is there the same emphasis upon individual control and achievement, moral respectability and sobriety. Instead there is socialization of the dominant values of society as Benton Johnson observed of the Holiness sects (Johnson, 1961, 309-16). Harold Fallding speaks of a tendency for sects to mellow with the social acceptance they enjoy or the accommodation to the world that accompanies their socialization of dominant values (Fallding, 1974, 153-54). Such mellowing of the sectarian is not always the case, however, as the instance of the Canadian Mennonite Brethren suggests.

Effects of Economic Prosperity upon the Sectarian Stance

Sociologists of religion have repeatedly shown that as sects achieve a greater degree of economic and social security, they not only tend to transform themselves into bodies of greater social respectability, but also shift on the continuum from sect to church. In other words, they lose their sectness. This chapter suggests that a religious movement can still retain its sectness despite the loss of the inner-worldly asceticism and the assimilation of the dominant values of society. The effect of prosperity upon the sectarian position needs, then, further to be examined. Russell R. Dynes has, for example, hypothesized that "sect-ness" is associated with low socio-economic status, and "churchness" with high (Dynes, 1955, 550-60). As indicated earlier, Niebuhr argued:

By its very nature the sectarian type of organization is valid for one genera-tion.... As generation succeeds generation, this isolation of the community from the world becomes more difficult. Furthermore, wealth frequently in-creases when the sect subjects itself to the discipline of asceticism in work and expenditure; with the increase of wealth the possibilities for culture also be-come more numerous and involvement in the economic life of the nation as a whole can less easily be limited. Compromise begins and the ethics of the sect approach the church type of morals. As with ethics, so with the doctrine, so also with the administration of religion. . . . So the sect becomes a church (Niebuhr, 1972, 20).

Despite this trend which has been observed in numerous sects, there can also be upward mobility without the concomitant de-nominationalizing. Bryan Wilson has shown that established sects in England, such as the Christadelphians, Salvation Army, and various Brethren groups, have grown stronger with age (Wilson, 1961). The Mennonite Brethren Church is some 115 years old, three generations of which have continued to flourish in Canada. The highly sectarian response on the empirical tests of religious beliefs and practice, simul-taneous with the increased upward mobility, suggest that Canadian Mennonite Brethren have not succumbed to the church-type religious movement. No doubt, the factors of religious continuity, surveyed in chapters five to nine, especially the strongly delineated cognitive and normative boundaries and the deliberate socialization through weekly worship and formal instruction, account for the persistence of the sectarian stance despite the vertical mobility.

Effects of Economic Prosperity upon the Stewardship of Resources

Whereas the effects of economic prosperity upon social class and upon the sectarian stance both fall into the purview of secularization, and hence, impede the continuity of sectarianism, the following two effects strengthen the religious movement both in its centripetal thrust of amassing and utilizing its resources, as well as in its more centrifugal concern of confronting and changing society. Not only has affluence given individuals economic security, it has also enlarged the church's material assets.

In a two-fold manner Canadian Mennonite Brethren have attempted to avert crass materialism and its accompanying curse. First, there has been instruction and exhortation on giving to the work of the church. The result of such teaching and preaching is that 47 percent of Mennonite Brethren (in the United States and Canada) give 10 percent or more and 32 percent give at least 5 but less than 10 percent; this compares to 40 percent and 26 percent, respectively, for (Old) Mennonites and 29 percent and 34 percent for General Conference Mennonites (Kauffman and Harder, 1975, 238). The per member giving from 1938 to 1959 had increased from $13.41 to $125.50 (*GCYB*, 1960, 104) and by 1974 it had increased to $310.68 (*GCYB*, 1975, 174). And yet, as Canadian Mennonite Brethren statistician George Epp notes, the annual per member contributions to Missions/Services do not keep up with the annual personal disposable income (Epp, 1974, 27).

A second attempt to avert materialism is in the careful disposal of the resources that are in fact mobilized. Who consumes the amassed wealth? Is it directed to the local church operating budget, new facilities, overseas missions, or to the starving world? On the one hand, interim editor Klassen argued that "if we build a church that is generally 'cheaper' than the very homes we live in, is this not robbing God of the glory due Him in this regard?" (Klassen, 1964, 3). On the other hand, editor Jantz lamented the materialistic attitude apparent in the construction of new churches. "We have often been tempted to build great monuments to our pride" (Jantz, 1967, 2). John Redekop extended the vision to the Third World. He argued:

In this land of abundance and often overabundance; in this land where so many of us have our petty tastes pampered and catered to; in this land plagued by both over-production and over-consumption; in this wonderful land it is a good thing for us, its inhabitants, to remind ourselves periodically of the plight of our fellowmen in the other countries (Redekop, 1964, 2).

Wealth, therefore, has not necessarily corrupted. While Canadian Mennonite Brethren expose themselves to the secularizing effects of affluence, they have also capitalized on the strengths that such affluence offers.

Effects of Economic Prosperity upon Social Reform

Prosperity may indeed lead to great self-indulgence, but it can also contribute positively to the promoting of social reforms. Contrary to the manner in which the social gospel seemed to emerge in Canada prior to the 1920s, among the Canadian Mennonite Brethren the emergence of the "social passion" is directly related to the problems of its fellow-believers. Prior to the immigrant influx of the 1920s, the *Kanadier* had supported relief efforts of Mennonite Central Committee in 1920 and became part of the Mennonite Board of Colonization in 1922 to assist in immigration and settlement. Subsequently, these agencies were instrumental in helping Mennonites with the *Reiseschuld*, conscientious objectors in time of war, coordinating mutual aid as in hospitalization, mental health, and burial assistance; and providing welfare to Mennonites overseas.

However, it was only with the increased urbanism, occupational change, and affluence that new problems were exposed and that there were new economic resources to assist in the solution of these problems. In 1965, F. C. Peters acknowledged the varied responses of Mennonite Brethren to labour unions and frankly stated, "The fact of the matter is that many—and I would venture to say the majority—of Mennonite Brethren labourers who are not working for themselves belong to a union" (Peters, 1965, 8). As a prominent leader of the denomination, he then stated that he did not object to union membership as such, but that each membership pledge should be carefully read to see whether or not it conflicted with the Christian's conscience. Again in 1968, John Redekop presented a forceful paper entitled "The Christian and Labor Unions" to the Conference on Discipleship and Evangelism in Winnipeg. Here he argued that unions have a place in our society and that there will be tensions for the Christian in the ethical-social relationships with non-Christians in society (Redekop, 1968, 10-11).

But it is not the editors, theologians, and professors alone who responded to these social problems that arise with modernization. Influential and well-to-do Christian businessmen also have addressed themselves to such involvement. Businessman Rudolph Dyck has courageously challenged the values commonly held—the popular perception of people, the bigness of success, and the survival of the fittest—which prevent a "comprehensive view of oneself as a servant of mankind with whatever means are at one's disposal." Dyck argues: "A total reversal from the usual values is what this is all about, coupled with a purpose for living. I am convinced that many of our most pressing problems—unemployment, inflation, pollution, work stoppage and overdevelopment can ultimately be attributed to failure at this point" (Dyck, 1977, 4, 5, 30). It was the willingness of businessmen to go that "extra mile" and their fundamentally different value systems which led to the formation of the Mennonite Economic Development Associates through which they contributed their expertise and financial resources to provide long-range solutions through industrial development, expansion of markets, and development of transportation facilities in the Third World countries. And so the prosperity of Canadian Mennonite Brethren was bringing about social and economic reform both within Canada and in the Third World.

Economic ascendancy brought with it vertical mobility. The secularizing impact of such upward mobility, however, was mitigated by the strength which such prosperity lent both to assist financially in religious causes at home and overseas, as well as to initiate reform centred in the very value system which itself had enhanced prosperity. Secularization was both accelerated and arrested by the economic ascendancy of Canadian Mennonite Brethren, and the tension provided an impetus to the sectarian movement.

Summary

The study of social analysts of the reciprocal relation between economics and religion finds ready application among Canadian Mennonite Brethren. Weber's thesis that religion affects economic behaviour found illustration not only among sixteenth-century Anabaptists but also among twentieth-century Mennonite Brethren. Yet, Niebuhr's analysis, however astute, cannot fully be illustrated by Mennonite Brethren, because sectarianism persisted beyond the second generation. Wilson's assertion that some sects can withstand the denominationalizing process and Lenski's findings that one can be socialized to withstand total convergence in attitudes, values, and behaviour explained the stubborn resistance by Canadian Mennonite Brethren to at least some of the secularizing effects of economic prosperity.

The seeds for such prosperity were implanted by the frontier spirit of early Mennonite settlers, and the beginnings were accelerated by the several waves of immigrants since 1920s. The work ethic has been a most tenacious motivating force, and the tendency to acquire economic assets has further contributed to the affluent state which could have serious secularizing consequences.

Empirical data reveal that the most affluent tend to be residents of cities, have usually received graduate or professional training, and likely belong to professional or business occupations. Despite these marks of material prosperity, the most affluent are not necessarily the least religious. It appears that the economically deprived have higher ratings in devotionalism, fundamentalist orthodoxy, and personal, moral issues. The affluent, at the same time, reveal higher responses in associationalism, Anabaptism, and social ethics. Neither group, the least affluent or the most affluent, can be said to be more religious, for each group excels in some of the measures of religiosity.

A further examination of the consequences of such material prosperity over a longer period of time indicates a decided upward social mobility with the usual results of class cleavage, accentuated values on worldly success, and a loss in inner-worldly asceticism. While there may be some mellowing of sectarianism, Mennonite Brethren have not shifted wholly to the right on the sect-church continuum, but the sectarian stance has persisted. This persistence can be explained in two further effects of prosperity—the ability to, and actuality of, using the material resources to promote religious causes, including assistance beyond one's own congregation, and taking the initiative to reform the secularized, economic structures of society. These latter effects not only demonstrate Weber's notion that religion motivates economic activity, but also suggest that religion has the vitality to overcome the secularizing effects of economic prosperity.

XIV

Assimilation and Identity Crisis

Canadian Mennonite Brethren are presently undergoing a crisis of identity. The discussion of the preceding chapters, ten to thirteen, helps to explain the current dilemma. The components of social change—education, urbanization, occupational advancement, and economic ascendancy—have exercised considerable secularizing stress upon the religious movement. Yet, the impact has not been unambiguously secular in the sense of producing a unilinear loss of faith or decrease in religious commitment. Education leads to increased differentiation in one's symbol system, but it also positively frees people to make their religious choices and commitments personally. Urbanization tends to relativize the most conservative beliefs and morals, but it also confronts a religious movement with new opportunities for exerting its influence. Occupational change opens new worlds which make one susceptible to new secularizing hazards, but such change with its enhanced penetration of society has also been more of an asset than a liability for religious vitality. And while economic affluence may have mellowed sectarian obstinacy, the secularizing effect has been arrested through rigorous socialization. The sacralizing processes, dealt with in chapters five to nine, have guarded the movement against excessive adaptability to such change. However, no single component of change has exercised such an insidious effect as assimilation itself. The tension generated by the dialectic of secularizing and sacralizing forces has been accentuated as the sectarian, immigrant movement gradually assumed the beliefs, attitudes, and behavioural patterns of its host society, making it even more difficult to be *in* the world while refusing to be *of* the world. Chapter fourteen concerns itself with this final component of social change and the resulting identity crisis.

Such variables of social change, however, cannot really be treated in isolation. All the while that changes in education, rural-urban residence, occupation, and economic status were taking place, the process of cultural diffusion has been at work. This chapter tests the degree to which assimilation, and the other variables of social change that con-

226

tribute to it, has led to a loss of faith and examines the viability of sectarianism in the face of the resulting identity crisis.

1. Assimilation and Its Evidence

Because the identity crisis is so closely related to the assimilation of the immigrant group, it will be helpful to analyse more closely the process of cultural diffusion and to be apprised of the historical and empirical data which explain the effects, and then to examine the identity crisis.

The Process of Cultural Diffusion

To recognize the sociological and psychological dynamics involved in the interaction between the dominant and minority groups of society is to understand somewhat the complexity of the process of cultural diffusion.

The continuum from conflict to convergence. The process of assimilation is perhaps best conceptualized by a continuum ranging from conflict with the dominant or host society at the one pole to total convergence at the other. Usually one views assimilation from the perspective of the dominant society, that is, the degree to which attachment to the host society has been achieved and one speaks in terms of social rejection or social acceptance. Total convergence, thus, represents the final state of assimilation, although the process leading to this state is also called assimilation. Kovacs and Cropley, however, have drawn attention to the simultaneous process of detachment or estrangement from the ethnic ways of an immigrant group with the resulting state of alienation, that is, "a state of estrangement from psychological props which, when shared by members of ethnic groups, make the world easily understandable and impart a sense of identity and belonging to the individual" (Kovacs and Cropley, 1972, 14). Viewed from the perspective of the ethnic group, then, the process of convergence with the ways of the dominant society can also be seen as a process of alienation with the removal of the psychological props and the resulting identity crisis. To view the process from one perspective alone, however, may lead to an ethnocentric interpretation. Kovacs and Cropley conclude that demands for excessively complete and rapid assimilation may cause otherwise avoidable traumatic experiences (1972, 21). The interplay of the psychological and sociological forces at work becomes quite obvious. For example, Hans Mol explains that a foreign church may hinder social integration, but at the same time facilitate personal integration. "The foreign church by being a home away from home is an effective antidote to the forces of personal disorganization and provides the immigrant with a sense of belonging and security necessary to his mental well-being" (Mol, 1961, 30). Sociologist E. K. Francis demonstrates this understanding when he suggests that "the aim of a rational immigration policy should be the integration of all ethnic components into the social body of the nation at the least cost in human suffering, rather than their assimilation at any price and with maximum speed" (Francis, 1955, 6). Perhaps the intensity of the current identity crisis among Canadian Mennonite Brethren results from too sudden and too excessive a shift on the continuum from conflict to convergence.

Distinguishing between acculturation and assimilation. The process of adjustment or adaptation in order to minimize conflict and maximize convergence has variously been referred to as accommodation, acclimatization, amalgamation, acculturation, and assimilation. While the last two terms, and particularly assimilation, are employed in this study, the first three warrant brief consideration. Park and Burgess deal exhaustively with the concept of accommodation and describe it as a process of adjustment to prevent or reduce conflict, control competition, and maintain a basis of security in the social order for persons and groups of divergent interests (Park and Burgess, 1970, 303-60). Obviously, accommodation of one kind or another will always need to occur when two cultures meet. Acclimatization is a form of accommodation which has to do with adapting to climatic conditions widely different from those to which a group was accustomed. No doubt, the first generation of Canadian Mennonite Brethren required a radical adjustment to climate in their moves from the mild Black Sea area to the continental extremes of the Canadian prairies. There is no evidence, however, that such a change in climate had adverse effects upon their religious commitment. Amalgamation has reference to the fusion of races through intermarriage. Such miscegenation, although rare among Canadian Mennonite Brethren, no doubt accelerates the process of assimilation between the parties which intermingle and especially among their offspring.

Acculturation, a term favoured by anthropologists, has been defined by Redfield, Linton, and Herskovits as comprehending "those phenomena which result when groups of individuals having different cultures come into continuous firsthand contact, with subsequent changes in the original cultural patterns of either or both groups" (Gordon, 1975, 61). Important to note is the reciprocal influence whereby the cultures of both groups are modified. Immigrants, hence, both accommodate themselves to their host society and also contribute culturally and modify it. Canadian Mennonite Brethren today appear to have successfully acculturated to their dominant society without having totally assimilated the value system and having withstood in a measure the secularizing effects.

Perhaps no one has so thoroughly studied American assimilation as Milton Gordon. In his discussion, he begins with Park and Burgess' definition of assimilation as "a process of interpenetration and fusion in which persons and groups acquire the memories, sentiments, and attitudes of other persons or groups, and by sharing their experience and history are incorporated with them in a common cultural life" (Park and Burgess, 1975, 360). Gordon isolates numerous variables of assimilation, but particularly cultural or behavioural (defined earlier as acculturation), identificational (development of a sense of peoplehood based exclusively on the host society), and structural (the large-scale entrance into cliques, clubs, and institutions of the host society, on a primary group level) (Gordon, 1975, 70). Gordon sees structural assimilation as the key variable.

For, if plural cultures are to be maintained, they must be carried on by subsocieties which provide the framework for communal existence—their own networks of cliques, institutions, organizations, and informal friendship patterns—functioning not only for the first generation of immigrants but for the succeeding generations of American-born descendants as well (Gordon, 1975, 158).

Gordon further develops three theories to explain American assimilation. "Anglo-conformity" demanded the complete renunciation of the immigrant's ancestral culture in favour of the behaviour and values of the Anglo-Saxon core group; the "melting pot" theory envisaged a biological merger of the Anglo-Saxon people with other immigrant groups and a blending of their respective cultures into a new indigenous American type; and "cultural pluralism" allowed for the preservation of the communal life and significant portions of the culture of the later immigrant groups within the context of American citizenship and political and economic integration into American society (Gordon, 1975, 85). It is cultural pluralism which is particularly suited to the preservation of Mennonite sectarianism. While ethnicity has largely disappeared, there are still some evidences of its sacralizing hold. The following historical overview will indicate how Mennonite Brethren have successfully assimilated structurally, much in the manner which Gordon articulates, to ensure the continuity of their sectarian stance.

A Brief Overview of Canadian Mennonite Brethren Assimilation

Two caveats are in place about the following historical survey: the first concerns its brevity and the second its arbitrary periodization. To facilitate brevity, only the most suggestive historical incidents are included and the documentation is highly selective. Not only is the division of the half-century into three generations somewhat arbitrary, but the appellations are also somewhat restrictive; yet both are intentional. The demarcations of time are not meant so much to define rigidly the boundaries between generations (for there will be much overlapping) as they are to suggest cross-sectional perspectives of separate generations for the purposes of comparison. And the suggested titles indicate predominant processes of assimilation rather than comprehensive designations.

First generation (1925-1945): accommodation despite conflict. On the continuum from conflict to convergence, the first generation (those who immigrated in the 1920s) encountered the anticipated conflict of any immigrant group. Yet, accommodation took place from the outset. Three events stand out during these years. The first is the settlement itself of the newly landed immigrants with the concomitant clash of cultures and initial adjustments. The conflicts had to do with land and livelihood, with acclimatization to new lows in temperature, and learning of a new language. As yet, there was no ideological conflict such as the earlier immigration of Old Colony Mennonites had faced with regards to education. The religious vitality which marked these immigrants fortified them in the isolation and led them to find a kindred group with which to worship and to meet their social needs.

A second noteworthy event is the depression of the 1930s. Crop failures, low prices, and burgeoning debts led many to abandon their farms in Saskatchewan and find employment in cities or resettle in the garden lands of the Fraser Valley or peninsular Ontario. Such dispersion from the isolated prairies to more populated communities led to increased exposure, acculturation, and eventual assimilation. Except for testing and often strengthening their religious commitment, the depression did not produce immediate, secularizing trends. It did, however, result in the eventual dissolution of a number of congregations across the prairies. As indicated above, such residential mobility had its own religious toll.

A third experience of conflict for the first generation was World War II. The ideological test of the movement's non-resistant stance has been outlined in chapter five. The failure of some Mennonite Brethren to take a conscientious objector's stand indicated some erosion of this religious distinctive, but led to increased efforts after the war to teach the doctrine more comprehensively. Despite some concessions to the host society during these first years, the conflicts but highlighted the rigorous religious commitment of Canadian Mennonite Brethren.

Second generation (1945-1965): acculturation and alienation. For the children of the early immigrants, the process of acculturation was somewhat easier, yet resulted in casualties of alienation which disrupted the cohesiveness of the religious community. Again three

events are highlighted to illustrate the accelerated tempo of acculturation following World War II together with the expected hazards of
alienation. The first of these has to do with the major components of
social change—the sudden interest in higher education, the rapid
urbanization, the entrance into a new vocational world, and the resulting affluence—as analysed in chapters ten to thirteen. By mid-century
the effects of the first three of these was especially noticeable. Expressions of dismay resounded from two of its most stalwart leaders, A. H.
Unruh and B. B. Janz. Unruh lamented that "slowly the flood of
conformity with the world and secularization infiltrate through the
broken dams, and we can identify our time as a period of the breaking
of the transmitted tradition in the Mennonite Brethren Church" (Unruh, 1953, 12). In his analysis, Unruh pointed to six factors which
contributed to the breakthrough: the influence of other (church) associations, the direct influence of the world, the opposition to unnecessary strictness, failure to understand youth, the lack of self-evaluation
among leaders, the laxity and worldliness of many church members. At
the same time, Unruh recognized both the liberating possibilities of this
"breaking" and proposed numerous ways to withstand the evil consequences of such a "breaking." Janz presented an analysis of the Mennonite Brethren Church to the annual session of the Canadian Conference. In doing so, he assessed its strengths and its liabilities. Among
the liabilities ("*schwersten Schattenseiten unserer Konferenz*"), he included materialism (with its craving for pleasure, ambition, and
amusements), the love of the world among youth, the problem of
language, and laxity in church discipline (Janz, 1954, 10-15). For these
leaders, not only assimilation, but also the secularizing effects of assimilation, had accompanied the acculturative process.

Another major occurrence for the second generation was the language transition. Church leaders who analysed the developments of
the Canadian Mennonite Brethren scene in the 1950s and 1960s
showed an awareness of this "language problem." Nonetheless, it was a
major factor in the acculturation process, but change in language did
not really retard the religiosity of the movement. Conducting services
wholly in English allowed the churches to become a "community
church" in fact, rather than a church serving but one ethnic subcommunity.

A third event worthy of note for the second generation is the centennial celebration of the Mennonite Brethren Church, which precipitated reflections on the impact of assimilation. At the special celebration in Reedley, California, at the time of the General Conference
session in 1960, several incisive statements in Conference sermons
drew attention to the effects of the acculturation process. Referring to
changes in language, vocation, and urbanization, J. A. Toews asserted:

The above changes provide new opportunities for an effective evangelistic outreach; they also provide occasions for the disastrous inroads of materialism and secularism. Can we unite as a brotherhood on ethical principles to keep out the floodtide of worldliness? A church that conforms to the world has no message that will transform the world (Toews, 1960, 6).

In a centennial publication, J. H. Quiring analysed the Mennonite Brethren at "the present" (1960) as increasing numerically, spreading and shifting geographically, prospering economically, standing firm doctrinally, and struggling ethnically. Quiring remarked: "Today complaints are pouring in that worldliness is wedging its way into our ranks. . . . One of the sinister wiles of the devil today is *die Verharmlosung* (making sin seem harmless) of that which is basically evil" (Quiring, 1960, 77). These interpreters of the Mennonite Brethren movement at the time of its centennial sensed the accommodation to the "world," the fragility in membership, and the preoccupation with materialistic pursuits—all indications of secularization—but invariably expressed confidence in the viability of the movement, despite these threats to its continuity.

Third generation (1965-1975): assimilation and convergence. What E. K. Francis predicted about the third generation has in fact become a reality. In 1954, he projected:

Sooner or later the Mennonites, too, would be absorbed into the general stream of Canadian life; hallowed traditions and customs would die away with the immigrant generation; at least their grandchildren would easily overcome the cultural lag in their mores and would embrace more up-to-date ideas; even attitudes towards religion would be modernized and religious taboos less restrictive, thus permitting more intimate conversation with and even conversion to other Protestant churches; English would become a primary means of communication, leaving their folk dialect a relic to be occasionally paraded by some old-timer before curious visitors or wide-eyed youngsters (Francis, 1955, 215).

Looking at the decade or more ahead of him in 1966, that is, at the grandchildren of the immigrants, Mennonite Brethren leader F. C. Peters projected to the annual session of the Canadian Conference that there would be a greater proportion of older people, increased wealth, further urbanization, higher levels of education, and great lay leadership potential (Peters, 1966, 4). Reflecting on the Conference proceedings almost a decade later, John Redekop observed: "For better or worse, we are becoming more acculturated. We have accepted fully the language and idioms of the land. The delegates no longer give the impression of being a massive, traditional church council" (Redekop, 1973, 11). Indeed, as these spokesmen intimate, the present generation represents a stage of structural assimilation in which there is little apparent conflict, because of the degree of acculturation, but much convergence. The conflict, however, is more inward and expresses itself in an identity crisis, as indicated below.

Testing the Effects of Assimilation

Measuring the effects of assimilation is a rather difficult undertaking. First, because assimilation has to do with basic values underlying cultural elements, measuring degrees of assimilation is a much more subjective process than determining the stage of outward conformity. Moreover, because an empirical test of a controlled group could not be administered diachronically to represent the gradual effects of assimilation, a single questionnaire used for the Church Member Profile becomes the measure as it is applied to three distinctly separated age groups. Hence, the following measures of the effects of assimilation are based on the assumption that intergenerational differences in religious practices, beliefs, and ethics suggest differences in degrees of assimilation.

Table XIV-1

Generational Differences and the Practice of Religion

	Percentage Response for Three Generations		
	Age 60 or more	40 to 50	15 to 25
Devotionalism			
Prayer	83.7 (n=36)	93.1 (n=94)	85.1 (n=63)
Bible study	90.2 (n=37)	92.2 (n=94)	79.7 (n=59)
Closeness to God	71.4 (n=30)	65.3 (n=66)	50.0 (n=37)
Seeking God's will	71.1 (n=27)	79.2 (n=80)	60.8 (n=45)
Subtotal of Rank Orders	8	11	5
Associationalism			
Church attendance	66.7 (n=28)	87.0 (n=87)	87.8 (n=65)
Sunday school attendance	41.5 (n=17)	74.5 (n=76)	73.0 (n=54)
Mid-week services	34.1 (n=15)	44.6 (n=45)	62.2 (n=46)
Leadership post	38.1 (n=16)	74.0 (n=74)	47.9 (n=35)
Subtotal of Rank Orders	4	10	10
Total of Rank Orders	12	21	15

Source: Church Member Profile, 1972.

Table XIV-2

Generational Differences and Religious Beliefs

	Percentage Response for Three Generations		
	Age 60 or more	40 to 50	15 to 25
Orthodoxy			
Deity of Jesus	100.0 (n=42)	97.1 (n=99)	93.2 (n=69)
Belief in miracles	97.6 (n=41)	97.0 (n=98)	95.9 (n=71)
Jesus' resurrection	100.0 (n=41)	100.0 (n=99)	93.2 (n=69)
Jesus' personal return	100.0 (n=44)	99.0 (n=101)	95.9 (n=71)
Personal devil	97.7 (n=43)	100.0 (n=102)	94.6 (n=70)
Subtotal of Rank Orders	13	11	5
Fundamentalism			
Inspiration of the Bible	95.3 (n=41)	100.0 (n=102)	90.5 (n=67)
Virgin birth of Jesus	100.0 (n=42)	99.0 (n=101)	97.3 (n=72)
Six-day creation	77.3 (n=34)	53.0 (n=53)	35.1 (n=26)
Universal flood	95.5 (n=42)	95.1 (n=97)	86.5 (n=64)
Eternal punishment	84.1 (n=37)	89.1 (n=90)	82.4 (n=61)
Subtotal of Rank Orders	13	12	5
Anabaptism			
Following Jesus	70.7 (n=29)	60.4 (n=61)	55.4 (n=41)
Against infant baptism	81.0 (n=34)	89.1 (n=90)	87.8 (n=65)
Church discipline	95.1 (n=39)	92.1 (n=93)	70.3 (n=52)
Non-resistance	85.7 (n=36)	73.5 (n=75)	47.3 (n=35)
Non-swearing of oaths	88.1 (n=37)	86.3 (n=88)	70.3 (n=52)
Subtotal of Rank Orders	13	11	6
Total of Rank Orders	39	34	16

Source: Church Member Profile, 1972.

Generational differences and the practice of religion.   Using the same measures of religion as in the preceding chapters and cross-tabulating the answers to specific questions from the Church Member Profile with distinctly separated age groups, one arrives at the following intergenerational responses to religion. Table XIV-1 reflects the generational differences and the practice of religion. The responses to measures of devotionalism and associationalism are distinctly different. In devotionalism, where surprisingly the second generation has the highest rating, followed by the first generation (except in "closeness to God," where possibly the advanced years make one feel "closer"), it is the third generation that is significantly less. In associationalism, the second and third generations rate decidedly higher than the first. Whereas in devotionalism, the third generation was consistently lowest, in associationalism the first generation was consistently lowest. This would momentarily not support the hypothesis that greater assimilation leads to more secularization. One might argue that in the case of the first generation the factor of physical vitality may be the intervening variable, and the lesser score on associationalism reflects decrepitude more than it does secularization.

Generational differences and religious beliefs.   Table xiv-2 indicates the cross-tabulations of measures of religious beliefs and generational differences. Here there is a remarkably consistent pattern for the three groups of measures. The first and second generations rate somewhat higher (with the first exceeding the second, but not significantly so). The third generation is significantly lower. Contrary to other variables of social change reflected in chapters nine to thirteen, the measures of Anabaptism consistently follow the other responses. The total results support the hypothesis that assimilation leads to secularization, especially between the second and third generations. Whatever factors account for it—ethnicity, socialization, or leadership involvement—the second generation shows little secularization despite its degree of assimilation.

Generational differences and ethics.   Table xiv-3 shows the cross-tabulations of measures of ethics and generational differences. Not surprisingly, in personal and moral issues, reflecting traditional taboos among Mennonite Brethren, the elderly generation ranks highest, the grandchildren rank decidedly lowest, and the middle-aged group in-between. The differences are significant. In the more liberal, social ethics, consistent with the findings in earlier chapters, the tables are turned, with the older generation ranking lowest and the younger generation ranking highest on the social ethics scale. As a result, the totals in ethics are not so different, for the extremes mentioned above balanced each other out. One would conclude that in conservative ethical practices, assimilation leads to secularization.

Summary of Empirical Findings

Table xiv-4 summarizes the crude, rank order ratings as used in the previous chapters. The summary by itself (and it must be kept in mind that the rank order method tends to exaggerate minimal differences) would suggest that there is no secularization or loss of religiosity between the first and second generations, but a significant decline between the second and third. This conclusion calls into question Will Herberg's thesis that the grandchildren of immigrant forbears return to their ancestral religious faiths, after the second generation had disassociated itself from the more ethnic first generation, rejecting also the church with which the ethnic subcommunity was inextricably linked (Herberg, 1960, 16-45). The findings of this study suggest that the second generation has retained its religious vitality and that the third generation is in fact, with the exception of associationalism, more secularized. The secularizing effects of assimilation are, thus, more apparent in the third generation than the second.

Table XIV-3
Generational Differences and Ethics

	Percentage Response for Three Generations		
	Age 60 or more	40 to 50	15 to 25
Moral Issues			
Drinking moderately	70.5 (n=31)	58.0 (n=58)	28.8 (n=21)
Smoking tobacco	88.4 (n=38)	87.0 (n=87)	59.5 (n=44)
Adult-rated movies	63.4 (n=26)	59.4 (n=60)	31.1 (n=23)
Premarital sex	97.7 (n=42)	99.0 (n=99)	89.2 (n=66)
Social dancing	90.2 (n=37)	74.3 (n=75)	40.5 (n=30)
Subtotal of Rank Orders	14	11	5
Social Ethics			
Race relations	27.3 (n=12)	54.9 (n=56)	85.1 (n=63)
Social welfare	27.9 (n=12)	31.4 (n=32)	44.6 (n=33)
Anti-Communism	19.5 (n=8)	24.0 (n=24)	23.0 (n=17)
Labour unions	25.6 (n=11)	12.7 (n=13)	6.8 (n=5)
Capital punishment	9.5 (n=4)	13.7 (n=14)	33.8 (n=25)
Subtotal of Rank Orders	7	11	12
Total of Rank Orders	21	22	17

Source: Church Member Profile, 1972.

Table XIV-4

A Summary of Scales of Generational Differences and Measures of Religiosity

	Total of Rank Order Ratings		
	Age 60 or more	40 to 50	15 to 25
Practice of Religion			
Devotionalism	8	11	5
Associationalism	4	10	10
Subtotal	12	21	15
Religious Beliefs			
Orthodoxy	13	11	5
Fundamentalism	13	12	5
Anabaptism	13	11	6
Subtotal	39	34	16
Ethics			
Moral Issues	14	11	5
Social Ethics	7	11	12
Subtotal	21	22	17
Total	72	77	48

Source: Church Member Profile, 1972.

2. Identity Crisis and Its Consequences

Assimilation of Canadian Mennonite Brethren has produced paradoxical results. While convergence with society has resulted in some toll to religious vitality, as the empirical findings indicate, such assimilation by no means represents a substantial loss of faith. Especially among the second generation, and even among the third generation, there is evidence of surprisingly vigorous religious life. However, on account of the rapid assimilation in recent decades, the tension of "being *in* the world but not *of* the world" has been accentuated and has contributed to the current identity crisis. In the case of the present-day Canadian Mennonite Brethren, however, religious identity is no longer determined largely by external, cultural behavioural patterns, but by association with those within a culturally pluralistic world who have a similar ideological intent, despite the varying external features of ethnicity. It is left, then, to show how the present search for identity is taking place and what the consequences of the newly forged identity might be.

The Search for Identity

The present search for an identity, which allows for maximal convergence with society culturally with minimal concession ideologically, becomes apparent in numerous ways.

Reformulating the theological and ethical stance.   Most important, it is marked by a deliberate rethinking and reformulation of doctrinal issues and ethical concerns. The current rethinking of theological issues is marked, first, by a return to the Anabaptist and, more significantly, the New Testament positions. It is important to the Anabaptist scholars to verify that the beginning itself of the Mennonite Brethren Church was characterized by this "return." That such restorationist thinking does not result in a static view, but is current and dynamic, is suggested by New Testament theologian John E. Toews, who maintains that Anabaptism calls us to "flesh out" our New Testament heritage. He avers, "Anabaptism means a profound commitment to take Jesus seriously in everyday life" (Toews, 1976, 2). It is marked, in the second place, by warning against the foreign influences that have shaped our current theology. J. A. Toews maintained: "Our present identity-crisis is largely the result of our exposure to 'every wind of doctrine' from various theological schools of thought. Our problem is perhaps not so much one of exposure to various theological views, as our indiscriminate acceptance of them" (Toews, 1972, 3). In the third place, such theological reformation is happening through careful restatement of the Confession of Faith and through in-depth studies of particular doctrines which represent the distinctives of the denomination. For example, in 1965 Delbert Wiens showed how the traditional understanding and description of the conversion of adults, who had had a crisis experience, did not fit children who had been "converted" between the ages of five and ten. He admits, "Because we have a theology of conversion appropriate to adults but no adequate theology of Christian nurture, we know what to do with pagans but not what to do with our own children" (Wiens, 1965). Finally, in ethical matters, Mennonite Brethren are reinterpreting their stance in keeping with contemporary issues. It appears, then, that in search for identity Mennonite Brethren are exploring a theology and an ethic which transcends ethnic boundaries.

Reconsidering the denominational designation.   A further indication of the current search for identity is the question of denominational designation. In his article to the *Mennonite Brethren Herald* constituency, J. A. Toews related the discussion of the name to a crisis in identity. "Mennonite Brethren are experiencing an *identity crisis* unprecedented in their history. Questions such as 'Who are we?' and 'What are we?' are surfacing in private discussions. The recent debate in our periodicals about the change of our denominational name is perhaps the clearest symptom of this crisis" (Toews, 1972, 2). Particularly in the last decade the discussion has been acute. In 1969, columnist John Redekop broached the question in his allegory of the "Two Bottles" in which he strongly suggested an appropriate change in labels to avoid being misrepresented as Amish (Redekop, 1969, 10). In a reply to Redekop, Professor Harry Loewen maintained that "Mennonite" is a "good label" (Loewen, 1969, 8). Again in 1971, Redekop contended that the name "Mennonite" was confusing and scared people off, and hence has lost its utility for evangelical Anabaptists (Redekop, 1971, 8). This article sparked off a good bit of debate and Professor Victor Doerksen argued, "We cannot slough off our history by changing our name; we can only add a potentially murky chapter by such an action" (Doerksen, 1971, 24). As Canadian Conference moderator, F. C. Peters in 1977 once again exposed the issue in his keynote address. Having himself at one time explained that "the Mennonite Brethren revival was meant to be a return to the Anabaptist vision rather than a deviation from it," he now told the delegates: "I'm at a point where I am asking whether the use of a name which has an ethnic connotation (as *Mennonite* Brethren) should not be reconsidered. . . . It is the biggest issue we have faced in fifty years" (Jantz, 1977, 2-4). It seems that for Canadian Mennonite Brethren Shakespeare's query "What's in a name?" has more than just passing significance; instead, it is a reflection of their own struggle with identity.

Rediscovering the heritage.   The crisis of identity is also particularly evident in the search for their roots. On the one hand, there is probing scholarship and Conference action which seeks to preserve their heritage. Already in 1945 and again in 1947, a first-generation scholar, A. H. Unruh, was requested to undertake the writing of history to preserve documents that already had been written. In 1960, a second-generation spokesman, Victor Doerksen, exhorted: "Just as it was long overdue that church historians should credit the Anabaptists within the whole Reformation, so it is incumbent upon each generation of Mennonites—and perhaps especially Mennonite Brethren—to examine afresh the heritage which is our gift and our responsibility" (Doerksen, 1960, 2). J. A. Toews' completion of a history was followed by a special symposium on Mennonite Brethren history in 1976. The search for roots is also marked by the establishment of historical societies and a new interest in archives.

On the other hand, there are words of caution which guard against excessive historical preoccupation at the risk of progressive forward action. In response to the building of a Mennonite museum, John Redekop maintained that "by glorifying our cultural peculiarity and ethnic separation, especially as it existed in the past, we are only making our evangelistic outreach more difficult" (Redekop, 1964, 2). Reflecting on the centennial celebrations of the 1874 immigration and of the 450th anniversary of the founding of Anabaptism, John E. Toews observed:

We, together with other ethnic Mennonites, are hungry for our roots. We want to know where we have come from. We are losing our ethnic shame and beginning to feel good about being Mennonite. "Mennonite is beautiful." After centuries of inferiority feelings we have experienced a moment of liberation... (Toews, 1976, 2).

Instead, Toews reminded Mennonite Brethren readers, "The 450th anniversary founding of Anabaptism judges all forms of Christian ethnicity and calls for rebirth of a radical faith and a church that is true to Jesus and the New Testament" (1976, 2). Rediscovering the heritage cannot simply be interpreted, then, as ethnic preservation, but ideological reorientation.

Reaffirming denominational and national separateness. Finally, the search for identity is also apparent in the confusion pertaining to denominational and national loyalties. Paradoxically, out of the ambivalence comes an affirmation of identity, both of sectarian separateness and national independence. While there is little empirical basis to pinpoint a peculiar constellation of symptoms which comprises the Mennonite reality, Mennonite Brethren have shown a measure of aloofness, ethnic self-hatred, and a sense of guilt which has led to severe self-criticism and abandonment of their denominational loyalties. Rudy Wiebe admitted a sense of confusion and suggested that after three generations the Mennonite Brethren may have served the purpose for which they came into being (Wiebe, 1970, 7). Even within the denomination there is strong nationalistic loyalty which makes the Canadian Conference reluctant to work at joint projects with United States. In his opinion column, John Redekop sensed in 1969 a "surprisingly widespread nationalistic identity which weakens our denominational unity" (Redekop, 1969, 10). Overtures to publish jointly a denominational periodical with the United States are resisted by Canadians. Despite much questioning, indecision, and withdrawal on a personal level, Canadian Mennonite Brethren are reaffirming their separate identity on both a denominational and national level. The search for identity is not in vain. Out of the dilemma of uncertainty and crisis of identiy new sectarian commitments seem to emerge.

The Consequences of the Crisis

What, then, are the consequences of this search for identity, and how is it strengthening sectarian commitment? While the outcome of the crisis is not yet fully known, it seems that the purging process is producing a newly forged identity which will lend even further continuity to the movement.

Purged of marginal commitment.   Assimilation has, doubtlessly, had its toll in secularization. There has been an erosion of values and a loss of faith with the consequential accommodation to, and almost total convergence with, the dominant society. There has been ambivalence of loyalty, and once faithful Mennonite Brethren have now capitulated to the syndrome of the "circulation of the saints" and have become members of the Missionary Alliance, Associated Gospel, Baptist, Evangelical Free, and a whole range of Gospel churches. There has been a weariness also with ethnic seclusion and introverted mentality with a resulting self-hatred, alienation, and defection from any and all sectarian affiliation. But out of the searching and questioning, self-examination and reformulation, there is also emerging a new commitment to the ideals of the movement.

Contrary to S. D. Clark's caution that today's sect "remains a movement of the socially unattached, and the foot-loose of the community" (Clark, 1971, 433), the purging of the marginally committed is resulting in a sect which is both socially attached and sure-footed. A new adherent, Tom Graff explained, "For me Mennonite does not mean social distinction: it is a way of living in God's grace" (Graff, 1973, 3). The newly forged identity is free of inhibitions about the name, unapologetic about being sectarian, and not intimidated about penetrating and witnessing to any sector of society. A new dedication to discipleship and missionary outreach characterizes the purged sect.

Purged of ethnic homogeneity.   Besides purging the sect of ambivalent loyalties, a further toll of secularization is the purging of remnants of traditionally Mennonite ethnicity. Such remnants of ethnicity had been a helpful identity factor in retaining the cohesiveness of the movement. As a result of convergence with society, however, the ethnic remnants are also disappearing.

For the religious analysts, the remants of ethnicity are a hindrance to the movement's ideological influence in society. Rudy Wiebe lamented as follows in 1970:

When the Canadian Broadcasting Corporation (1963) or the Columbia Broadcasting System (1967) do TV shows on Mennonites they show thousands of pictures backed by thousands of words but the name of Jesus or the witness of the church is not mentioned except by preachers. On the whole, we have remained ethnic in the eyes of the public. And often young people leave simply to get away from old-fashioned ethnicity ... rather than because the claims of Jesus Christ are presented too rigorously in our church (Wiebe, 1970, 6).

Canadian Baptist theologian Jerald Zeman warned Mennonites, "Unless you can shed the ethnic image, you will have difficulty growing and eventually surviving" (Kroeker, 1975, 5). The secularizing effects of assimilation have facilitated a liberation from such hindrances.

With the liberation and the disappearance of Mennonite ethnic solidarity, the sixteenth-century Anabaptist ideal comes closer. John E. Toews reminded Mennonite Brethren of the proximity of this ideal. "Except for the problem of ethnicity the issues facing us are not different from those which confronted the 16th century Anabaptists. Then as now the great temptation is christianized conformity to a pagan society" (Toews, 1970, 6). The new identity which is being forged through the double purging process should help Mennonite Brethren in their dilemma to preserve their ideological purity and religious vitality as a sect while outwardly being assimilated to the dominant society. If secularization has meant some loss to the movement, paradoxically, it has also meant some gain, for the purging of the cohesive, external homogeneity is helping to restore a cohesive, internal homogeneity held together by ideological commitment alone. The result is a religious vitality which can continue despite ethnic heterogeneity. Original Anabaptism, adaptable to a heterogeneous environment, is thus restored for a structurally assimilated sub-society. As Milton Gordon maintained, such sub-societies will endure beyond the first generation in a culturally pluralistic society. And while Driedger admits there may be some assimilation at the urban end, he also affirms that there is a process of changed identification which has been able to cope without assimilation for centuries. "Tradition and modernity are in tension; that tension must remain intact" (Driedger, 1977, 286, 291).

Summary

In the dialectic of sacralization and secularization, assimilation stands out as a most significant component of social change for an ethnic community. Assimilation can best be conceptualized by viewing the process of cultural diffusion on a continuum from conflict to convergence, the final state of convergence being the end product of assimilation. Simultaneous to the process of assimilation is the alienation from the props of the ethnic group which imparted a sense of identity. Such removal of the props, especially when it is too rapid and too excessive, results in an identity crisis. It is also important to distinguish between acculturation (the process of simply accepting strange cultural elements, which might be quite external) and assimilation (the process of accepting basic values underlying the cultural elements). Secularization occurs when there is an exchange of sacred and profane values. Milton Gordon's theory of cultural pluralism, particularly, allows for the preservation of sectarian ideology.

At least three phases mark the assimilation of Canadian Mennonite Brethren from 1925 to 1975. The first generation encountered its severest conflict, socially, in the initial adjustments as immigrants, economically, during the depression, and ideologically, during World War II. The second generation rapidly acculturated in the decades after the war, but encountered casualties of alienation. Upward social mobility accelerated the assimilative process. Change of language, while culturally traumatic, has but given the sectarian movement greater religious credibility, and centennial celebrations helped precipitate the identity crisis. The third generation in the last decade of study shows signs of convergence with the dominant society, thus, accentuating the identity crisis.

Empirical data, based on the response of different generational groups to variables of religiosity, suggest no loss of faith or secularization between the first and second generations, but a significant decline between the second and third generations. Herberg and Hansen's thesis that "what the son wishes to forget, the grandson wishes to remember" is called into question.

Despite the toll of assimilation on the third generation, the current identity crisis has consequences in secularization which augur well for the continuity of sectarianism. The search for an identity has generated a self-examination which is resulting in a reformulation of theological and ethical statements (an updating, as it were, without sacrificing the sectarian separateness), a reconsideration of the denominational designation (which does not mean a change necessarily), a rediscovery of the true, spiritual heritage (not confusing it with mere traditionalism), and a reaffirmation of denominational and national separateness. The consequence of the crisis of identity can then be summarized as a purging of marginal commitments (those who have ambivalent loyalties defect or are renewed in their commitment) and a purging of ethnic homogeneity (restoring the ethnic heterogeneity of sixteenth-century Anabaptism). The secularizing effect of assimilation, once again, has had both negative and positive effects. Despite the loss of faith and loss through defection, the membership continues to grow as the dialectic between sacralization and secularization stimulates religious vitality. Canadian Mennonite Brethren seem to persist in their sectarianism in the face of seductive secularization.

Part Five

VIABILITY OF SECTARIANISM

XV

Conclusion: Sectarian Persistence

The foregoing essay has attempted to combine a study of the sociology of religion with religious sociology, that is, to examine scientifically a sociological theory of religion and, at the same time, to analyse a religious movement in order better to understand it. To determine the degree of success achieved in this venture, this final chapter is meant to accomplish three purposes: to summarize the findings in an all-inclusive manner, to assess the support ascertained for the separate hypotheses, and to respond to several of the principal spokespersons in the sociology of religion who concern themselves with sectarianism.

1. Summation of Findings

The essay applies the Troeltschian church-sect typology to the Mennonite Brethren of Canada today. The shift or lack of shift on this church-sect continuum represents the degree of sacralization, which in turn reflects continuity, and the degree of secularization, which reflects change, in the religious movement. Viewing sectarianism simply as a movement of religious protest against or dissent from the social order, this study hypothesizes that sectarianism is a viable alternative where the processes of sacralization (the stabilizing quality of religion) and secularization (referring to religious decline and/or change) are in tension. Expressed in sociology-of-knowledge terminology, where the strongly integrated and taken-for-granted plausibility structures begin to totter, the status of objective reality also disintegrates and the sectarian strength erodes. To avoid excessive accommodation in which decreased transcendence results in increased immanence in the symbol system, the sect takes a defensive stance in deliberately perpetuating essential plausibility structures at the ideological level of religious continuity. In other words, in order to ensure continuity the movement does not simply devise more structures or program more inspirational sessions, but wrestles with the applicability of its Anabaptist distinctives

246

for the present time. Chapters one and two are concerned with such methodological and theoretical considerations.

A quick survey of the origins and the development of the sect prior to 1925, as chapters three and four attempt, intimated the repeated tension between dissent and accommodation. The Anabaptist-Mennonite movement itself, out of which the Mennonite Brethren emerged in 1860, represents a similar, rigorous separatism from a church which had become coextensive with society and where, in keeping with its attempt to recapture the New Testament model, such factors as the purity of the church, voluntarism, and the separation of church and state became normative. However, in subsequent generations the Anabaptist-Mennonite movement encountered a "routinization of charisma" and the prosperous, self-governing religious colonies in South Russia themselves became coextensive with society. Consequently, the resulting transformation of a believers' church to a parish church led to the birth of the Mennonite Brethren. The vigour of the pious movement, tempered only briefly around the turn of the century by success in terms of numerical growth, cultural achievements, and material prosperity, was restored by a religious revival which erupted in the midst of religious persecution, widespread epidemics, and famine following World War I and the Bolshevist Revolution. Large numbers of the purged sect emigrated to Canada in the mid-1920s and there joined the smaller beginning of Mennonite Brethren who had come from United States, themselves descendants of immigrants of the 1870s. The mid-1920s, therefore, constitutes the beginning of the more intensive study of the interaction of those forces which account for the persistence of sectarianism one-half century later: the tension between *Kanadier* (partly assimilated) and *Russlaender* (newly arrived immigrants), between routinized charisma and revived sectarianism, between conversionists and introversionists, and between those eventually defecting from their Mennonite roots and those rediscovering their heritage—themes so common to the dialectic of integration and differentiation, basic to an identity theory of religion which explains such persistence.

Analysing the integrating side of the dialectic, chapters five to nine isolated those components of continuity which facilitated the sacralization of the movement. The more ideological, cognitive, and normative boundaries have been not only delineated, but largely maintained. Empirical measures of belief indicate the highest scores in orthodoxy and evangelicalism, comparing favourably with Southern Baptists. In Anabaptism, they lag behind other Mennonite groups in several of the indices. Such retention of beliefs through one-half a century is explained in terms of its emphasis upon restorationist thinking, biblicist orientation, voluntarism, and separatism. Empirical measures of ethics indicate a more restrictive life-style in personal issues than the General Conference Mennonites from whom they seceded. In social ethics, however, they generally fall behind. While in some issues Mennonite Brethren have refused to change their ethical stance, on other issues they have accommodated themselves to society, or remain open to several points of view. Despite some give and take, ethical decisions are not lightly made and the church is greatly influential in the shaping of the stance it adopts.

In the more biological and cultural spheres, the church has again successfully maintained a cohesiveness in family and group ethnicity despite rather rigorous erosion and change. Through largely endogamous marriages and emphasis upon the indissolubility of marriage, few separations and divorces occur. Moreover, at various levels of socialization, such as study sessions, official statements, family periodicals, and family assemblies, attempts are made to offset the erosion caused by an industrial-urban society. For most of the half century, ethnicity has strongly contributed to the cohesiveness of the group, especially the common experience of immigration, the collective *Reiseschuld*, the retention of the *Muttersprache*, and the many commemorations. Only recently have the cultural components which made the group homogeneous been replaced by ideological ones which transcend and unite heterogeneous groups. The religious movement has been particularly conscious of the impact of change and the need to cohere religiously in spite of such change.

Analysing religiosity both psychologically on a personal level and sociologically on a group level, one can view conversion and charisma as consolidating the respective personal and sociological identities. Empirically, almost all Mennonite Brethren witness to a conversion experience. Moreover, they continue to seek intense religious experiences subsequent to conversion and a rather active devotional life and personal witness. Sporadic renewals through revival have further brought vitality. Widespread involvement in leadership roles guarded against hierarchy; yet distinctly local and national leaders give its many organizational structures needed directives. Charisma is most apparent among the managerial and pastoral figures, who exercise influence in conference sessions or local churches. While societal change has enhanced such problems of leadership as those which relate to elitism, the role of the professional pastor, and the role of women, the emerging pattern is one which encourages congregational involvement together with professional leadership and increased, though restricted, involvement of women. Charisma has enabled the brotherhood's notion of leadership to prevail.

The movement is further perpetuated by the careful socialization of its families and membership both through participation in weekly services and attendance at its various schools. Empirical measures of associationalism and participation yield very high scores, exceeding even the sect groups measured by Stark and Glock. Such regular assemblies provided occasion for worship, instruction, fellowship, and preparation for outreach. Increasingly tension accompanies the change that occurs in modes of worship, models of instruction, and the forms of fellowship and witness. Parochial training has been increasingly aggressive through the half century, in excess of one-half of Mennonite Brethren having attended its own high schools or Bible institutes. While interest in higher theological education has increased in the last three decades, the Christian liberal arts college finds little support among Canadian Mennonite Brethren. Since each institution testifies to tensions unique to its own purpose and manner, such aggressive socialization does not occur without its inherent countervailing forces.

A final synthesizing component of integration is the structural networks and service agencies of the denomination. Serving as ideological, primary groups, the organizational structure of the Canadian Mennonite Brethren allows for both centripetal (the preserving of the old) and centrifugal (the recruiting of the new) forces to operate simultaneously without the former yielding to the petrifaction of an ingrown group and the latter to total assimilation with society. Conference structures at provincial, national, and international levels provide a covenant relationship of interdependence which allows the autonomy of the local church in local affairs while at the same time ensuring subordination of the local church to the larger body in decisions reached by this larger body and in matters crucial to faith and polity. While participation in conference sessions enhances fellowship and brotherhood and inspires further commitment and service, it also tends to promote elitism and bureaucratization through its centripetal hold. At the same time, however, these structures enable evangelism and service-oriented agencies to extend themselves beyond the denominational boundaries and guard against fragmentation despite the centrifugal tug.

Chapters five to nine have thus indicated that, despite the operation of countervailing, differentiating forces, the overwhelming impact of these components of religiosity was integrating and helped to sacralize the identity of Canadian Mennonite Brethren.

Analysing the differentiation side of the dialectic, chapters ten to fourteen isolated those components of social change which particularly affected the continuity of the sectarian movement. Initial reluctance to change and persistent resistance to secularization have given way to extensive change and tacit approval to considerable conformity to the world. Education was discovered not only to enhance some variables of religiosity (such as devotionalism and associationalism in the practice of religion and Anabaptist belief and ethics), but also to relativize fundamentalist and orthodox beliefs and personal ethics. Education does in fact lead to increased differentiation in the symbolic system, but by facilitating personal choice, it simultaneously encourages the voluntarism of Anabaptism.

Urbanization similarly has its erosive effects, but also provides for new religious challenges. Most urban among Mennonite groups, Mennonite Brethren are being secularized through urbanization in both a negative and a positive way. The practice of religion, as measured by devotionalism and associationalism, is not only less rigorous in urban than rural residence, but especially so in general and fundamentalist orthodox beliefs, as well as in personal, moral issues. Curiously, at the same time, the Anabaptist belief variable is enhanced by urban residence. Consciously Mennonite Brethren have faced their increasingly urban environment and have aggressively confronted it with their sectarian strengths.

The secularization accompanying occupational change seems to have promoted the continuity of the movement. While measures of religiosity suggest the machine operator to be the most religious, followed by the housewife and farmer, the shift to the non-farming occupations has enabled Mennonite Brethren to penetrate a much broader spectrum of society with their Christian witness. At the same time, increased residential mobility and a new appreciation for the arts and leisure have caused considerable defection. Despite the loss, however, the change from the rural, farming vocation to the urban, non-farming occupations has given the sectarian movement increased credibility for survival in an otherwise hostile world.

Economic ascendancy, itself the result of the frontier spirit and work ethic accompanying the immigrant flux, has been shown to have a powerful secularization impact, yet not totally to the discredit of the movement. While the more affluent score lower in such measures of religiosity as devotionalism, fundamentalist orthodoxy, and personal moral issues, at the same time in associationalism, Anabaptism, and social ethics they have higher responses. Upward mobility does not necessarily mean loss of sectarianism, as Niebuhr has hypothesized. While economic prosperity does tend to increase class cleavage, places undue emphasis upon worldly success, and results in a loss of "inner-worldly asceticism," such prosperity also provides the resources to promote religious causes and to initiate reform of the secularized, economic structures which affect their fellow-believers and society at large.

Finally, the process of secularization is occurring in an ongoing way through the assimilation of the predominantly immigrant group. It appears, however, that Canadian Mennonite Brethren have successfully acculturated to their dominant society without having totally assimilated the value system. Three phases characterize this shift on the continuum from conflict to convergence: the first generation prior to World War II made social and economic adjustments and encountered the ideological factor mainly when their pacifism was tested during World War II; the second generation suffered some casualties of alienation with the rapid social change after World War II; the third generation suffered a greater loss of faith with its further convergence with the dominant society, and, particularly as a result of the rapidity of assimilation, has most seriously encountered an identity crisis. The crisis manifests itself in the articulation of a theology and ethic which transcends ethnic boundaries, in the rethinking of the denominational designation, the rediscovery of their roots, and reaffirmation of denominational separateness. The result of such purging of marginal commitment and ethnic homogeneity is a newly forged identity. Secularization through assimilation has undoubtedly meant some loss to the movement. At the same time, it suggests a gain as well, since it demonstrates the ability of the movement to survive within an ethnically heterogeneous society.

Chapters ten to fourteen have shown that the overwhelming impact of these components of social change has been a secularizing effect upon religion; nevertheless, the sectarian movement has persisted because of the deeply rooted sacralizing components that were simultaneously operative.

2. Ascertaining the Support of the Hypothesis

The study has postulated the viability of sectarianism. The support for such an hypothesis lies neither in upholding the synthetic process of sacralization, which ostensibly explains the continuity of the movement, nor in disclaiming the analytic process of secularization, which accounts for the gradual disintegration of the movement, but in the interaction of these opposing forces. To understand the nature of the interaction, one should be reminded first of the cumulative impact of these opposing forces.

Chapters five to nine have demonstrated that, despite repeated concessions to the erosive forces of secularization, the overwhelming impact is in fact integrating. For instance, in 1975 Canadian Mennonite Brethren still upheld theological convictions and ethical positions, the unique constellation of which made Mennonite Brethren quite sectarian in outlook. Hence, a strong measure of ideological homogeneity, which can successfully straddle ethnically heterogeneous groups, has gradually emerged to offset the erosion of the biological and cultural cohesion which provided such a strong measure of integration until recent times. Both on a personal, as well as on a group level, identities have been consolidated through conversion and charisma, respectively, throughout the half century under scrutiny, regardless of new ways of responding to the psychological and sociological dimensions of these religious phenomena. Moreover, the increased sophistication in the socialization endeavours has more than offset the relativizing effects of the encounter with the pluralism of the world. Finally, conference structures and service opportunities continuously reinforced the integration which was being challenged by increased privatization and competing appeals for loyalties. The sacralization of the Canadian Mennonite Brethren identity after a half century of testing is unambiguously clear despite the countervailing forces of secularization apparent within each of these mechanisms of sacralization.

Chapters ten to fourteen have shown that through numerous, rather insidious means the secularization process has been active throughout the half century. Yet Mennonite Brethren have been quite aware of this force and have consciously responded and withstood the negative implications. An examination of Mennonite Brethren openness to education has demonstrated both the marked impact of education upon social change, as well as the deliberate socialization that simultaneously occurs with such change. Urbanization undoubtedly has erosive effects upon conservative beliefs and life-styles, but affords new challenges of outreach for a movement which is capable of exercising influence beyond its own people. While a study of occupational change suggests the white-collar worker to be more secularized than the blue-collar workers, such change nevertheless allows for a broad spectrum of vocational penetration with the Christian witness, more than compensating for any loss of commitment in faith by becoming white-collar groups. Again, since economic ascendancy likewise results in lower scores in some variables of religiosity, while at the same time it produces higher scores in other variables, its impact is not unilinear. And while assimilation of the largely immigrant group has continuously produced a shift on the continuum from conflict to convergence, the identity crisis which eventually erupts enables the movement to discover itself and purge itself of those elements not conducive to ongoing religiosity in a pluralistic world. The end product of these five major forces of secularization is not total convergence with the host society, but an adaptation to the forces of differentiation which is restricted by the checks and balances rooted in the Archimedean point. Each group of chapters represents an overwhelmingly major thrust of sacralization and secularization, respectively, with a significant and sometimes not so significant counter-thrust simultaneously at work. This see-saw relationship needs further examination.

Having ascertained the cumulative impact of the synthetic process of sacralization and the analytic process of secularization, one can further assess how both of these forces are essential to a viable form of sectarianism. By itself, the integrating process of sacralization may lead to continuity, but without adequate checks such continuity would result in a rigidification which would stifle the vitality of such sectarianism in contemporary society. So also, by itself the differentiating process of secularization may rapidly lead to change in the religious movement, but again, without adequate checks, such change would result in total convergence with the host society and loss of the sectarian stance. Both sacralization and secularization are essential, therefore, to lend viability to sectarianism in contemporary society. The forces of integration and differentiation constitute a yin/yang complementarity, the dialectic of which keeps a sectarian movement alive in an age otherwise known for decreased transcendence and increased immanence in religious symbolism.

Within the dialectic of sacralization and secularization, one can further discover a yin/yang complementarity in which religion is treated as both an independent and dependent variable. In keeping with the thesis of Max Weber, chapters five to nine have demonstrated how religion can serve as an independent variable and consequently influence forces in society. A sectarian theology accounts for the Archimedean fulcrum which helps define the boundaries. The biological and cultural links have been given sacred meaning because of their significance. The individual and group identity have also been sacralized, even as socialization has been thoroughly saturated with religious content, while the structural network and action-oriented bases are religiously legitimated. Religion is treated as an independent variable to account for the continuity. At the same time, it also becomes the dependent variable, in which society determines religion (or lack of it), as Emile Durkheim would have us believe. Education relativizes religious beliefs and conservative ethics, urbanization makes a movement accessible to the hazards of fragility, occupational change exposes the proponents of religious beliefs to new testings, upward social mobility leads to less reliance on religious motivation, and assimilating with society tends to disguise the religious distinctive. It is only as one views religion simultaneously as an independent and dependent variable that one more fully understands the complexity of the forces at work and how Canadian Mennonite Brethren have persisted in the face of continuity and change. The viability of sectarianism is explained, therefore, in terms of the ongoing dialectic between integration and differentiation.

3. Responding to Studies of Sectarianism

As a result of the foregoing study of sectarianism, one responds to both the theoreticians and empirical investigators of sectarianism in the following manner. Responding first to the two European "founding fathers" who first employed the typology, Max Weber and Ernst Troeltsch, one affirms that despite extensive use, repeated elaboration, and rigorous critique of the church-sect typology, one can still today use this heuristic device if one is alert to its limitations. The Canadian Mennonite Brethren Church and the Anabaptist-Mennonite movement from which it emerged are good examples of a sect not only in its early stage of conflict with the host society, but also in its later refusal to be entirely assimilated by the church type. Moreover, as chapter thirteen indicates, Mennonite Brethren in the twentieth century constitute a case study of Weber's thesis of the "Protestant ethic" both in the asceticism which marked the early years after immigration and in the loss of the "inner-worldly asceticism" of recent times.

Responding further to the two North American spokesmen on sectarianism, H. Richard Niebuhr and S. D. Clark, whose works became classics in the United States and Canada, respectively, one appreciates their insights on sectarian growth on the frontier setting, but recognizes also their limitations. Contrary to Niebuhr's hypothesis, Mennonite Brethren have demonstrated sectarian continuity beyond the second generation. Contrary to Clark's conclusion that contemporary sectarianism serves principally to provide a sense of solidarity for those who have lost a sense of belonging and are "socially unattached" and "foot-loose" in the community, Mennonite Brethren in Canada today have integrated culturally, demonstrating upward social mobility and vocational and intellectual penetration of all spheres of society, and yet maintained sectarian separateness while reshaping a new identity rooted in ideological issues.

Responding briefly to those American sociologists who have done extensive empirical studies in religion and whose conclusions bear upon this study, one might single out Herberg, Lenski, Glock and Stark. On the basis of the findings concerning Mennonite Brethren, one disagrees with Herberg's conclusion that the second generation disassociates itself more from the first with a subsequent recovery in the third. Secularization among Canadian Mennonite Brethren was decidedly more apparent in the third than the second generation. So also one takes exception to his view that Protestantism is but a sanction for the American values of individualism, activism, and self-improvement; instead, one sides with Lenski who contends that through training from early childhood persons can internalize different values which result in a behavioural pattern that does not converge with society. Today's Mennonite Brethren provide considerable evidence of the latter. Stark and Glock's grouping of sects into one collapsed category does violence to the serious study of a particular sectarian group, because the uniquely different groups have been blended into a nonreality through statistical averaging. In some empirical measures, Mennonite Brethren score even higher than Glock and Stark's findings indicate; in other measures, the findings are quite the reverse. Consequently, as chapter one suggests, these authors fail to come to grips with sectarian viability and are too ready to predict religion's imminent demise.

The findings of this thesis are more supportive of Berger and Greeley's notions. As Berger might suggest, the study of sectarianism not only provides empirical data which contrast with the beliefs and practices of established churches, but supplies significant evidence of transcendence. Religion persists, and so does "unsecular man," as Greeley purports. Repeatedly one returns to the findings of E. K. Francis in his study of Manitoba Mennonites. Whereas his insights on the acculturation and assimilation of an immigrant group are indeed helpful, he would find contemporary, urban Mennonite Brethren very different from the largely homogeneous communities he studied in rural Manitoba. This would not come as a surprise, for he himself detected the openness to education and middle-class origins of many of the newly immigrated *Russlaender* who constituted the core group of this study. Furthermore, the recent identity crisis highlights his caution that assimilation should occur at the least cost to human suffering. Kauffman and Harder, whose Church Member Profile of 1972 provided the data for the secondary analysis, enabled the attainment of the second goal of the study, that is, to do an analysis of the religious movement so as to provide a better understanding of it than current studies provide. While their own comparative interpretation of the data provided insights into the religious sociology of Mennonite Brethren, they contributed as well to the theoretical framework of the identity theory in religion by isolating the key variable of Mennonite reality. This isolation of the key variable, which is the belief variable, including the distinguishing principles of Anabaptism, strengthened the conclusion that cognitive boundaries constitute the most significant component of religious continuity.

Responding, finally, to the primary architects of the theory which is being tested, one singles out Bryan Wilson and Hans Mol. Despite Wilson's elaborate typology, Mennonite Brethren do not quite fit either his introversionist or his conversionist types. Nonetheless, it is these types that explain the tension between those in the sect who tend to provide continuity and those who aggressively confront change, yet refuse to be assimilated by the world. More significant than finding a model, however, is Wilson's definition of a sect as an ideological and social unit, a protest against wider society. In addition to Wilson's examples from Great Britain, the Canadian Mennonite Brethren have demonstrated their ability to retain their protest without withdrawing from society. Like Wilson's, these findings indicate that economic determinism does not explain such a sectarian phenomenon. Unlike Wilson's, these findings indicate that psychological and sociological reasons are also inadequate. What is needed is the ideological component, for which Wilson finds an illustration in the Christian Science movement which is among the socially and economically privileged. Mol's theoretical framework is helpful in that he isolates the mechanisms of sacralization—objectification, ritual, commitment, and myth. More importantly, he views the sacralization/secularization process as a dialectic, as part of the see-saw relationship of integration and differentiation, for it is in this dialectic that the sect finds its viability in the contemporary world—maintaining the necessary integration to give continuity and allowing sufficient adaptability to provide change. The findings of this study affirm the utility of Mol's theory.

Epilogue

Some 450 years after the birth of Anabaptism, some 115 years after the renewal movement which spawned the Mennonite Brethren, and 50 years after the major immigration of the core group in Canada today, Mennonite Brethren show signs of distinctive religious vitality despite outward society. Such vitality is explained, not merely through theological and ethical tenets held by the group, but in terms of a scientific theory of religious identity which hypothesizes the viability of sectarianism. Forces constituting sameness and continuity and forces constituting differences and change hold one another in balance. It is this dialectic of integration and differentiation, expressed in the religious terms of sacralization and secularization, which accounts for the continued viability of Canadian Mennonite Brethren.

BIBLIOGRAPHY

The bibliography includes the books, articles, and documents used in the preparation of the text. The works listed are classified as "Primary Sources" and "Secondary Materials" with several types in each category, that is, books and pamphlets, articles, and theses. The following abbreviations are used:

BOMAS   Board of Missions and Services

CMECP   *Consultation on Mennonite Educational and Cultural Problems*

GCYB   *Year Book of the General Conference of Mennonite Brethren Churches*

JSSR   *Journal for the Scientific Study of Religion*

K-J   *Konferenz-Jugendblatt*

MBBC   Mennonite Brethren Bible College

MBH   *Mennonite Brethren Herald*

MO   *Mennonite Observer*

MQR   *Mennonite Quarterly Review*

MR   *Mennonitische Rundschau*

YB   *Year Book of the Canadian Conference of the Mennonite Brethren Churches of North America*

1. Primary Sources

Books, Official Documents, Pamphlets

Acts of Incorporation and By-Laws of the Alberta Conference of Mennonite Brethren Churches. 1957. Winnipeg: Christian Press.

Bekker, Jacob. 1973. *Origin of the Mennonite Brethren Church.* Trans. by D. E. Pauls and A. E. Janzen. Hillsboro, Kans.: Mennonite Brethren Historical Society of the Midwest.

Calendar: Mennonite Brethren Bible College, 1945-46. 1945. Winnipeg: Christian Press.

Charter and By-Laws of the Canadian Conference of the Mennonite Brethren Church of North America. 1945. Winnipeg: Christian Press.

Church Directory: The Mennonite Brethren Churches of Winnipeg, 1976. Winnipeg: Christian Press.

Confession of Faith of the Mennonite Brethren Church of North America. Hillsboro: Mennonite Brethren Publishing House, n.d. (See also revised Confession in *GCYB*, 1975, pp. 17ff.)

Confrontation: Triennial Report, 1969. Hillsboro: BOMAS.

Constitution and By-Laws of the Ontario Conference of Mennonite Brethren Churches, 1971. Mimeographed copy in MBBC archives.

Constitution of the Canadian Conference of the Mennonite Brethren Churches of North America, 1970. Winnipeg: Christian Press.

Constitution of the General Conference of Mennonite Brethren Churches, 1963. Hillsboro: Mennonite Brethren Publishing House.

Friesen, P. M. 1911. *Die Alt-Evangelische Mennonitische Bruederschaft in Russland (1789-1910).* Halbstadt, Taurien: Raduga Verlagsgesellschaft.

Glaubensbekenntnis der Vereinigten Christlichen Taufgesinnten Mennonitischen Brüdergemeinde in Russland. 1902. Halbstadt, Russia: P. Neufeld.

Hamm, Martin. 1971. *Aus der alten in die neue Heimat.* Winnipeg: Christian Press.

Impact: Triennial Report, 1975. Hillsboro: BOMAS.

Kauffman, J. Howard, and Harder, Leland. 1975. *Anabaptists Four Centuries Later: A Profile of Five Mennonite and Brethren in Christ Denominations.* Scottdale, Pa.: Herald Press.

Klassen, A. J. c. 1964. *The Bible School Story: Fifty Years of Mennonite Brethren Schools in Canada.* N.p., n.d.

————, ed. 1975. *The Seminary Story.* Fresno, Calif.: Mennonite Brethren Biblical Seminary.

Lohrenz, J. H. 1950. *The Mennonite Brethren Church.* Hillsboro: Mennonite Brethren Publishing House.

Mission Report, 1960. Hillsboro: BOMAS.

Obedience in Partnership, 1963. Hillsboro: BOMAS.

Open Doors: Report to General Conference, 1966. Hillsboro: BOMAS.

Servanthood: Triennial Report, 1972. Hillsboro: BOMAS.

Die Statuten der Mennoniten Bruedergemeinde von Manitoba, Canada, 1953. Winnipeg: Christian Press.

Twenty-fifth Anniversary Publication of MBBC, 1944-1969. 1969. Winnipeg: Christian Press.

Unruh, A. H. 1955. *Die Geschichte der Mennoniten-Bruedergemeinde.* Winnipeg: Christian Press.

Wenger, J. C., ed. 1956. *Complete Writings of Menno Simons.* Scottdale: Herald Press.

Wiebe, Walter, *et al.* 1960. *Century of Grace and Witness.* Hillsboro: Mennonite Brethren Publishing House.

Wiens, Delbert. 1965. *New Wineskins for Old Wine: A Study of the Mennonite Brethren Church.* Hillsboro: Mennonite Brethren Publishing House.

Year Book of the Canadian Conference of the Mennonite Brethren Churches of North America. 1910-1976. Winnipeg: Christian Press.

Year Book of the General Conference of the Mennonite Brethren Churches. Hillsboro: Mennonite Brethren Publishing House, 1894-1908, annually published; 1909-1915, triennially published; 1919, 1921-1939, triennially; 1943, 1945-1975, triennially.

Articles in Denominational Periodicals and Year Books

Adrian, Victor. 1965. "Born Out of Anabaptism and Pietism," *MBH,* IV (March 26). (Insert in *MBH.*)

Classen, Paul. 1970. "Statistics on Mennonite Central Committee Personnel," *MQR,* XLIV (July), 324-29.

Doerksen, Victor. 1971. "A Clarification," *MBH*, X (Oct. 22), 24.

Dueck, Abram. 1972. "Retrospect and Prospect: Reformatio or Restitutio," *Direction*, I (April), 42-43.

Duerksen, David D. 1968. "The Legacy of the Elmwood Bible Conference," *MBH*, VII (Jan. 12), 7, 18-19.

Dyck, Cornelius J. 1975. "1525 Revisited? A Comparison of Anabaptist and Mennonite Brethren Origins." Unpublished paper presented to the Symposium on Mennonite Brethren History, Fresno, May 1975. See MBBC archives.

Dyck, Rudolph. 1977. "Being Christian in Business," *MBH*, XIII (May 17), 4, 5, 30.

Epp, George. 1974. "What the Statistics Tell," *MBH*, XIII (Mar. 22), 27.

Erb, Paul. 1959. "Status Seeking," *MO*, V (June 26), 2.

Ewert, David. 1954. "Some New Testament Teachings on the World," *Voice*, III (Jan.-Feb.), 6-9.

————. 1960. "Reflections on Bible Reading in the Mennonite Brethren Church," *Voice*, IX (Jan.-Feb.), 3-6.

————. 1962. "What About our Liberal Arts College?" *MBH*, I (Aug. 24), 11.

————. 1967. "An Approach to Problems of Christian Ethics," *MBH*, VI (Mar. 24), 1-25.

————. 1974. "The Christian Woman in the Church and the Conference," *YB*, 30-43.

Giesbrecht, Herbert. 1965. "Teaching the Liberal Arts," *Voice*, XIV (Sept.-Oct.), 4-8.

————. 1976. "In Search of Discipline: Ethical Covenants and Codes in the Local Church," *Direction*, V (Jan.), 3-10.

Graff, Tom. 1973. "Why I Became a Mennonite," *MBH*, XII (April 6), 3.

Hein, Marvin. 1966. "The Church in Flux," *MBH*, V (Nov. 25), 1, 8-9.

————. 1968. "The Church, Its Regulations, and the Individual Member," *MBH*, VII (Jan. 26). (Insert in *MBH*.)

Hiebert, Lando. 1960. "Our Sacred Trust Is a Spiritual Trust," *GCYB*, 2.

Hostetter, Charles. 1967. "Work Addiction," *MBH*, VI (Dec. 8), 5, 6.

Janz, B. B. 1954. "Die Konferenz Botschaft," *YB*, 10-15.

Janzen, Edmond. 1974. "The Church and the Urban Frontier," *MBH*, XIII (Oct. 18). (Insert in *MBH*.)

Jantz, Harold. 1965. "Devotional Guide for the Family," *MBH*, IV (Jan. 8), 2.

————. 1966. "Separated unto God for an Effective Witness," *MBH*, V (May 27), 3.

————. 1967. "Our Materialistic Society," *MBH*, VI (Nov. 10), 2.

————. 1968a. "Revival," *MBH*, VII (Jan. 5), 3.

————. 1968b. "Winnipeg Study Conference," *MBH*, VII (April 26), 3.

————. 1973. "What Holds Us Together?" *MBH*, XII (Nov. 30), 11.

————, and Siebert, Allan. 1971. "Mennonite Name—Biggest Issue in Fifty Years," *MBH*, XVI (July 22), 2-4.

Jantz, Hugo. 1965. "Time for Change, *MBH*, IV (Feb. 26), 9, 18.

Just, L. Roy. 1953. "An Analysis of the Social Distance Reactions of Students from the Three Major American Mennonite Groups," Ninth *CMECP*, 73-77.

Kehler, Larry. 1970. "The Many Activities of the MCC," *MQR*, XLIV (July), 298-315.

Klassen, Peter. 1963. "Conference Spirit," *MBH*, II (July 12), 3.

————. 1964a. "Turning the Sod," *MBH*, III (May 15), 3.

————. 1964b. "A Philosophy of Change," *MBH*, III (June 26), 3.

————. 1964c. "On Being Agreeable," *MBH*, III (July 3), 3.

Konrad, Abe. 1955. "B.C. Teachers' Witness Expands," *MO*, I (Sept. 21), 3.

Konrad, George. 1967. "Education and the Mission of the Church," in A. J. Klassen, *The Church in Mission*. Fresno: Board of Christian Literature of General Conference of Mennonite Brethren, pp. 205-21.

————. 1971. "Christian Families—Another Look," *Voice*, XX (April), 12-20.

Kroeker, Dave. 1975. "Catholic and Baptist Speak at Anabaptist Anniversary Celebration," *Mennonite Reporter*, V (Feb. 3), 5.

Loewen, Harry. 1969. "A Good Label," *MBH*, VIII (Feb. 21), 8, 20.

————. 1973. "University Education Dangerous," *MBH*, XII (June 15), 11.

Loewen, Jacob, and Loewen, Anne. 1969. "Can Child Conversion Last? Socialization and Child Conversion: A Personal Record," *MBH*, VIII (Oct. 17), 2-6.

Neufeld, H. 1925. "Eine Einwanderungstatistik," *MR*, XLV (Apr. 22), 5, 8.

Penner, Peter. 1958. "The Heritage of M.B. Young People," *MO*, IV (May 30), 8.

Peters, F. C. 1959. "Mennonite Brethren Church Polity," *Voice*, VIII (Nov.-Dec.), 17-21.

————. 1962. "Living in the World as Strangers," *Voice*, XI (July-Aug.), 1-3.

————. 1963. "The Local Church—And Cultural Influences," *MBH*, II (Jan. 18), 7.

————. 1965a. "Act or Motive?" *MBH*, IV (Jan. 8), 7.

————. 1965b. "Work—Biblical View," *MBH*, IV (Aug. 6), 8.

————. 1965c. "Mennonite Brethren and Labour Unions," *MBH*, IV (Nov. 5), 8.

————. 1965d. "I'm Tired, I've Been Resting All Day," *MBH*, IV (Nov. 26), 6.

————. 1966. "Faith of our Fathers in the Day of our Children," *MBH*, V (Sept. 9), 4.

————. 1968. "Consensus and Change in our Brotherhood," *MBH*, VII (Jan. 12), 6. (Insert in *MBH*.)

————. 1969a. "Families in a Secular Society," *MBH*, VIII (Apr. 4), 6, 7.

————. 1969b. "Needed—A Sense of Identity for Christian Families," *MBH*, VIII (May 2), 4.

————. 1971. "Two Worlds," *Voice*, XX (July), 21-23.

————. 1976. "Capital Punishment," *MBH*, XV (Jan. 9), 17.

Quiring, J. H. 1952. "The Challenge of the Public School," *Voice*, I (May-June), 15.

————. 1957. "Konferenze und Gemeinde," *Voice*, VI (May-June), 7-9.

————. 1968. "Dealing Redemptively with the Divorced and Remarried," *MBH*, VII (Feb. 23). (Insert in *MBH*.)

————. 1972. "Do We Create an Elite among Our Ministers?" *Voice*, XIII (Sept.-Oct.), 6.

Redekop, John H. 1964a. "A Starving World," *MBH*, III (Apr. 24), 2.

————. 1964b. "Museum or Missions?" *MBH*, III (June 19), 2.

————. 1965a. "College Training—Where are we heading?" *MBH*, IV (Feb. 19), 2.

_____ . 1965b. "Reflections on Hepburn," *MBH*, IV (Aug. 6), 2.

_____ . 1966a. "Capital Punishment," *MBH*, V (Jan. 7), 2.

_____ . 1966b. "Anabaptism," *MBH*, V (Sept. 30), 2.

_____ . 1968a. "Reflections on Television," *MBH*, VII (Mar. 22), 2.

_____ . 1968b. "The Christian and Labor Unions," *MBH*, VII (June 28), 10-11.

_____ . 1968c. "Crowds at Clearbrook," *MBH*, VII (Aug. 23), 3.

_____ . 1969a. "Two Bottles," *MBH*, VIII (Jan. 24), 10.

_____ . 1969b. "Understanding the Brethren," *MBH*, VIII (Aug. 22), 10.

_____ . 1971. "Evangelical-Anabaptist but not Mennonite," *MBH*, X (July 9), 8.

_____ . 1973a. "Casualties of Urbanization," *MBH*, XII (May 18), 2.

_____ . 1973b. "An Assessment," *MBH*, XII (Aug. 3), 11.

_____ . 1975a. "The Council of Boards," *MBH*, XIV (Mar. 7), 8.

_____ . 1975b. "Christian Class Consciousness," *MBH*, XIV (Sept. 19), 12.

Regehr, Henry. 1972. "Patterns of Leadership in the M.B. Conference," *Direction*, I (Oct.), 112-21.

Schroeder, William. 1959. "The Teacher as a Missionary," *MO*, V (Dec. 4), 10.

Siemens, Leonard. 1970. "To Be Christian in the 'Secular City'," *Voice*, XIX (Jan.), 11-18.

_____ . 1974. "The Christian and His Material Possessions," *MBH*, XIII (Oct. 18), 21-27. (Insert in *MBH*.)

Stobbe, Leslie. 1957a. "A Step in the Right Direction," *MO*, III (Apr. 5), 2.

_____ . 1957b. "Will You Be There?" *MO*, III (May 31), 2.

Toews, John A. 1953. "Mangelhafte Betonung der konfessionellen Eigenart in unserer religioesen Erziehung," *Voice*, II (July-Aug.), 21-23.

_____ . 1955a. "On Attending the Conference," *Voice*, IV (Mar.-Apr.), 9-11.

_____ . 1955b. "The Church as a Brotherhood: A Study in Early Mennonite Theology," *Voice*, IV (Sept.-Oct.), 13-16.

_____ . 1956. "Die Stadtgemeinde in der Mennonitischen Bruderschaft," *Voice*, V (July-Aug.), 1-4.

_____ . 1961. "A Legitimate Compromise," *MO*, VII (Apr. 7), 2.

_____ . 1972. "In Search of Identity," *MBH*, XI (Mar. 10), 2-4, 25.

Toews, John B. 1966. "Have We Really Seen the City?" *MBH*, V (Nov. 25), 4-5.

Toews, John E. 1965. "Secularized Times and Places," *MBH*, IV (June 11), 19.

_____ . 1976. "Where to, Mennonite Brethren . . . ?" *The Christian Leader*, XXXIX (Jan. 6), 2.

Unruh, A. H. 1951. "Die Gleichstellung mit der Welt," *K-J*, VII (May-Aug.), 3-8.

_____ . 1953. "Das Durchbrechen der ueberlieferten Ordnung in der Mennoniten Bruedergemeinde," *Voice*, II (July-Aug.), 12-17.

Unruh, Benjamin. 1926. "Die Wehrlosigkeit," *MR*, XLIX (July 14, 21, 28).

Voth, H. H. 1957. "Love not the World," *K-J*, XIII (Mar.-June), 29-30.

Wiebe, Katie Funk. 1974. "Faith and Art: A Compatible Team," *MBH*, XIII (June 28), 2-4, 30.

Wiebe, Rudy. 1962. "New Faces Needed at the Conference," *MBH*, I (May 25), 4.

_____ . 1963a. "Counting on the Conference," *MBH*, II (Feb. 8), 3.

_____ . 1963b. "Gratitude for Canada," *MBH*, II (Mar. 15), 3.

_____ . 1963c. "The Rule Book and the Principle," *MBH*, II (June 28), 3.

_____. 1964. "Tombstone Community," *Mennonite Life*, XIX (Oct.), 150-53.

_____. 1970. "The Meaning of Being Mennonite Brethren," *MBH*, VIII (Apr. 17), 2-4.

Wiens, Delbert. 1974. "From the Village to the City," *Direction*, II (Jan.), 98-149.

2. Secondary Materials

Books and Pamphlets

Bainton, Roland H. 1956. *The Age of the Reformation*. Princeton, N.J.: D. Van Norstrand.

Becker, Howard. 1968. *Through Values to Social Interpretation: Essays on Social Context, Actions, Types, and Prospects*. New York: Greenwood Press.

Berger, Peter L. 1969a. *A Rumour of Angels: Modern Society and the Rediscovery of the Supernatural*. Baltimore, Md.: Penguin Books.

_____. 1969b. *The Sacred Canopy: Elements of a Sociological Theory of Religion*. New York: Anchor Books.

_____, and Berger, Brigitte. 1975. *Sociology: A Biographical Approach*. New York: Basic Books.

_____, and Luckmann, Thomas. 1967. *The Social Construction of Reality*. New York: Doubleday (Anchor Books).

Blanke, Fritz. 1961. *Brothers in Christ: The History of the Oldest Anabaptist Congregation, Zollikon, near Zurich, Switzerland*. Trans. by Joseph Nordenhaug. Scottdale: Herald Press.

Broom, Leonard, and Selznick, Philip. 1973. *Sociology: A Text with Adapted Readings*. New York: Harper and Row.

Budd, Susan, 1973. *Sociologists and Religion*. London: Collier-Macmillan.

Clark, Elmer T. 1929. *The Psychology of Religious Awakening*. New York: Macmillan.

_____. 1937. *Small Sects in America*. Nashville: Abingdon-Cokesbury Press.

Clark, S. D. 1971. *Church and Sect in Canada*. Toronto: University of Toronto Press.

Cox, Harvey. 1971. *The Secular City: Secularization and Urbanization in Theological Perspective*. New York: Macmillan.

Crysdale, Stewart. 1965. *The Changing Church in Canada*. Toronto: United Church Publishing House.

Davis, Kenneth Ronald. 1974. *Anabaptism and Asceticism: A Study in Intellectual Origins*. Scottdale: Herald Press.

Durkheim, Emile. 1965. *The Elementary Forms of the Religious Life*. Trans. by Joseph Ward Swain. New York: Free Press.

Dyck, Cornelius J., ed. 1967. *Introduction to Mennonite History*. Scottdale: Herald Press.

Ehrt, Adolf. 1932. *Das Mennonitentum in Russland von seiner Einwanderung bis zur Gegenwart*. Berlin: Verlag von Julius Beltz.

Eliade, Mircea. 1958. *Patterns in Comparative Religion*. New York: Sheed and Ward.

Epp, Frank H. 1962. *Mennonite Exodus*. Altona, Man.: D. W. Friesen.

_____. 1974. *Mennonites in Canada, 1786-1920: A History of a Separate People*. Toronto: Macmillan.

Estep, William R. 1963. *The Anabaptist Story*. Nashville: Broadman Press.

Ewert, D. 1975. *Stalwart for the Truth*. Winnipeg: Christian Press.

Fallding, Harold. 1974. *The Sociology of Religion: An Explanation of the Unity and Diversity in Religion*. Toronto: McGraw-Hill Ryerson.

Francis, E. K. 1955. *In Search of Utopia: The Mennonites in Manitoba*. Altona: D. W. Friesen.

Gerth, H. H., and Mills, C. Wright, trans., ed. 1974. *From Max Weber: Essays in Sociology*. New York: Oxford University Press.

Glock, Charles Y. 1973. *Religion in Sociological Perspective: Essays in the Empirical Study of Religion*. Belmont, Calif.: Wadsworth Publishing.

_____, and Stark, Rodney. 1969. *Christian Beliefs and Anti-Semitism*. New York: Harper and Row.

Goerz, H. 1949. *Die Molotschnaer Ansiedlung*. Steinbach, Man.: Echo-Verlag.

Goode, William J. 1964. *The Family*. Englewood Cliffs, N.J.: Prentice-Hall.

Gordon, Milton M. 1975. *Assimilation in American Life: The Role of Race, Religion, and National Origin*. New York: Oxford University Press.

Greeley, Andrew M. 1969. *Religion in the Year 2000*. New York: Sheed and Ward.

_____. 1974. *Unsecular Man: The Persistence of Religion*. New York: Dell

Herberg, Will. 1960. *Protestant, Catholic, Jew*. New York: Anchor Books.

Hershberger, Guy F. 1962. *The Recovery of the Anabaptist Vision: A Sixtieth Anniversary Tribute to Harold S. Bender*. Scottdale: Herald Press.

Hillerbrand, Hans J. 1969. *The Protestant Reformation*. New York: Harper and Row.

Janzen, A. E. 1966. *Mennonite Brethren Distinctives*. Hillsboro: Mennonite Brethren Publishing House.

Kanter, Elizabeth Moss. 1973. *Commitment and Community: Communes and Utopias in Sociological Perspective*. Cambridge, Mass.: Harvard University Press.

Kelley, Dean M. 1972. *Why Conservative Churches are Growing: A Study in Sociology of Religion*. New York: Harper and Row.

Klapp, Orrin E. 1969. *Collective Search for Identity*. Toronto: Holt, Rinehart & Winston.

Klaassen, Walter. 1973. *Anabaptism: Neither Catholic nor Protestantism*. Waterloo: Conrad Press.

Klassen, William. 1968. *Covenant and Community: The Life, Writings, and Hermeneutics of Pilgram Marpeck*. Grand Rapids, Mich.: W. B. Eerdmans.

Krahn, Cornelius. 1968. *Dutch Anabaptism: Origin, Spread, Life and Thought (1450-1600)*. The Hague: Martinus Nijhoff.

Lenski, G. 1963. *The Religious Factor: A Sociological Study of Religious Impact on Politics, Economics, and Family Life*. Garden City: Anchor Books.

Littell, Franklin Hamlin. 1972. *The Origins of Sectarian Protestantism: A Study of the Anabaptist View of the Church* (formerly, *The Anabaptist View of the Church*). New York: Macmillan.

Luckmann, Thomas. 1967. *The Invisible Religion: The Problem of Religion in Modern Society*. New York: Macmillan.

Martin, David. 1969. *The Religious and the Secular: Studies in Secularization*. London: Routledge and Kegan Paul.

Marx, Karl, and Engels, Friedrich. 1964. *On Religion*. Introduction by Reinhold Niebuhr. New York: Schocken Books.

Mol Hans J. 1961. *Churches and Immigrants*. R.E.M.P. Bulletin, IX (May).

_____. 1976. *Identity and the Sacred*. Agincourt, Ont.: Book Society of Canada.

Newbigin, Lesslie. 1966. *Honest Religion for Secular Man*. London: SCM Press.

Niebuhr, H. Richard. 1972. *The Social Sources of Denominationalism*. New York: World Publishing (Meridan Book).

Nisbet, Robert A. 1966. *The Sociological Tradition*. New York: Basic Books.

O'Dea, Thomas F. 1966. *The Sociology of Religion* (Foundation of Modern Sociology Series). Englewood Cliffs: Prentice-Hall.

Oyer, John S. 1964. *Lutheran Reformers Against Anabaptists: Luther, Melanchthon and Menius and the Anabaptists of Central Germany*. The Hague: Martinus Nijhoff.

Park, Robert E., and Burgess, Ernest W. 1970. *Introduction to the Science of Sociology*. Chicago: University of Chicago Press.

Parsons, Talcott. 1949. *The Structure of Social Action*. Glencoe: Free Press.

_____ . 1950. *The Social System*. Glencoe: Free Press.

Peachey, Paul. 1963. *The Church in the City*. Newton: Faith and Life Press.

Penner, Peter. 1959. *Reaching the Otherwise Unreached: An Historical Account of the West Coast Children's Mission of B.C.* Winnipeg: Christian Press.

Peters, G. W. 1952. *The Growth of Foreign Missions in the Mennonite Brethren Church*. Hillsboro: Board of Foreign Missions.

Pope, Liston. 1942. *Millhands and Preachers*. New Haven: Yale University Press.

Popenoe, David. 1974. *Sociology*. Englewood Cliffs: Prentice-Hall.

Scharf, Betty. 1970. *The Sociological Study of Religion*. New York: Harper Torchbooks.

Simmel, Georg. 1959. *Sociology of Religion*. Trans. by Curt Rosenthal. New York: Philosophical Library.

Sorokin, Pitirim. 1957. *Social and Cultural Dynamics: A Study of Change in Major Systems of Art, Truth, Ethics, Law and Social Relationships*. Boston: Porter Sargent Publisher.

Stark, Rodney, and Glock, Charles Y. 1968. *American Piety: The Nature of Religious Commitment*. Berkeley and Los Angeles: University of California Press.

Toews, John A. 1959. *Alternative Service in Canada During World War II*. Winnipeg: Christian Press.

_____ . 1975. *A History of the Mennonite Brethren Church*. Fresno: Board of Christian Literature of General Conference of Mennonite Brethren Churches.

Toews, John B. 1967. *Lost Fatherland*. Scottdale: Herald Press.

Troeltsch, Ernst. 1960. *The Social Teaching of the Christian Churches*. Vols. I, II. Trans. by Olive Wyon; intro. by H. Richard Niebuhr. New York: Harper Torchbooks.

Wach, Joachim. 1971. *Sociology of Religion*. Chicago: University of Chicago Press.

_____ . 1977. *Types of Religious Experience Christian and Non-Christian*. Chicago: University of Chicago Press.

Weber, Max. 1958. *The Protestant Ethic and the Spirit of Capitalism*. Trans. by Talcott Parsons; foreword by R. H. Tawney. New York: Charles Scribner's Sons.

_____ . 1964. *The Theory of Social and Economic Organization*. Trans. by A. M. Henderson and Talcott Parsons; intro. by Talcott Parsons. New York: Free Press.

_____ . 1968. *Economy and Society: An Outline of Interpretive Society*. Vols. I, III. Ed. by Guenther Roth and Claus Wittich. New York: Bedminster Press.

_____ . 1969. *The Sociology of Religion*. Trans. by Ephraim Fischoff; intro. by Talcott Parsons. Boston: Beacon Press.

Williams, George Huntston. 1962. *The Radical Reformation*. Philadelphia: Westminster Press.

_____ , and Mergal, Angel M. 1957. *Spiritual and Anabaptist Writers: Documents Illustrative of the Radical Reformation* (Library of Christian Classics, Vol. XXV). London: SCM Press.

Wilson, Bryan R. 1961. *Sects and Society: A Sociological Study of Three Religious Groups in Britain*. London: William Heinemann.

_____ . 1966. *Religion in Secular Society: A Sociological Comment*. London: C. A. Watts.

_____ . 1967. *Patterns of Sectarianism: Organization and Ideology in Social and Religious Movements*. London: Heinemann Educational Books.

_____ . 1970. *Religious Sects: A Sociological Study*. London: Weidenfeld and Nicolson.

_____ . 1973. *Magic and the Millennium: A Sociological Study of Religious Movements of Protest among Tribal and Third-World Peoples*. New York: Harper and Row.

Winter, Gibson. 1961. *The Suburban Captivity of the Churches*. Garden City: Doubleday.

Yinger, J. Milton. 1969a. *Religion, Society, and the Individual: An Introduction to the Sociology of Religion*. New York: Macmillan.

_____ . 1969b. *Sociology Looks at Religion*. Toronto: Collier-Macmillan.

_____ . 1970. *The Scientific Study of Religion*. New York: Macmillan.

Scholarly Articles

Bellah, Robert N. 1964. "Religious Evolution," *American Sociological Review*, 29, 358-74.

Berger, Peter L. 1958. "Sectarianism and Religious Sociation," *American Journal of Sociology*, LXIV, 41-44.

_____ . 1967. "A Sociological View of the Secularization of Theology," *JSSR*, VI, 3-16.

_____ . 1974. "Some Second Thoughts on Substantive and Functional Definitions of Religion," *JSSR*, XIII, 125-33.

Bibby, Reginald W., and Brinkerhoff, Marlin B. 1973. "The Circulation of the Saints: A Study of People Who Join Conservative Churches," *JSSR*, XII (Sept.), 273-82.

Blumenfeld, Hans. 1973. "The Process of Urbanization," in *The City: Canada's Prospects, Canada's Problems* by L. Axworthy and J. M. Gillies (eds.), Toronto: Butterworth, pp. 16-19.

Currie, R., Driedger, L., and Linden, R. 1979. "Abstinence and Moderation: Mixing Mennonite Drinking Norms," *MQR*, LIII, 263-81.

Currie, R., Linden, R., and Driedger, L. 1980. "Properties of Norms as Predictors of Alcohol Use Among Mennonites," *Journal of Drug Issues*, IX, 93-107.

Demerath III, Nicholas J. 1967. "In a Sow's Ear: A Reply to Good," *JSSR*, VI, 77-84.

Dobbelaere, Karel, and Lauwers, Jan. 1973-74. "Definition of Religion—A Sociological Critique," *Social Compass*, XX, 535-51.

Driedger, Leo. 1968. "A Perspective on Canadian Mennonite Urbanization," *Mennonite Life*, XXIII, 147-52.

————. 1975a. "Canadian Mennonite Urbanism: Ethnic Villagers or Metropolitan Remnant?" *MQR*, XLIX, 226-41.

————. 1975b. "In Search of Cultural Identity Factors: A Comparison of Ethnic Students," *Canadian Review of Sociology and Anthropology*, XII, 150-62.

————. 1977. "The Anabaptist Identification Ladder: Plain-Urbane Continuity in Diversity," *MQR*, LI, 278-91.

————. 1980. "Fifty Years of Mennonite Identity in Winnipeg: A Sacred Canopy in a Changing Laboratory," in *Mennonite Images* by H. Loewen (ed.), Winnipeg: Hyperion Press, 123-35.

Driedger, L., Currie, R., and Linden, R. 1983. "Dualistic and Wholistic Views of God and the World: Consequences for Social Action," *Review of Religious Research*, XXIV, 225-44.

Driedger, L., Fretz, J. W., and Smucker, D. E. 1978. "A Tale of Two Strategies: Mennonites in Chicago and Winnipeg," *MQR*, LII, 294-311.

Driedger, L., and Kauffman, J. H. 1982. "Urbanization of Mennonites: Canadian and American Comparisons," *MQR*, LVI, 269-90.

Driedger, L., and Peters, J. 1973. "Ethnic Identity: A Comparison of Mennonite and Other German Students," *MQR*, XLVII, 225-44.

Driedger, L., Vogt, R., and Reimer, M. 1977. "Mennonite Intermarriage: National, Regional and Intergenerational Trends," *MQR*, LI, 227-40.

Dyck, William, and Sawatsky, John. 1968. "Psycho-Social Changes Within a Metropolitan Religious Minority," *Mennonite Life*, XXIII (Oct.), 172-76.

Dynes, Russell R. 1955. "Church-Sect Typology and Socio-Economic Status," *American Sociological Review*, XX, 555-60.

Eister, Allan W. 1967. "Toward a Radical Critique of Church-Sect Typology," *JSSR*, VI, 85-90.

Fretz, J. Winfield. 1957. "Social Trends Affecting the Mennonite Family at Mid-Century," in *Proceedings of the Eleventh CMECP*, 131-35.

Friesen, Jim, and Vogt, Reinhard. 1964. "The Mennonite Community in Winnipeg," *Mennonite Life*, XIX (Jan.), 13-15.

Friesen, John W. 1971. "Characteristics of Mennonite Identity: A Survey of Mennonite and Non-Mennonite Views," *Canadian Ethnic Studies*, III (June), 25-41.

Goode, Eric. 1967. "Some Critical Observations in the Church-Sect Dimensions," *JSSR*, VI, 69-77.

Harder, Leland. 1971. "An Empirical Search for the Key Variable in Mennonite Reality," *MQR*, XLV (Oct.), 331-51.

Hillerbrand, Hans J. 1971. "Anabaptism and History," *MQR*, XLV, 107-22.

Johnson, Benton. 1961. "Do Holiness Sects Socialize in Dominant Values?" *Social Forces*, XXXIX, 309-16.

————. 1971. "Church and Sect Revisited," *JSSR*, X, 124-37.

Kauffman, J. Howard. 1977. "Boundary Maintenance and Cultural Assimilation of Contemporary Mennonites," *MQR*, LI, 227-40.

Klaassen, Walter. 1971. "The Nature of the Anabaptist Protest," *MQR*, XLV, 291-311.

Kovacs, M. L., and Cropley, A. J. 1972. "Assimilation and Alienation in Ethnic Groups," *Canadian Ethnic Studies*, IV, nos. 1-2, 13-24.

Krahn, Cornelius. 1935. "Some Social Attitudes of the Mennonites in Russia," *MQR*, IX, 170-74.

————. 1968. "Research on Urban Mennonites," *Mennonite Life*, XXIII (Oct.), 189-90.

Kreider, Robert. 1953. "Vocations of Swiss and South German Anabaptists," *Mennonite Life*, VIII, 38-43.

Loewen, Harry. 1980. "The Anabaptist View of the World: The Beginning of a Mennonite Continuum?" in *Mennonite Images* by H. Loewen (ed.), Winnipeg: Hyperion Press, 85-95.

Mobert, David O. 1961. "Potential Uses of the Church-Sect Typology in Comparative Research," *International Journal of Comparative Sociology*, II, 47-58.

Mol, Hans. 1974. "Some Major Correlates of Churchgoing in Canada," paper presented at McMaster University, March 1974.

Peachey, Paul. 1955. "Early Anabaptists and Urbanism," *Tenth CMECP*, 75-83.

Redekop, Calvin. 1974. "A New Look at Sect Development," *JSSR*, XIII, 345-52.

Shiner, Larry. 1967. "The Concept of Secularization in Empirical Research," *JSSR*, VI, 207-20.

Stayer, James M., Packull, Werner O., and Deppermann, Klaus. 1975. "From Monogenesis to Polygenesis: The Historical Discussion of Anabaptist Origins," *MQR*, XLIX, 83-121.

Vogt, Roy. 1980. "The Impact of Economic and Social Class on Mennonite Theology," in *Mennonite Images* by H. Loewen (ed.), Winnipeg: Hyperion Press, 137-48.

Wiebe, Don. 1980. "Philosophical Reflections on Twentieth-Century Mennonite Thought," in *Mennonite Images* by H. Loewen (ed.), Winnipeg: Hyperion Press, 149-64.

Wilson, Bryan R. 1959. "An Analysis of Sect Development," *American Sociological Review*, XXIV, 3-15. (Also in *Patterns of Sectarianism*, pp. 22-45.)

Wirth, Louis. 1938. "Urbanism as a Way of Life," *American Journal of Sociology*, XLIV (July), 1-25.

Yinger, J. Milton. 1967. "Pluralism, Religion, and Secularism," *JSSR*, VI, 17-30.

Dissertations

Doerksen, John G. 1968. "Mennonite Brethren Bible College and College of Arts: Its History, Philosophy, and Development." Ph.D. dissertation, University of North Dakota.

Hamm, Peter M. 1978. "Continuity and Change Among Canadian Mennonite Brethren, 1925-1975." Ph.D. dissertation, McMaster University.

Harder, Leland. 1962. "The Quest for Equilibrium of an Established Sect." Ph.D. dissertation, Garrett Biblical Institute.

Rempel, David G. 1933. "The Mennonite Colonies in New Russia: A Study of their Settlement and Economic Development from 1789 to 1914." Ph.D. dissertation, Stanford University.

Ross, John Arthur. 1973. "Regionalism, Nationalism and Social Gospel Support in the Ecumenical Movement of Canadian Presbyterianism." Ph.D. dissertation, McMaster University.

INDEX